SEEING THROUGH ABSTRACTION

Seeing Through Abstraction

LITERARY ENCOUNTERS WITH INFORMATION
IN MODERN CHINA

Anatoly Detwyler

Columbia University Press
New York

Columbia University Press wishes to express its appreciation for assistance given by the Wm. Theodore de Bary Fund in the publication of this book.

Columbia University Press
Publishers Since 1893
New York   Chichester, West Sussex

Library of Congress Cataloging-in-Publication Data
Names: Detwyler, Anatoly author
Title: Seeing through abstraction : literary encounters with information
in modern China / Anatoly Detwyler.
Description: New York : Columbia University Press, 2025. | Includes bibliographical
references and index.
Identifiers: LCCN 2025008879 (print) | LCCN 2025008880 (ebook) | ISBN 9780231219891
hardback | ISBN 9780231219884 trade paperback | ISBN 9780231562959 ebook
Subjects: LCSH: Chinese literature—20th century—History and criticism |
Abstraction in literature | Communication in literature | LCGFT: Literary criticism
Classification: LCC PL2302 .D48 2025 (print) | LCC PL2302 (ebook) |
DDC 895.109/005—dc23/eng/20250428

Cover design: Chang Jae Lee
Cover image: © Shutterstock

GPSR Authorized Representative: Easy Access System Europe, Mustamäe tee 50,
10621 Tallinn, Estonia, gpsr.requests@easproject.com

CONTENTS

CONTENTS

ACKNOWLEDGMENTS

In the opening to Liang Qichao's *Intellectual Trends in the Qing Period* (清代學術概論), the writer and military strategist Jiang Fangzhen (1882–1938) wryly recounts: "When I finished composing my history of the European Renaissance, I asked Liang Qichao to write the foreword. But his foreword ran as long as the original book, so it became in itself a separate, general account of Qing learning. He then asked me to write the foreword."[1] I, too, find myself simultaneously on either side of a book. Between conceiving this project during my graduate study at Columbia and now, I had the fortune of coediting two volumes on "information" and its history in scholarship and Chinese literary history—projects that seemed to me necessary to help establish this new subject of humanistic inquiry. As a relative latecomer, my monograph feels at once like a provocation and a response to this expanding subfield. But better late than never.

Many contributed to this book by shaping me into the reader and thinker I am today. Above all, I'm grateful to Lydia H. Liu for her generous guidance and support in my researches. Her seminar on "The Technologies of Empire" introduced me to the possibility of studying something like "information" in the first place. Her encouragement, feedback, and intellectual inspiration have pushed me (and so many others!) to think about Chinese literature in interdisciplinary ways. I can't imagine a better mentor.

At Columbia, I'd also like to thank Eugenia Lean, whose work on the history of science and technology was foundational for me. One of the marks of Eugenia's generosity is her willingness to wade into the weeds of early chapter drafts. Later on, I came to realize that I had internalized her editorial voice, telling me to "concretize" and "clarify." Without her help and boundless intellectual energy, I might still be wandering. Bao Weihong inspired my interest in media studies and set the high bar for contributing to it. Tomi Suzuki helped me reframe this project substantially and gave me comparative perspective. Equally important, her warmth and humor made Columbia a fun place to work. And Shang Wei helped me to situate this project within a broader historical and cultural context and served as a model of intellectual breadth. Madeleine Zelin not only offered sage advice but also sponsored several workshops I co-organized that stimulated this project. Richard John's feedback was critical to my understanding of the field of communications history writ large. Li Tuo's studies of modern and contemporary Chinese literature gave me the spark to revisit canonical writers in new ways. Haruo Shirane, David Lurie, and Bob Hymes offered invaluable feedback and collegial support. And I couldn't have asked for a better neighbor and friend than Liz Irwin, whose encouragement helped me through more than a few rough patches. I'm also grateful to the many Columbia staff and administrators who made my research possible: Tamara Kachanov, Josh Gottesman, Anri Vartanov, Petya DeVallance, Jeffrey Cousino, Ken Harlin (an institution in his own right!), Rich Jandovitz, Wang Chengzhi, and, once upon a time in a galaxy far away, Alexander Sasho Donovan. Laura Schein deserves special mention as a friend and trench mate. Catherine Lasota and Kelly Lemons at the Institute for Comparative Literature and Society also provided key assistance at a critical stage.

At the University of Minnesota, I knew there'd be no going back after studying the *Shijing* with Joe Allen, well before my Chinese was good enough to read the poems in the original. The formal and linguistic issues raised in that class, coupled with Joe's unique mix of scholarliness and playfulness, inspired me to become a lifelong learner of Chinese. I'm deeply thankful to Ann Waltner for introducing me to the history of print in China and for allowing me to sit in on her longstanding classical Chinese reading group. A hallowed tradition that has continued to meet regularly for a marvelously long time, the group instilled in me a profound appreciation of the complexity of late imperial history. And it also cemented my love of reading groups! I'm equally grateful to Paul Rouzer for his guidance and training. One can't truly repay an intellectual debt so great, but I hope this book brings my teachers some small satisfaction in having planted its seed.

At Penn State's Center for Humanities and Information, I'd particularly like to thank Eric Hayot for taking me under his formidable wing. Working with him and Lea Pao on *Information: A Reader* was as a uniquely fun project and an ideal introduction to academic publishing. I'm also grateful to my cohort at CHI: Laura Helton, Sara Grossman, Victoria Salinger, and especially Bonnie "No Chains" Mak, along with my Penn State colleagues: Jessamyn and Jon Abel, Kate Baldanza, Darwin Tsen and Victoria Lupascu, Michele Kennerly, Sam Frederick, Nico Volland and Chang Tan, Sam Frederick, Lea Pao, Kate Merkel-Hess, Erica Brindley, and Shuang Shen. CHI provided support for early planning sessions for *Literary Information in China: A History*, the other cornerstone for this book. I thank my coeditors: Liu Xiao, Chris Nugent, Bruce Rusk, and particularly Jack Chen, whose generosity as a thinker and friend never fails to amaze.

The core support for this research was provided by the Social Science Research Council, as well as by the University of Wisconsin-Madison Office of the Vice Chancellor for Research with funding from the Wisconsin Alumni Research Foundation. In China, the occasional frustration of accessing materials was more than offset by the guidance and friendship of the wonderful scholars I encountered there. Wang Zhongchen at Tsinghua University opened countless doors for me and, more important, was the first to encourage me to work on Mao Dun. At Peking University, I benefited immensely from the support of Wang Feng, Zhang Lihua, Chen Pingyuan, and Wu Xiaodong. Participating in Wu's intensive reading group proved to be a deeply inspiring challenge, and his advice to bring Shen Congwen into my project was invaluable. I also thank Liu Daxian and He Jixian at CASS, Sun Yu at Renmin University, Huang Qiaosheng from the Beijing Lu Xun Museum, and Bao Kun for their respective help over the years. Thanks, too, to the archivists, librarians, and staff at Tsinghua, Peking University, the National Library, the Institute for Modern Chinese Literature, the Shanghai Municipal Library, the Lu Xun Museum, and the Mao Dun Former Residence in Beijing. Their patience, humor, and in some cases, shared *danwei* lunches and badminton sessions made colorful what were otherwise frequently gray days of research.

Over the years, I've benefited immensely from conversations with numerous colleagues. Paola Iovene, Jacob Eyferth, Tom Mullaney, Andrew Jones, Bryna Goodman, Hoyt Long, Tamara Chin, Paize Keulemans, Ariel Fox, Jake Werner, Charles Laughlin, Peng Hsiao-yen, Hilde De Weerdt, and Kai-Wing Chow all offered instrumental feedback at various points. A special shoutout goes to Rebecca Karl, who graciously allowed me into her reading group in New York. Rebecca's dedication to her students is humbling ("When I commit, I commit," she once told me—and how true!). Her sharp analysis and frank feedback provided a level of aid I had no right to expect. My wonderful colleagues at the University of Wisconsin, especially Rania Huntington, Bill Nienhauser, Steve Ridgely, Adam Kern, Hieyoon Kim, Joe and Laurie Dennis, Yuhang Li and Viren Murthy, Charo D'Etcheverry, Wei-hua Zhu, Judd Kinzley, and Jennifer Hekman, have made my institutional home warm and supportive. And, of course, my students at Wisconsin deserve special thanks as well. I'm especially grateful to Liu Ruikang and Li Yuzhe for their help in the closing stages of preparing the manuscript.

Something feels naggingly inadequate about a list's ability to capture one's gratitude toward each person named therein. Acknowledgments gather uniquely heartfelt relations and condense them into a series of gestural blips. So much more of the iceberg is underneath the water! When we encounter lists, most of us are in the habit of scanning rather than pausing to reflect. (Conversely, so much pop culture writing creates "content" merely through the activity of listing: best albums, top moments, worst gaffes, and so on.) Still, without resorting to the form of the list, this section might rival the length of the book itself. It goes without saying that inadequacy/necessity of the list form is hardly a new one. Indeed, this book is about lists, along with other forms of information management like data tables, telegrams, and encyclopedias. Quaint as they may seem in our era of quantum computing and AI, these information genres profoundly reshaped literary identity and expression in Republican China (1912–1949). The mixture of skepticism, anxiety, and fascination with which modern Chinese writers and artists regarded the incompatibility between genres of information, on the one hand, and sentiment or knowledge, on the other, still resonates today. We still share an epoch with our counterparts from the early twentieth century.

Among my friends, I'd especially like to thank Arunabh Ghosh, a wonderfully stimulating co-organizer and fellow traveler in China; Chen Kaijun, an intellectual inspiration; and Greg Patterson, my heady drinking companion. I am also grateful to my Columbia cohort in modern Chinese literature, particularly Zhong Yurou, Gal Gvili, and Chloe Estep—and some really cool cats in Japanese literature: Nate Shockey, Ariel Stillerman, Daniel Poch, and my fellow Packers fan, Pau Pitarch-Fernandez. Thanks also to my friends across the world who have sustained me along the way: Soonyi Lee, Jeongmin Kim, Ksenia Chizhova, Yumi Kim, Tracy Howard, Liza Lawrence, Ti-kai Chang, Andy Liu, Sixiang Wang, Wulan, Tracy Howard, and Elizabeth Reynolds in New York; Jesse Field, Du Weihong, and Qin Fang in Minneapolis; Aiwen Wang-Huddleston, Rivi Handler-Spitz, Quinn Javers, and Timothy O'Neill in Taipei; Jiang Wentao, Liu Lu, Zeng Rong, Liu Kai, Zhao Wei, Angie Baecker, Chen Jie, Song Ming, and Sang Hai in China; and my Point crew—particularly Jesse Stroik. Myra Sun, my better half for much of this journey, deserves special thanks. This book is as much yours as it is mine.

I'm beyond thankful to Christine Dunbar, my editor at Columbia University Press, for taking this project on, as well as to the two reviewers for their invaluable feedback. Anna Paretskaya, Danielle Ogno, and Stephen Billingham all played an important part in pulling this book (and me) together in its final stages, as well.

Finally, I'm grateful to my core people. My family provided unwavering love throughout a writing process filled with self-doubt. Thank you to my amazing brothers, Dmitri and David; my sister, Laura, who didn't live to see me finish the project; and my nephew, Nick. To Charlie, for helping me look up and outward. And to my father, for encouraging me to pursue a scholarly career, and my mother, for inspiring my love of foreign languages. Besides my family, I dedicate this book to three dear comrades: Richard Jean So—my model; Uluğ Kuzuoğlu—my muse; and Eric Marx—my North Star.

A NOTE ON ROMANIZATION
AND TRANSLATIONS

Nearly all the Chinese names, titles, phrases, and words in this book follow the pinyin system of romanization. An exception is made for two political figures, Sun Yat-sen (Sun Zhongshan) and Chiang Kai-shek (Jiang Jieshi), who retain the transliterations that were conventionalized before the advent of pinyin. At their first mention, titles of works are typically given first in pinyin along with the original Chinese characters, followed parenthetically by the title of the English-language translation in italics (if one has been published) or a nonitalicized English gloss of the title. This book centers on the Republican Period (1912–1949), before the standardization of simplified characters. As such, any name or term that appeared before the foundation of the People's Republic of China is rendered in traditional Chinese characters.

INTRODUCTION

Literary Encounters with Information
in Modern China

In 1936, the author and literary critic Mao Dun (1896–1981) published a brief "sketch" (*suxie* 速寫) of the Shanghai China Merchants Stock Exchange, then the largest exchange in China and an emblem of economic modernity.[1] This vignette's description of the hectic trading and speculation at the exchange might be read as a retrospective study for Mao Dun's earlier novel *Midnight* (*Ziye* 子夜, 1933) and its influential account of finance capitalism's emergence and inevitable domination over industrial capital. Indeed, in a few strokes, the sketch captures *Midnight*'s central insight into the working of finance as a process of extraction and accumulation of capital through its symbolic inscription as stocks, bonds, or futures contracts—various forms of "fictitious" capital (to use Karl Marx's term) seemingly uncoupled from tangible assets.[2] Following the narrator's gaze upon the scene, we see a complex performance unfolding in a large hall, where

> everyone is standing: the outer ring has come to watch the market conditions, prepared to buy or sell—likely the majority of them are individual traders with small amounts of capital, though naturally there's also no shortage of "inside traders." But these are not the source of the ear-piercing shouts of numbers. Among them, some raise their heads and look toward the stage—though please don't be mistaken, the men on the clapper-board

stage who roll up their sleeves all the way to their shoulders are not at all handsome, and one can't spot anything of guiding value. Rather, the traders are looking at the "background" on the stage that is exhibiting "XXXX Treasury Bonds," "X period of time" . . . a sort of "theater program" [*ximu* 戲目] (if I may make such a comparison), especially the constantly changing, electrically lit number board atop the "program." Located on a small horizontal rectangle inlaid high on the wall, behind the platform, are rapidly jumping red Arabic numerals, lined up four in a row, where two are the decimal places of the yuan, like the format we frequently see on an invoice; under the decimal numbers there is a horizontal line, also red. Their size isn't small, such that one can clearly make them out from anywhere in the pit. These small, red, electrically lit digits are created by people, and it is people that make them change every moment, but they control people's "fate."

The theatrical likeness of the scene elicits a feeling of unreality crossed with familiarity: behold the proscenium of the exchange space, legible as such, but occupied by a nonhuman and disembodied "actor" that for all its strangeness is nonetheless recognizable as at once both like a written theater program and like an odd banknote (odd because its face value changes continuously). The sketch's unfolding theater metaphor and its emphasis on forms of symbolic representation underscores the fictitiousness of the value at play, where the pitched buying and selling of stocks offer a simulacrum of the supply and demand of tangible things. While the dancing numbers described here also appear as a central plotline in Mao Dun's *Midnight*, which tells of the reorganization of social and economic relations under capitalism, as the sole descriptive focus of this shorter auxiliary piece, the stock exchange is described in greater detail than in the novel. It offers a unique look at the spectacle of modern abstraction.

Such a spectacle proved far more significant than merely appearing as a documentary accessory to its author's earlier novel. Rather, the importance of this visual encounter with the dancing numbers approaches that of a far better-known one, described in Lu Xun's autobiographical preface to his collection of short stories, *Call to Arms* (*Nahan* 吶喊). In the latter, Lu recounts his experience as a foreign student in Japan. When one day after class the instructor projected a propaganda slide that showed a Japanese soldier beheading a Chinese spy while a group of Chinese passively look on, Lu experienced a self-awakening as a Chinese national and, so inspired, abandoned his path toward becoming a doctor in favor of attending to matters of the "soul" through modern literature. Rey Chow has observed how this momentous encounter binds the birth of modern Chinese literature with the advent of film and photography, in which Lu Xun is confronted with the "transparent effect of a new medium that seemingly communicates without mediation."[3] In a similar manner, Mao Dun's epiphany extends beyond a realization about the nature of financial capitalism to an insight about two interrelated phenomena—hypermediation and the illusory, quasi-magical essence of abstract information. Telephone, courier deliveries, balled-up notes, gestures, rumors: the many modes of communication at the stock market together assemble into an immense apparatus for producing and processing market data.[4] Its "face," where the clapper board numbers float above the cacophony of the pit, fascinates by its dual nature—both as a product of the mixture of practices and instruments that make up the apparatus of the market, but also as purely numeric symbols that appear to be uncoupled from material reality.

What Mao Dun sees in this spectacle, and brings back to his readers, is an encounter with *information* in its very essence. "A kind of abstract stuff present in the world, disconnected from the situation that it is *about*," the linguist Geoffrey Nunberg calls it.[5] Likewise for Mao Dun, for whom seeing information made it both a thinkable thing and a thing to think with—he would devote much of his output during the 1930s to exploring the significance of its abstractness. At stake in his encounter at the exchange was Mao Dun's realization that people's "fate" was bound up with the arrival of a new era of abstraction, one which in turn called for innovations in literary practice to critically address it. *Seeing Through Abstraction* examines the ways in which writers during China's Republican era (1912–1949) responded to that call: how they came to know information when they saw it, and how such seeing shaped the development of modern literature.

The historical backdrop to the development of new forms of literary knowing and seeing was a rapid expansion of information—its volume, velocity, variety, veracity, and value[6]—that had been underway in China since the late nineteenth century, in large part precipitated by new communications technologies and practices arising in urban centers from the capital of Beijing to port cities such as Shanghai and Tianjin. For example, China's blooming network of telegraph lines, installed alongside train tracks, integrated cities and regions both domestically and internationally:

it grew from 5,030 kilometers in 1884 to 27,750 by 1900 and nearly doubled to 45,000 by the fall of the Qing dynasty in 1911.[7] These electrified wires brought fresh news—latest developments at the imperial court in the capital, the price of silver in Britain, revolution in the Philippines—that was subsequently disseminated through the burgeoning institution of the modern newspaper. As an early scholar of modern communication would dub it in 1934, the modern newspaper, coupled with wires, connected readers to a global "present instance" (*cike xianzai* 此刻現在) by delivering information at the speed of electricity—for the first time in history outpacing the movement of people and material transportation.[8] Other networks further pushed the reach and speed of information's circulation. The telephone, sporadically installed in major cities beginning in the 1890s was consolidated into a national system in the 1920s.[9] A centralized national post joined it.[10] These distributed networks of transmission were supplemented by new forms of mass media, from radio and phonography to film and photography, and, perhaps most prominently, the growth of industrial print culture that brought with it a deluge of books, magazines, and journals in addition to the newspaper.[11] Of course, this era of burgeoning information hardly emerged out of nowhere. New modes of producing and communicating information developed on top of older ones, including a field of woodblock print that had flourished for centuries, along with systems of political communication in the form of traditional court gazettes coupled with an intricate mechanism of centralized imperial administration.[12] But the collective result of this swath of new technologies was an architectonic shift in China's long-standing information order, whereby older institutions and sources of knowledge production became decentered or altogether superseded by new ones.[13]

Looking back from our vantage point today, we can recognize such developments as a part of a modernity global in scope (if not always in reach), propelled by its humming engine formed by industrialism, capitalism, and imperialism. But the explosion of information around the turn of the century posed challenges and opportunities distinct from these related dynamics. For Mao Dun and other writers during the Republican period, the unprecedented compression of time and space effected by information technologies would demand changes in literary expression and even a reckoning of what "literature" was in relation to "information" (terms that will need to be historicized here). The literary encounter with information ultimately formed a kind of extended zone of experimentation. Composed of both familiar and long-overlooked works, this zone offers a unique view into the broader history of information in modern China, for literature and art are uniquely capable of picking up on the psychic and social implications of material change before it is fully articulated in other spheres of life. Indeed, the works discussed here function as "antennae" of the changing information order by reflecting new experiences and perceptions in ways that other genres of information such as a telegram or newspaper could not.[14]

Here I take a cue from Richard Menke, who, in his study of the telegraph's impact on literary realism in Victorian England, observes that "an informatic history of literature also offers a literary history of information."[15] With one key difference in the present study: in the case of Republican China, "literature" and "information" were not stable or well-articulated categories. Instead, they helped shape one another in both surprising and lasting ways, for as writers sought to understand how new forms of and growing access to information shaped both individual and social forms of knowing, there emerged a tightly recursive relation between literature and information whereby each could mediate the other and "know" it. By investigating this historical and formal coupling, *Seeing Through Abstraction* argues that we cannot know modern Chinese literary history without knowing it informatically.

"INFORMATION": KNOWING AND SEEING

One basic premise of this book is that the category of information reveals China's modern literary history in a new light. But what is "information," exactly? Mao Dun's "Sketch of the Stock Exchange" offers some instructive clues: a mobile and morselized "thing" whose meaning or content remains the same even as it passes through different media. But Mao doesn't directly name it in his text, leaving us to infer its importance to the stock market. In this opening example, information appears as both present and absent— prosaic to the point that it can be left unarticulated within the narrative, yet at the very heart of the demonstrative spectacle of modern technologies and practices of communication. In the literary culture of early twentieth-century China, the representation of information alternated between direct and indirect depictions, explicit and implicit invocations. As an object of historical analysis, information in this context presents some significant methodological challenges regarding language and identity. In order to help us "see" information in the chapters that follow, I trace its definition here within three interrelated frames: through, first, a brief reflection of the treatment of *information* as a concept and as a word within the field of information history (which will help clarify my own approach and contribution); second, an examination of the historical formation of an information discourse in modern China, and how this discourse was both connected with and distinct from roughly concurrent developments in the West; and, finally, a consideration of information's specific relation with literature. From atop this trilevel scaffolding, we will be in a position to examine the historical, aesthetic, and comparative stakes of studying modern Chinese literature's encounter with information.

Speaking of Information

Any academic discipline or scholarly subfield operationalizes its key terms through analysis and definition. But from the 1980s to the present, the incipient field of "information history" has devoted an outsized share of its energy toward the challenges of defining and leveraging a term that is as fuzzy as it is central. Information has been assigned a wide range of meanings, spanning the mundane (per the *Oxford English Dictionary*, "knowledge communicated concerning some particular fact, subject, or event; that of which one is apprised or told; intelligence, news") to the technical (as a measurement of uncertainty or entropy) and the philosophical or even cosmological (a "difference which makes a difference").[16] This broad range of definitions demands that any inquiry into information history (including the present one) grapple with questions of its identity and how to study it in contexts outside of our present age of digital computing and big data.

Ann Blair reflects on the problem of definition in her foreword to a recent volume on the long history of literary information in China. Positioning information as an object of direct study, she observes, frequently necessitates choosing between approaching it as a *word* or as a *concept*. Borrowing a dyad of terms from linguistics, she characterizes the choice as one between emic and etic approaches. Originally coined to distinguish between "phonemics" (sounds meaningful within a specific language, an internal system of meaning) and "phonetics" (physical properties of sound in a universal sense, external to and objective of a specific language), for the historian the emic refers to terms that appear directly in source materials, while the etic is an analytical category imposed by the historian from the outside. The latter, in Blair's words, is "applied by current scholars to historical contexts where there was no equivalent term or concept. [Here] the point is not to seek such equivalents in Chinese language and writing [for example] but rather to examine how what we today call information [in English] in a demotic, nontechnical sense was stored, sorted, and retrieved in contexts distant from our own, both geographically and chronologically."[17] Conceiving information as something that is transcultural and transhistorical, the etic argument goes, makes it possible to illuminate historical experiences and conditions of knowledge that otherwise remain unarticulated by historical actors themselves. So equipped, we can study an endless variety of contexts and transformations: the Chinese literary tradition as an evolving set of forms of information management, the feeling of information overload among late Renaissance readers (as Blair has done), the emergence of a "library of public information" amidst the explosion of print in Tokugawa-era Japan, and so on.[18] By doing so, such histories effectively dislodge the cliché that ours is the first age of information: every era is an information age, characterizable by specific practices and media.[19]

Although Blair rightly specifies that information history primarily adopts a nontechnical understanding of its subject, the consolidation of information as an etic category cannot be separated from the rise of information science in the wake of the 1948 publication of "A Mathematical Theory of Communication" by the mathematician and engineer Claude Shannon (1916–2001).[20] In it, Shannon proposed a formula for calculating the amount of information within a message in thermodynamic terms as a form of negative entropy. (For example: coming across a cup of coffee on a table, if the liquid is still hot, its energy is highly differentiated from the surroundings; we thereby gain more information about it: someone must have only recently placed it there. If the coffee is room temperature, we cannot guess as precisely how long it has been there: such entropic cooling thus carries less information.)[21] Shannon originally sought to solve a relatively narrow problem of how to transmit a greater amount of information along a channel without increasing the latter's bandwidth or compromising the fidelity of the communication. But by conceiving of information quantitatively, his formula transformed "something already quite familiar in war, bureaucracy, and everyday life into a concept of science and technology. Information was no longer raw data, military logistics, or phone numbers; it [became] the principle of the universe's intelligibility."[22] In the postwar West, this new science seemingly had something to offer to nearly every discipline of knowledge, including biology, psychology, physics, and linguistics.[23] It has even been adopted in literary studies in order to measure a piece's creativeness by its amount of information, and, more recently, to analyze texts or corpora as sets of observable data.[24] On the whole, the highly abstract nature of information together with its historical uptake across so many disciplines should make us see it not just as one etic term among many, but as the ultimate instantiation of etical thinking.[25]

But we must be wary of the universalist claims of the etic category of information, argues John Durham Peters, for it is "a word which has a history full of inversions and compromises. *Information* is a term that does not like history . . . [yet] is, after all, a word with a history: it is a cultural invention that has come to prominence at a certain point in time, in a specific constellation of interests."[26] In his essay "*Information*: Notes Toward a Critical History," Peters traces its etymology from Latin to its jump to English in the fourteenth century, where it denoted the force that imbues all physical objects or matter with their form; expansion in the eighteenth century, where the rise of empirical science transformed information into a sensory impression on the mind, arriving from the outside world; and modern evolution, where it denotes a bit of knowledge—analogous to the contemporaneous emergence of the "fact"—reified as an entity and which gained prominence thanks to the development of bureaucratic systems and new ways of transmitting it such as the telegraph.[27] This genealogy exposes a conceit regarding the divisibility between etic concepts and emic words, for the former originate in the latter, whose sediments continue to inflect the imagination and leverage of etic universalism from below.

What remains to be addressed is how conceptual and linguistic articulations of information are historically entangled as part of the global advent of modernity. When and how did information (including as an English term) gain etic traction outside of Europe and North America? What role has translation played in demonstrating the supposed universalism of information by way of particular, emic terms? In a footnote to *Empire and Information*, the historian C. A. Bayly touches upon this dynamic in the context of colonial India by laying out his definition of information:

No "information" can, of course, be perceived and ordered unless the observer has conceptual paradigms within which to apprehend it. Our use of the word "information," however, implies observations perceived at a relatively low level of conceptual definition, on the validity of whose claims to truth people from different regions, cultures, and linguistic groups might broadly agree. "Knowledge" implies socially organized and taxonomized information about which such agreement would be less sure. In north Indian languages "information" would be rendered by words such as *khabr* and *suchna*; knowledge by *ilm* or *vidya*, though under some circumstances vidya might mean something more akin to "occult" knowledge, while spiritual knowledge would be represented by *gyana* or *jnan*.[28]

Despite his brief gesture toward emic equivalents of *khabr* and *suchna*, information, for Bayly, is primarily an etic category; he does not pursue further what possible role these local words played within the formation of the colonial "information order" that was co-created by English colonial administrators and Indian subaltern groups. The specific conceptual paradigms by which the latter perceived this order *as such* are thus left unattended in favor of adopting information as a "heuristic device, or a field of investigation, which can be used to probe the organization, values, and limitations of past societies."[29] Nonetheless, Bayly's note calls attention both to the issue of language in historicizing the perception of information outside of Europe (and English) and to the key role of translation in spreading etic categories across national and colonial boundaries. To a degree, any time we work comparatively and across languages, we must work out the specific balance between our (etic) terms of analysis and the language(s) of our historical interlocutors. But the significance of this balance is redoubled when translation is itself a significant part of the story.

With this in mind, I pursue a hybrid strategy for defining information as my object of analysis. While retaining the leverage of a soft and inclusive understanding of information as a transhistorical term, I aim to historicize how it became conceived of and discussed as a universal term through acts of translation. In her influential study of modern Chinese literature, Lydia Liu demonstrates that translation should not be taken for granted as mere equivalence-finding, where one matches words with foreign counterparts; instead, translations are always made within specific historical contexts, frequently at the bidding of authority, and occasionally leading to unintended consequences.[30] If the English term "information" is itself not transparent but one that is instead embedded within particular social, material, and political practices at a given historical moment, it is all the more important to look carefully at its movement across and encounters with other languages and cultures. Paying attention to the complexity of this encounter in early twentieth-century China (a context that was linguistically shaped by the outsized influence of European languages, along with Japanese, due to the spread of imperialism, colonialism, and capitalism) helps reveal the process by which information became synonymous with modernity and prompted newly urgent reflections regarding the changing nature of knowledge.

Articulations of Information in Modern China: From *Xiaoxi* to *Xinxi*

Within the last decade, scholars of Chinese history and culture have begun to address the myriad of roles that information management played in the bureaucratic mechanisms of governance and the formation of social identity and everyday life, from the early unification of the empire under the Qin dynasty (221–207 BCE) through the late imperial era of the Qing (1644–1911).[31] In dialog with adjacent subject fields like the history of the state, political communication, print and book culture, and the history of knowledge, this growing body of work conceives of Chinese culture (broadly speaking) as the outcome of "socially transmitted information," showing how China's "broader culture apparatus . . . has responded to problems of its own scale" vis-à-vis different modes of information management.[32] Along these lines, cultural innovation and continuity are rewritten as forms of information practice (and vice versa, of course). Fast-forwarding to a more recent era, Xiao Liu has highlighted the popularization of information theory (*xinxilun* 信息论) and cybernetics by tracing their influence on the film and literature of the early postsocialist period (1978–1989), a moment when "information"/*xinxi* 信息 had largely come to denote the digital bits of Shannon's mathematical model.[33] Collectively, these studies flank either side of my own focal point, namely, the Republican era (1912–1949), a pivotal three and a half decades during which there developed a set of terms for recognizing information as a reified unit of abstraction. The process by which these terms developed was as complicated as it was uneven, but it ultimately resulted in a "discourse of information" through texts and images featuring a range of new forms and themes. And it is this discourse that distinguishes the modern literature of the early twentieth century from the earlier tradition, where an emic expression of "information" is largely absent.

One influential dimension of this development involved the establishment of translational counterparts between Chinese and Western word-concepts. In English, the two senses of information that we colloquially associate it with today were established by the mid-nineteenth century: information as statistical facts and as an index of communication. Both senses came into view in China by the early twentieth century, in part because of the active conduit that Western missionaries and their Chinese counterparts established for the introduction of new words and ideas. For example, in its former meaning as empirical knowledge in the form of modern facts or numeric figures, information was matched with *tongji* 統計, indicating information of a statistical nature. *Tongji* featured prominently in early missionary newspapers, such as the Chinese name of *East-West Examiner and Monthly Recorder* (*Dongxiyang kao meiyue tongji zhuan* 東西洋考每月統計傳), established by the German missionary Karl Gützlaff (1803–1851) and published first in 1833–1834 and again in 1837–1838. Illustrating information's importance as a front for transcultural exchange and even geopolitical struggle, in its second run, the *East-West Examiner* served as the publication arm of the recently formed Victorian group, the Society for the Diffusion of Useful Knowledge, a number of whose members were missionaries and merchants in China working to transmit "Western scientific, technological, and cultural information to the Chinese in the hope that it would impress them sufficiently with the achievements of the West to induce them to open more positive and productive exchanges with the foreign 'barbarians.'"[34]

By the early twentieth century, the spread of surveys as a technology for measuring social aggregates turned statistical data and its visualization into a widely adopted lens for looking at the nation. Tong Lam shows how this development ushered in a new era of the "fact" and factored into the broader epistemological changes at the turn of the twentieth century as intellectuals abandoned traditional Confucian knowledge in favor of modern—that is, "scientific" and "democratic"—forms of knowledge production. The "fact" became recognizable as a bit of empirical knowledge that was both socially mobile (circulating, for example, in the form of the widely quoted stock figure of China's population as four hundred million) and mobilizable, too, as evidence or rationale in support of an argument, serving ultimately as a new medium for understanding society and modern subjectivity.[35] As I show in the first chapter, during the 1920s this medium was extended to remake another medium, literature, as a range of writers reenvisioned literary texts as an important source for collecting social, psychological, and even aesthetic information.

While there is no firmly singular Chinese counterpart for the English meaning of information as the object of communication, the term *xiaoxi* 消息 comes closest. *Xiaoxi* is one of the innumerable, easily overlooked terms caught in the undertow of the sea change of language in modern China. Unlike prominent whitecaps such as *wenming* 文明 ("civilization") and *kexue* 科學 ("science") or the medium-sized terms bubbling along the surface like *qunzhong* 群眾 ("crowds") and *dazhong* 大眾 ("masses"),[36] *xiaoxi* is hardly weightier than the token bit of knowledge that it denotes. And to be sure, *xiaoxi* was not a purely modern coinage invented for the purpose of translating "information" into Chinese—for instance, one finds *xiaoxi* circulating as messages in late Ming novels such as *The Plum in the Golden Vase* (*Jin Ping Mei* 金瓶梅, c. 1610).[37] But in the wake of the communications revolution, *xiaoxi* became an object of a more sustained interest, inspiring, for example, an entire novel devoted to the social life of information amidst a remote village located far from China's urban centers and a short story about how city elites manipulation news coverage to shape public opinion (both by the writer Shen Congwen, more conventionally known for his lyrically ethnographic descriptions of western Hunan), as I examine in chapter 4. In the literary readings that follow, my approach toward information is hardly limited to discourse analysis of this emic term: many of the works I read describe information without explicitly naming it at all, like in Mao's "sketch" or in the case of a curious poem on the experience of gazing upon a data table (chapter 1). But insofar as *xiaoxi* forms a significant part of the backdrop against which information became a sensible and contestable entity, the term deserves special attention here as one of the primary, visible vectors for the growth of interest in information at the turn of the twentieth century.

Xiaoxi marks the transmission of minor knowledge. Its contents are ephemeral (useful or valuable for a limited period), contextually bound, and oftentimes actionable. Its social circulation is much more visible in everyday life than deeper forms of knowledge such as bodily skill, wisdom, or learning. Often informal and personal in nature—gossip counts—*xiaoxi* is the communicational lifeblood of a community. The scale of this community expanded radically in the late nineteenth century with the arrival of new media to China, when *xiaoxi* definitively surpassed its oral connotations by naming the news sent over telegraph wires. By the 1880s *xiaoxi* began appearing as the title of a new genre of the modern newspaper as special morsels of international news that had been acquired from the news wires. Whether it moves from person to person or over a telegraph or postal network, *xiaoxi* indexes a transmission (*chuan* 傳—a verb that is closely associated with *xiaoxi*). Like a snapshot that captures a moment in time, the invocation of *xiaoxi* makes communication itself visible.

When separated into its two antonymous components, the compound reveals something of a cosmological view of communication: *xiao* 消 means "decay," while *xi* 息 means "to flourish" or "growth." Etymologically, one of its earliest appearances is in the hexagram descriptions of the abstruse Zhou dynasty divination book, the *Classic of Changes* 易經, as in the line "The superior man takes heed of the alternation of *decrease* [*xiao*] and *increase* [*xi*], fullness and emptiness; for it is the course of heaven" 君子尚消息盈虛，天行也.[38] Like its more famous antonymous cousin *yin/yang* 陰陽, the compound of *xiaoxi* in its earliest sense thus refers to the principle of opposing forces that in tandem form a cycle of fortune that fluctuates without end. This binary cycle of *xiao/xi* inspires the compound's eventual accumulation of another layer of meaning when it came to denote a bit of transmitted news or knowledge around the dissolution of the Han dynasty (220 CE).[39] The first modern dictionary of Chinese, the *Ciyuan* 辭源 (literally, the "source of words"), shares this genealogy:

> *Xiaoxi*: A verbal message (*yinxin* 音信). The *History of the Three Kingdoms* 三國志 records that Zhuge Ke (202–253 CE) laid siege to the city of Hefei. One of the city's remaining soldiers, Liu Zheng, escaped to transmit a message, but he was captured by bandits. In the *Book of Jin* 晉書 it is written, "Lu Ji mused to his dog, 'There have been no letters from home. Is it possible for you to take a letter there, and bring some *xiaoxi* back?'" Among human affairs there is only auspicious or evil, good or bad, thus an oral message was called *xiaoxi*.[40]

Accordingly, from the third century on, *xiaoxi* indexed communication between parties, an update from one to the other about their status that boils down to a yes/no or good/bad indication.

Today *xiaoxi* still primarily denotes personal news, but its role as a translation of "information" has largely been supplanted by the related term *xinxi* 信息—a compound indirectly deriving from *xiaoxi* that gained contemporary currency with the introduction of information science since the 1950s.[41] A reader literate in modern Chinese knows that *xiaoxi* denotes an update in a situation and may wonder how my study delineates "news" from "information" in *xiaoxi*—are the chapters that follow in fact more about "news" instead of "information" per se? The two are closely related materially and conceptually, but distinct. Here I find clarifying the work of the communications critic Xie Liuyi 謝六逸 (1898–1945), whose career as a scholar straddling the emergence of modern literature and journalism studies led him to reflect extensively about the entity of information itself. Xie saw "news" as a distinct practice of reportage that could be traced back at least as far as the Tang and Song dynasties.[42] Following his genealogy, in the nineteenth century, in the wake of the publication of Adam Morrison's *Canton Register* in Guangdong in 1827, and influenced by the translation of "news" as *shinbun* 新聞 and "newspaper" as *shinbunshi* 新聞紙 in late Tokugawa Japan (ca. 1853–1867), the Chinese word *xinwen* came to correspond with the Western meaning of news. Crucially, this development was inseparable from the modern medium of the newspaper. This is the key difference: in contrast to news/*xinwen*, *xiaoxi* is not limited to what is printed for broad consumption. This much Xie made clear in a 1942 article on different kinds of correspondence networks, in which he reflects upon the historical emergence of information as a peculiar entity. The passage is worth quoting at some length thanks to the range of historical contexts in which Xie judges *xiaoxi* to have obtained:

> Primitive people knew to use drums, fire beacons, gestures, and paintings as methods of transmitting *xiaoxi*. In more recent times the consciousness of communication passed from the Orient to Europe. In 200 BCE, when the Egyptian empire was established, in the coffee shops of Cairo and the market of Baghdad there were already "couriers" [*chuanxinzhe* 傳信者] specializing in the profession of transmitting *xiaoxi*. Later, in medieval Europe there flourished a sort of "news communication," where gentry and the rich

resided at their own fiefs or villas, and hired people to [transmit] letters and reports of *xiaoxi* from the cities; afterward, because of increasing demand, an individual could hire several people, and when the master received a "letter" [*tongxin* 通信], he had manuscript copies [*chuanchao* 傳抄] made and sent out, and from this gradually developed a sort of communications industry. At this time there also steadily developed in the church such an industry for the sake of proselytizing [*chuanjiao* 傳教], also employing communication, whereupon priests also became involved in communications work.[43]

This communications field would further expand in the modern industrial era thanks to the invention of technologies such as the steam engine, telegraph, linotype, airplane, and radio (along with "all literary works, paintings and photographs, critical writings, and specific reports").[44] We need not dwell on the accuracy of Xie's account. Rather, what is important to recognize is his usage of *xiaoxi* as clearly contrastive with news: *xiaoxi* is what could be transmitted via various media (as opposed to one medium, the printed newspaper). Crucially, Xie's explication shows that *xiaoxi* covers more than simply gossip or tidbits of news and can carry value as a commodity or as the lifeblood of bureaucratic mechanisms. Writing for the retrenched literary institution in the wartime hinterland of the early 1940s, Xie was particularly attuned to the cultural and strategic importance of information flows and the need for apparatuses of what he termed "mutual spiritual communication" (*jingshen jiaotong* 精神交通) between authors and readers who had previously worked in proximity to one another in Shanghai but were now scattered across Guiyang, Guiling, Chongqing, and Kunming.[45] Overall his discussion is reflective of a growing general interest in and urgency toward the entity of information among writers during the Republican era.

The information discourse that can be glimpsed through the term *xiaoxi* was not limited to changes in language and writing but extended to visual culture as well, where information surfaced as an abstract object of graphic or pictorial representation. Here two representative examples demonstrate the sustained interest in *xiaoxi* and its political stakes as a visible trace of the communications and social infrastructures through which it moves. In the first image (figure 0.1), an illustration from China's leading newspaper, *Shenbao*, the subject is the transmission of secret

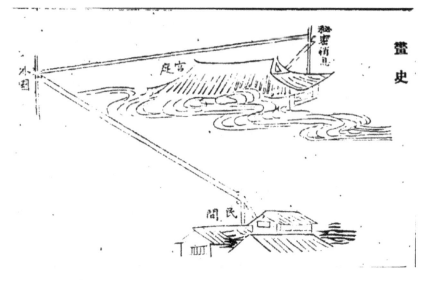

FIGURE 0.1 Movement of "secret information" (*mimi xiaoxi* 秘密消息) from the imperial court to the public via the telegraph. From *Shenbao*, October 1907

xiaoxi (*mimi xiaoxi* 秘密消息) and the role of foreign technology in mediating news from the court palace at the top of the register to the public (*minjian* 民間) located below.[46] Rather than depict an actual event or a specific incident, the image offers a simple scheme of information flow, all laid out on an ethereally non-Euclidean space. By capturing the movement of *xiaoxi* across a basic network, it figures the *process* of communication (rather than an instance of it) in the attempt to illuminate an information order composed of infrastructures (telegraphy), institutions (the Qing Court, foreign newspapers), and groups (rulers, the Chinese public, foreigners).

In contrast to this schematic visualization of *xiaoxi* in figure 0.1, the realism of the woodcut representation of *xiaoxi* in figure 0.2 captures information as a social phenomenon. One of the most vibrant art forms in the 1930s, woodcut prints commonly thematized information as part of their broader reflection on modern propaganda (itself a key form of information management) and its increasing dominion over cultural production (see chapter 3). In this instance, one peasant whispers into the ear of another, exuding a strongly oral quality that is further augmented by the background figures chatting animatedly in the village lane. Like with the first image, we can only speculate about the content of the message transmitted before

FIGURE 0.2 *A Bit of News* (alternative title: *Xiaoxi*), woodcut print by Ge Yuan. From *Zhongguo banhua ji* (Shanghai: Chenguang chuban gongsi, 1948), 94

us. The historical rise of woodcut art was closely bound up with leftist politics and the propagation of political consciousness, and the artist, Ge Kejian 葛克俭 (1923–2020), was an avowed Communist. Given the date of 1948—Communist forces were making immense territorial gains over the Nationalists in the civil war raging in the northeast—this image likely suggests peasants' delighted anticipation of the arrival of People's Liberation Army. But the question of the contents of the whispered message is quite beside the point. Indeed, by not explicitly expressing the message itself, the picture shifts our attention from the ephemerality of the moment to the nature of information "itself" and its social function.

By pictorially representing *xiaoxi*—as well as naming it directly in their titles—both figures 0.1 and 0.2 reify the abstract entity of information. As a thing, information is here embedded in two spaces at once. On the one hand, there is the implied meaning within the diegetic space of the image: a bit of specific knowledge known to the parties that share it, but not to the viewer standing outside the frame. On the other hand, precisely because we are not privy to its content, the exchanged token of information indexes something else—the larger social systems and communications infrastructures within which such tokens move—that might be partially visible, imperceptible to, or entirely occluded from the individuals who are shown circulating it. As such, insofar as they purport to depict information head on, these images reflect both the abstraction of information and the abstraction of infrastructures and social systems that generate information in the first place.

Figures 0.1 and 0.2 serve as important reminders that the proliferation of the modern information discourse extended well beyond literature to include a variety of accompanying images expressing or picturing information. In addition to literature and graphic art, the discourse of information emerged through other media, as well. A comprehensive account of the breadth of this discourse would need to extend to film, photography, and painting. While it is my hope that the present study will also help open new avenues for exploring the history of information in Chinese cinema and abstract modernist art, I here cleave primarily to literary articulations, with several significant forays into the pictorial and graphic representation of information. In part this is due to the close entanglement between text and image in modern print culture. In many instances images appeared directly alongside literature in contemporary print culture, as, for example, the great number of modern data visualizations—tables, graphs, diagrams—that proliferated in literary journals, where they vernacularized tenets of Western science such as measurability and commensuration while also shaping ideas of literary creation and reading. Printed texts and images also constitute a relatively durable archive that records and remediates more ephemeral media like telegrams or the radio.[47]

This is, then, a study of how literature came to know information. Such knowing involved naming, too. And wherever it shows up—whether as *xiaoxi*, *xinxi*, *qingbao*, or otherwise—the object of information captures a moment of communication in the act. Articulation of information *as such* makes an otherwise ephemeral event or relationality recordable and open to inspection. In other words, information lifts out the object of transmission (a piece of knowledge) from its original context and tokenizes it into an abstracted, reified "stuff." To refer to "information" is thus to make a representation of a representation. Information is inherently nonmimetic because it does not exist in the physical world. Rather, it is in the eye of the beholder, an abstract or virtual entity that is created through the very practices of managing it.[48] And, crucially, the conjuration of information in modern Chinese literature posed more than the introduction of a new object of knowledge and representation at the turn of the century. It also contributed to the emergence of a new perceptional apparatus in its own right: a mode of "seeing through abstraction." If seeing is one means of knowing, then this apparatus represents nothing short of an epistemological revolution.

After first detailing different attempts to see through abstraction in the main chapters, I will have more to say about the specifics of this apparatus in the conclusion. For now, my adoption of visuality as my primary frame for this literary history deserves a few further words of explanation. Visuality may seem like an odd choice given *xiaoxi*'s close genealogical association with oral exchange. Already in evidence in figure 0.2 and Mao Dun's "Sketch of the Exchange," an interest in conversation—along with related phenomena like sound waves, noise, and hearing—underlies many of experiments discussed here. But the overlap between vision and epistemology (seeing as a form of knowing, insight versus blindness, and so forth) made visual perception an especially vital site for modern Chinese literature's investigation of information and its impact on knowledge. Indeed, a trope of seeing forms of abstraction and information runs through all four chapters, in effect constituting a kind of "literary visuality" where texts "not only talk about [an] observer, but actually stage his or her acts of seeing."[49] Abstraction, I thus argue, served as a kind of figural lens or medium through which the world could be apprehended in fresh ways. Like the many visual technologies newly proliferating in the nineteenth and early twentieth centuries such as microscopy, photography, and film, information expanded the perceived world beyond the limitations of the individual subject's naked eye.[50] If the inventions of microscope and camera revealed some fragment of the physical world that the naked eye could not physiologically register, what the figurative lens of information made newly available was a kind of totalizing, abstracting view of something at scale.

To a degree, the mold for this lens was shaped by traditional Chinese aesthetics, which viewed the central function of literary narrative and visual art to be the expression of something's inner essence. As conceived, such an essence is an idealized abstraction that could be only indirectly rendered through mimetic details of its outer appearance.[51] The qualities of brushstrokes in a painting or the ups and downs of a character in the plot of a novel reveal the universe's moral order or a philosophical principle. The modern lens of information is similarly sublime, but its telos is this-worldly rather than cosmological. Instantiations of information—the observable detail—add up to a different sort of abstract construct: a population, an infrastructure, or some society-wide process such as a rumor's spread or a speculation scheme at the stock market. Seen partly as the basis for successfully modernizing society, these constructs were the characteristic subjects of new literature. At the same time, in considering these abstractions, modern literature also frequently and self-referentially turned toward the material technologies and practices of abstraction itself.

The reshaping of visuality effected by the modern discourse of information inspires my title, Seeing Through Abstraction. "Seeing through" in both senses of the phrase: on the one hand, abstraction reveals (or refracts) the world in new ways, as I have illustrated, and thus serves as a modality for formal experimentation in text and image. This sense of seeing is meant quite literally. In addition to this lens-like aspect, I also mean "seeing through" in the figurative sense of penetrating a façade or getting to the bottom of something. Here it captures writers' skepticism toward or even unmasking of this informatic lens and its epistemic claims. By this token, literature and art attempted to "see through" modern abstraction by probing the limitations of its promises of transcendence and totalizing control.

The Information Order and the Making of Modern Literature

In 1928 the enduring author and arbiter of China's modern literary scene Lu Xun 魯迅 (1881–1936) observed in a letter: "It is true that all literature and art is propaganda, but definitely not all propaganda is literature and art; it's just like saying that all flowers have color (including white as a color), but not all colors are flowers. The reason that revolutions use literature and art in addition to slogans, placards, reports, telegrams, textbooks, and so on is because literature and art is literature and art."[52] Lu Xun invokes an idea of literature's aesthetic value that separates it from the purely utilitarian realm of propaganda, a field of technical knowledge that was emerging as a key vector of information discourse in modern China (see chapter 3). But his division equally works to draw a line between literature and information: any literary work is, or contains, information about the world that it builds (whether that world accords with our own is another matter). But not all information is literary: clearly, we don't read a phone book or a menu with the same expectations that we might a novel or poem.

It does not take too big of a conceptual leap to recognize literature as a source and form of textual information (a reality that is plain to anyone who has visited a library or used a search engine to find a passage in a novel), though doing so also brings with it a series of interrelated shifts in emphasis, from literature's narrative to its "stuff-ness" as a work, from the individual experiences of absorptive reading to the forms of information management that have accompanied these experiences from the very beginning: the collection, categorization, and reproduction of texts.[53] But a work of literature is in excess of the information that it contains. This excess leads to questions of identity: When and where is literature something more than information, and what is contained in this *more*? Lu Xun's division between literature and propaganda harbors a set of ideological and epistemological positions: that literature's aesthetic qualities cannot be squared with the purely utilitarian drive of propaganda (a similar distinction can be made between literature or art and the commodity). Here again, the same might be said of the opposition between literature and information—that literature is blood to information's water: thicker, more vital, less ephemeral.

The inherent tension between literature and other genres of information is already manifest in one of China's earliest works of self-avowedly modern or "new" fiction (*xin xiaoshuo* 新小說), *A Future Record of New China*

(*Xin Zhongguo weilai ji* 新中國未來記, 1902), by Liang Qichao 梁啟超 (1873–1929). The body of the novel is presented through a lecture series by one Master Kong, an esteemed reformist and direct descendent of Confucius whose chronicle of China's rise over the previous sixty years imparts the story with a "future anterior" perspective to chart the path by which China will have been successfully modernized.[54] Liang's novel renders this future attainable by emphasizing how the story is itself very much a product of its present—and rapidly transforming—information order. The opening details how, rather than offering a direct reproduction of the words of Mr. Kong's speech, the narrative situates itself as the output of a chain of mediations. To begin with, the lecture itself is given in front of a mass audience numbering twenty thousand. The speech is concurrently transcribed by a stenographer, then hastily transmitted by telegraph to the Japanese port city Yokohama (*The wiring fee is indeed huge*, notes the narrator), where the text is subsequently printed in Liang's journal, *New Fiction* (*Xin xiaoshuo* 新小說)—the physical copy of which the original "we" of Liang's intended audience would hold before it. These details present a remarkable and unprecedented moment in the history of Chinese literature: for the first time, a narrative presents itself *as a piece of information*, one message among the many that circulate amid the rapidly transforming landscape of new communications technologies and practices. But although (or because) it is imagined as a technological achievement, such a narrative framing results in a literary failure. The amalgamated style of the text, described self-deprecatingly by Liang as "like a novel, but not a novel, like an unofficial history, but not an unofficial history, like a treatise, but not a treatise . . . [with] many instances of legal regulations, lecture theses, etc., that are lengthy and tedious and completely lacking in appeal,"[55] appears as an effect of this technologized flow of communication, by which different genres and styles are flattened into the homogenized "stuff" of information. The work ultimately falls short of the popular novels of its day, let alone the lofty powers that Liang attributed to "new fiction."[56] It is no surprise, then, that Liang abandoned the project after its serial publication of five chapters, leaving a fragment that today is occasionally mentioned but seldom read.

Liang's broader idealization of literature's role in shaping the reader's ideology would heavily influence a following generation of authors who believed that the key to modernizing the nation and saving it from dissipation lay in the invention of a "New Culture" composed of new literary styles and forms. But if his novelistic experiment left little mark on cultural history, its failure nonetheless reveals a crisis of literary identity that New Culture writers and critics such as Lu Xun and Mao Dun would face head on in the coming decades: Could literature be rendered *as* information and yet remain literary? How could literature "know" the information order and reveal something of its social importance and individual impact? Most important, how was literary writing—including genres of prose fiction and new, free-verse poetry—itself constitutive of an information order? Exploring the zone where literature and information intersect, writers, critics, scholars, and artists variously worked out questions of information's potentially literary qualities (and vice versa). Such questions were crucial to the making of modern literature itself, a category that in the 1920s and 1930s was still very much in formation, as Chinese writers negotiated between longstanding and newly imported ideas about the boundaries, value, and purpose of literary writing.[57] The task of literary self-fashioning, meanwhile, bore the hefty responsibility of transforming Chinese society, for, as Marston Anderson observes, modern literature was a conduit for modernization at large, and "offered a necessary grid through which to view the vast quantity of new ideas and new information that suddenly became available when the doors to the West were opened."[58]

Corresponding to the dual definition of information as both medium and object of communication, the following case studies present two types of convergences between literature, on the one hand, and forms of data or communication, on the other. On one side are instances where writers sought to merge literature with nonliterary forms of information management such as account books or data tables, thereby precipitating new modes of creative literary composition. On the other side were those skeptics intent on probing the limits of incorporating information into literature and even making self-conscious attempts to use literary form to expose or intervene in the contemporary information order. This body of information-conscious work collectively attempts to "see through" modern abstraction. And in both cases, the relationship between information and literature was especially relevant to the development of realism: Did seeing through abstraction provide new ways of constructing the real—or should literary realism be directly opposed to the disembodying qualities of information? Whatever one's response, the encounter with information left an indelible mark on modern Chinese writing.

Rather than provide an exhaustive account of this encounter, the following chapters examine more sustained experiments with "seeing through" abstraction through the lens of information. Although the cases I discuss follow a loosely chronological order, my account is episodic instead of linear. Chapter 1 opens with two commonplace forms of information visualization, the table (*biao* 表) and the diagram (*tu* 圖), which proliferated across New Culture print media, including numerous journals devoted to literature and culture. Mundane as these modest graphics may be, they constitute an important vernacular form of scientific modernism that familiarized abstract statistical information and data to a broad audience. Intriguingly, these graphics also inspired new modes of reading and producing knowledge about literature and language, as critics used *biao* and *tu* to see through textual corpora and thus make visible formal or narrative patterns that otherwise remained out of the reader's view. The chapter explores three distinct areas of this zone of experimentation. The first introduces Liang Qichao's now-forgotten project of "historical statistics," an attempt to data mine China's massive historiographical tradition to expose its statistical unconsciousness. The second part turns to a group of young psychologists who, inspired by the power of the data table to generate and organize empirical knowledge, contributed to the analysis of the psychologized and interiorized subject of the May Fourth individual. To do so, they turned to both traditional and contemporary literature as a treasure trove of psychological facts, inventing what I call a form of "enumerative survey" of texts. The chapter ends with the story of "diagrammatic criticism," developed by leftist critics in the 1930s to abstract literary narrative into basic formal elements visualizable in diagram form. Collectively, these experiments with *tu* and *biao* foregrounded literature's informatic dimension in an unprecedented way, making it appear that data had always been part and parcel of China's literary tradition. At the same time, the information visualizations produced in this vein were also recognized as objects of beauty in their own right, capable of further inspiring small moments of literary play—a kind of recursive process whereby information drawn from literature was used to generate new literature.

Chapter 2 details a germinal moment in the intersection between literary experimentation and visuality in modern China by revisiting literary realism as developed by its most influential advocate, Mao Dun. I read a set of his 1930s fiction and criticism that deals with markets and finance capitalism. What greatly interested Mao Dun about the latter was its essential dependence upon forms of symbolic abstraction, whereby capital is increasingly converted into economic figures and circulated through modern media, including the telegraph and the financial section of the newspaper. Mao Dun recognized that finance capital, and in particular the game of speculation, is inextricable from the rise of information as a key commodity in its own right. Financial capitalism's impact on the information order was essential for the elite industrialists and financiers populating Shanghai's stock exchanges, but to Mao Dun, it was furthermore instructive for understanding changes in the epistemology of the modern individual at large. I argue that we read this imagined individual, as Mao Dun interpolates them, as a kind of modern *Homo informaticus* who, like Marshall McLuhan's figure of the "information-gatherer,"[59] explicitly relies on hunting, gathering, and cooking information management for survival. To this end, I read Mao Dun's practice of literary realism as a direct attempt to teach readers how to make sense of financial statistics and news by his effort to unmask economic abstraction as the grounds for the exploitative leverage of advanced capitalism. Mao Dun's didactic project, I show, revolves around experimentation assimilating the information-rich form of account book into realist narrative, dramatizing the encounter between the ledger and fiction as one between capitalist and revolutionary forms of knowledge production.

Chapter 3 is devoted to the visualization of broadcast information in the leftist literature and art of the 1930s. A crucial backdrop to this practice is the rise of modern propaganda science during the Nanjing Decade (1927–1937), a period during which the Nationalists' consolidation of governance over a reunified China quickly came to include experimentation with new techniques of social mobilization and propaganda war. Even more than statistics or financial figures, propaganda foregrounds the information order and its stakes for individual and societal knowledge during the modern period. Like the discourse of information of which it forms a central pillar, propaganda science appears as medium-neutral. As an overarching suite of techniques for managing information for the masses, it serves as a stand-in for all broadcast technologies. Technologized and politically agnostic, propaganda science appears in manuals, literature, and woodcut art of the Nanjing Decade as a matter of broadcast-signal engineering, whereby the propagandist reaches their target with messaging by successfully channeling it through various fields of noise in the form of counterpropaganda or atmospheric impedance. I show how this conception of propaganda undergirds the modernist fiction of Ding Ling 丁玲 (1904–1986) after her turn to writing politically inflected mass fiction and, furthermore, how her evocation of this abstract signal is echoed within the field of avant-garde woodcut art. Here text and image alike make the propaganda apparatus and its abstract field of signals/countersignals sensible by foregrounding how information moves through physical and social space. By doing so, these works do not merely thematize propaganda; they also reflect on the changing dispensation of their own media ecology and its implications for a revolutionary intervention into the information order. If, at the outset of the Nanjing Decade, Lu Xun could draw a distinction between literature and art, on the one hand, and propaganda as a central genre of information, by the end of the 1930s this division became neither politically nor aesthetically tenable within the institution of modern literature: literature and art were reconceived as forms of politicized information work like any other. This reduction would prove to be a lasting one with the pervasive dispensation of propaganda in Maoist China after 1949.

While propaganda and the interpellation of politically charged mass society through broadcast media was becoming an inevitability in China during the Nanjing Decade and into the fraught conditions of Japanese territorial encroachment at the end of the 1930s, this trend did not go entirely uncontested. Chapter 4 turns to the case of Ding Ling's close friend Shen Congwen 沈從文 (1902–1988) as a uniquely critical response of one individual to the emergent propaganda era. More than any other author, Shen documented the information order of his day, in particular through his last—and unfinished—major creative literary project, *Long River* (*Changhe* 長河, 1945). What makes Shen relevant here—and has been overlooked in studies of his work—is his critical interest in *xiaoxi* and the social life of information (including propaganda) in the countryside, far from China's urban centers. Per his informatic view of society, where Ding Ling sees masses, Shen sees networks, intricately connected together through delicate threads of individual communication and miscommunication. In his adoption of network-inspired narrative structures to investigate social connectivity, Shen problematizes the propagandist's fantasy of direct transmission to the masses via broadcast media (that is, the hypodermic needle model of political messaging) and instead highlights how the local circulation of *xiaoxi* mediates all social understanding, above all that of propaganda from outside the community.

In the book's conclusion I delve further into the perceptual mode that is entailed by seeing through abstraction. I also provide in an appendix translations of three key literary pieces—Mao Dun's "Sketch of the Stock Exchange" and his essay "Old Accounts," along with Shen Congwen's short story "Unemployed"—which deserve further attention, in no small part because they demonstrate the degree to which some of the best-known figures of the modern Chinese literary canon were concerned with the changing information order of their day.

In closing, it should be noted that negotiations of the literature/information divide in modern China paralleled concurrent developments elsewhere in the world. Perhaps the clearest example comes to us from Walter Benjamin (1892–1940), who in his well-known essay "The Storyteller" (1937) lays out an essential opposition between the psychological depth of literary art and, on the other hand, the ephemerality and superficiality of information or, in German, *Mitteilung* (he had in mind the newspaper). Focusing on the writer Nikolai Leskov (1831–1895), Benjamin laments the decline of storyteller's wisdom and "good counsel" to their audience in the face of a glut of information:

> If the art of storytelling has become rare, the dissemination of information has played a decisive role in creating this situation. Every morning, news reaches us from around the globe. And yet we lack remarkable stories. This is due to the fact that no incident any longer reaches us not already permeated with explanations. In other words: almost nothing occurs to the story's benefit anymore; instead it all serves information. In fact, at least half of the art of storytelling consists in keeping one's tale free of explanations. Leskov was a master at this (think of stories like "The Deception" or "The White Eagle"). Extraordinary and miraculous events are recounted with great precision, but the psychological context is not forced on the reader. He is left the freedom to interpret the situation as he understands it, and the story thus acquires a breadth that information lacks. . . . Information is valuable only for the moment in which it is new. It lives only in that moment. It must be completely subject to it and explain itself immediately without losing any time. A story is different: it does not use itself up. It preserves its inherent power, which it can then deploy even after a long period of time.[60]

Of course, Benjamin's framework cannot be tidily transposed to the context of Republican China. But the terms by which he envisioned the fate of the polysemic literary narrative amid the advent of a modern information age would have at least been legible to writers such as Lu Xun and Shen Congwen, who shared similar concerns as Benjamin. Along similar lines, the engagement with genres of information by authors like Liang Qichao and Mao Dun certainly resonates with contemporaneous experiments abroad, including Rudyard Kipling's survey of the information order of British-ruled India in *Kim* (1901), the Japanese writer Kataoka Teppei's investigation into the materiality of telecommunications infrastructures in his 1930 short story, "The Linesmen," and Jamaican creole poet Louise Bennett (1919–2006) and her sustained play with the local uptake of global events in her "metanews" poetry during the 1940s.[61] This transnational constellation of individuals who respectively engaged with different facets of information attests to an overarching (though as yet perhaps underappreciated) dimension of modernism, one both global in its reach and local in its stakes when it came to the definition and function of literature vis-à-vis information.

Acknowledging this transnational scope lets us see that Chinese literature was by no means late to arrive at this modern moment. For although they may have been guilty of embracing nineteenth-century Western literary modes such as realism as current (or at least as a necessary stage according to the logic of an evolutionary ladder of progression), by grappling with the modern information order, Chinese writers and artists found themselves at the front of a global present that is still unfolding into today. As vital as the episodes explored here are for expanding our comparative perspective of the cultural history of information, they are perhaps all the more relevant for how they call out to our conditions in the twenty-first century, where the rise of digital media has so greatly expanded apparatuses of surveillance, misinformation, and permanent mobilization that the strangeness of modern abstraction has become second nature.

Chapter One

"DISTANT READING" AND THE PULL OF LITERARY ABSTRACTION IN NEW CULTURE CHINA

The role of information graphics in the changing visual culture of early twentieth-century China is a history that awaits telling. Tables, graphs, charts, diagrams—forms that proliferated so widely among the period's print culture as to appear banal—are today all too easily overlooked as natural features of the graphic landscape, mere outcroppings against a background of spreading interest in empiricism and the social sciences.[1] Upon the initial appearance of information graphics, however, their operation and significance were not taken as entirely self-evident, prompting introduction and explanation.[2] What happens if, in revisiting the periodicals and books of this period, we defamiliarize ourselves with such visualizations in order to encounter anew the strangeness of their essential hybridity—where text intersects with image, science with art, sensual perception with intellectual abstraction? Do such visualizations index new ways of seeing and knowing? How was their adoption in China influenced by older, established forms of visualization such as *tu* 圖 ("diagrams" or "visual schemes" constituting "templates for action")[3] and *biao* 表 ("tables" or even "data frames" organizing sets of observations)? Overall, what did such visualizations contribute to the broader project of pursuing modernity, especially under the guise of the expanding promotion of a New Culture and its democratic and scientific ideals?

The complexity of the introduction of information graphics into China is demonstrated in a little-remembered project on "historical statistics"

省别	前汉		后汉		汉		唐		北宋		南宋		宋		明	
	人数	%	人数	%	人数	%	人数	%	人数	%	人数	%	人数	%	人数	%
陕西	22	10.58	73	15.91	95	14.96	248	21.60	63	4.31	6	0.99	69	3.34	80	4.51
直隶	21	10.10	28	6.12	49	7.36	212	18.48	212	14.51	7	1.16	219	10.60	128	7.22
山西	10	4.92	16	3.50	26	3.91	176	15.33	141	9.65	17	2.81	158	7.65	56	3.16
河南	39	18.75	170	37.20	209	31.43	203	17.68	324	23.80	37	6.12	361	17.58	123	6.94
山东	61	29.33	57	12.47	118	17.75	89	7.83	156	10.68	13	2.15	169	8.17	93	5.25
江苏	23	11.06	12	2.84	36	5.41	76	6.62	97	6.63	49	8.20	146	7.07	241	13.61
浙江	2	0.96	14	2.99	16	2.40	32	2.78	84	8.74	136	22.50	220	10.65	288	14.51
湖北	7	3.36	11	2.48	18	2.70	23	2.00	19	1.30	14	2.32	33	1.60	76	4.29
四川	4	1.92	26	5.68	30	4.51	9	0.78	93	6.36	71	11.75	164	7.94	57	3.21
安徽	3	1.44	24	5.25	27	2.06	19	1.65	53	3.62	38	6.29	91	4.40	199	11.24
江西	1	0.49	2	0.42	3	0.45	2	0.17	81	5.54	83	13.40	164	7.94	204	11.52
湖南	0	0	2	0.42	2	0.30	2	0.17	12	0.82	12	1.98	24	1.16	27	1.52
福建	0	0	1	0.21	1	0.15	0	0	95	6.50	88	14.60	183	8.80	92	5.19
广东	0	0	0	0	0	0	3	0.26	3	0.20	4	0.66	7	0.33	50	2.82
广西	0	0	1	0.21	1	0.51	0	0	2	0.13	6	0.99	8	0.38	13	0.73
贵州	0	0	0	0	0	0	1	0.08	0	0	0	0	0	0	10	0.56
云南	0	0	0	0	0	0	0	0	0	0	0	0	0	0	14	0.79
甘肃	10	4.92	17	3.72	27	4.06	50	4.35	19	1.30	23	3.89	42	2.03	23	1.29
奉天(汉人)	0	0	0	0	0	0	3	0.26	0	0	0	0	0	0	0	0
内蒙古(汉人)	3	1.44	1	0.21	4	0.60	0	0	0	0	0	0	0	0	0	0
外族	2	0.96	1	0.21	3	0.45	40	3.48	7	0.61	0	0	7	0.34	14	0.79
总数	208		457		665		1,149		1,461		604		2,065		1,771	

FIGURE 1.1 Demonstration of historical statistics with a table of the geographic distribution of historical personages by Liang Qichao and Ding Wenjiang. Republished in *Liang Qichao quanji*, ed. Yang Gang and Wang Xiangyi (Beijing: Beijing chubanshe, 1999), 4,045–50

(*lishi tongjixue* 歷史統計學) introduced by Liang Qichao in a 1922 speech at Southeastern University.[4] With this method, Liang proposed to advance China's well-established tradition of historiographic research by treating its extensive record as a source of data that, once extracted, could be explored using statistics. To illustrate his method's promise, Liang, with the help of his Tsinghua University colleague, the geographer Ding Wenjiang 丁文江 (1887–1936), compiled from the lengthy dynastic histories all details of personages' places of birth. The summary of results, organized by province and laid out as a dense table of numerical figures (figure 1.1), charts the *longue durée* rises and declines in China's population—a subject that had preoccupied reformers since the turn of the century and a flashpoint in what Tong Lam characterizes as the period's biopolitical "enumerative imaginary."[5] For

Liang, the included table was not merely a visual enticement but instead an integral demonstration of both the method and the outcome, of rendering numeric data from text. Its success inspired Liang's grand vision for a twenty-four-volume set of "general tables," or *tongbiao* 通表, that would supplement the texts of the standard histories. Though this expansion never came to fruition, in a later articulation of historical statistics, Liang's student Wei Juxian 衛聚賢 (1899–1989) added to Liang and Ding's original table an assortment of finely crafted graphs and charts dealing with classical texts, showing, for example, the narrative distribution of events in classical sources, such as the *Spring and Autumn Annals* (*Chunqiu* 春秋), the *Zuozhuan* 左傳 (Zuo tradition), and the *Guoyu* 國語 (Dialogues of the states). These were collectively published in an article in the popular journal *Dongfang zazhi* 東方雜誌 (Eastern Miscellany) in 1929 (figures 1.2 and 1.3).[6]

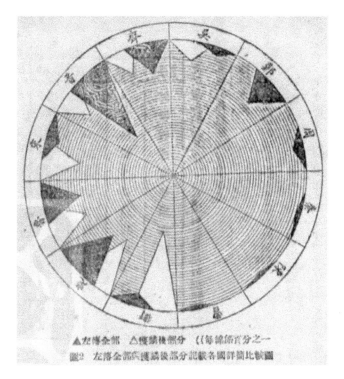

FIGURE 1.2 Graph of the distribution of narrative attention in the *Zuozhuan* by state before and after the capture of the *lin* unicorn in 481 BCE, an event Confucius took as the sign of the decline of sage governance. Wei Juxian, "Yingyong tongjixue de fangfa zhengli guoxue," *Dongfang zazhi* 26, no.14 (1929): 73–84

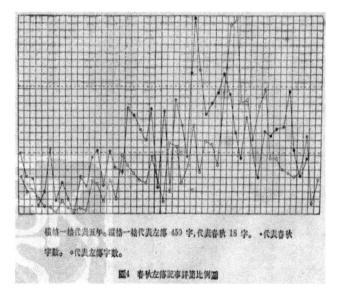

FIGURE 1.3 Graph comparing coverage of chronological events in the *Zuozhuan* and *Spring and Autumn Annals*. Wei Juxian, "Yingyong tongjixue de fangfa zhengli guoxue," *Dongfang zazhi* 26, no. 14 (1929): 73-84

Much more deserves to be said about this dust-covered method and its place within the modern field of "National Studies" (*guoxue* 國學) historiography. For the purposes of this chapter, what must here be highlighted is Liang's appeal to a sense of statistical *vision* as an expedient form of knowing and discovery. As he puts it:

> if one wants to know the true face of history [*lishi zhenxiang* 歷史真相], one absolutely must not be satisfied with only examining great figures and events on the surface level; the most important thing is to identify the active changes happening throughout an entire society. Such active changes in society can only be identified by accumulating and comparing them. Usually very small affairs [*hen xiao de shi* 很小的事] are totally overlooked by most people. But if one aggregated all the events on this scale, sorting them into categories and then researching them, one could discover wondrous phenomena and invent invaluable theorems. . . . The usefulness of statistics lies in its ability to "observe macroscopic trends" [*guan qi da jiao* 觀其大較; quotation marks in the original]. In other words, it focuses on the average state of various matters, distributing them evenly to calculate a comprehensive account.[7]

Accordingly, below the surface of recorded events lies an invisible realm of greater historical significance. This model of textual depth anticipates what the historian Fernand Braudel would later develop as the "unconscious" layer of history, sensible "beyond the reach of [recorded] illuminations and their brief flashes . . . at some distance, a social unconscious . . . belonging half to the time of conjunctures and wholly to structural time."[8] "Regular" reading is diminished by Liang as a barrier to a more comprehensive understanding. To unlock the narrative's latent truth that lies unperceived by readers in their series of encounters with its separate details, one needs to move to a plane of greater abstraction. The tool is datafication, which allows the researcher to aggregate details, enumerate them, and then analyze them using calculation. To this end, Wei Juxian offers a formal process of textual datafication to the historical statistician, in the form of an index card template, suitable for recording and organizing individual observations within a text (figure 1.4).[9] The payoff for this reduction of text into data is

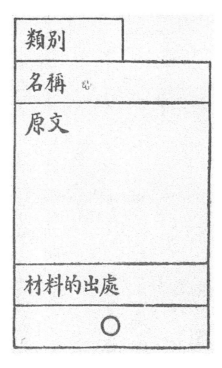

FIGURE 1.4 Notecard format for extracting and organizing data from historical texts. Wei Juxian, *Lishi tongjixue* (Shanghai: Shangwu yinshuguan, 1934), 15

nothing short of a new level of textual mastery, where seeing (rather than reading) is equated with knowing and made all the more attractive by the method's associations with scientific rationality and efficiency.[10]

Liang's application of statistics to large-scale textual analysis feels oddly familiar today. The recent consolidation of the so-called digital humanities has brought with it a cascade of computational methods in scholars' search for the laws and patterns that shape a text, oeuvre, corpus, or even a culture at large. The methodological emphasis on scale is accompanied by a shift to visual knowing, nowhere captured better than in the influential formulation of "distant reading" by Franco Moretti (himself inspired by Braudel). Moretti might as well be describing Liang's historical statistics in his observations of scale as "a condition of knowledge . . . [which] allows you to focus on units that are much smaller or much larger than the text: devices, themes, tropes—or genres and systems."[11] And, as he goes on to say in *Graphs, Maps, Trees*: "a field [he means world literature] this large cannot be understood by stitching together separate bits of knowledge about individual cases [i.e., national histories or stand-alone works], because . . . it's a collective system, that should be grasped, as such, as a whole."[12] With his proposal to tabulate data from the relatively large textual corpus of the standard histories, Liang's project offers an earlier "abstract model for literary history" (to use the subtitle of Moretti's book). In both cases, "raw" textual data is progressively cooked for the sake of rendering trends and patterns sensible and thereby intelligible.

Hearing historical statistics as a century-old echo to "distant reading" calls into question the rhetoric of novelty that pervades much of the digital humanities today.[13] By the same token, Liang's method invites a further consideration of both the techniques of information management in scholarly labor and literary culture in China leading up to the twentieth century and the ways in which such techniques have shaped today's digital humanities tools in the study of China's cultural tradition.[14] The present chapter tacks a more modest course by charting the modern turning point of the history of textual datafication and visualization in China. In what follows I add to the example of historical statistics two further attempts to read at a distance. The first, which I call "enumerative survey," emerged at the margins of the literary field, in the disciplinary formation of experimental psychology in the early 1920s, as psychologists undertook word counting and statistical analysis in the pursuit of new linguistic and psychological knowledge. Despite this social-scientific orientation, frequent engagement with traditional and modern literature made such surveys a dynamic site for producing literary facts, criticism, and even the occasional poem. The second approach explored here, called "diagrammatic analysis" (*tujie* 圖解) by its proponents, emerged in the early 1930s as a means of picturing narrative elements, such as plot structure or character relations, using diagrams.

In both "enumerative survey" and "diagrammatic analysis," the knowledge created from the intersection between literature and information visualization was, on the whole, little more than a cabinet of curiosities, but what makes these methods interesting is the light they cast upon the profound instability of disciplinary knowledge during its formative period in the early twentieth century. This includes modern science, which was newly brought to bear upon fields of experience previously considered outside its reach, such as emotion and history. But it also extends to "literature," which, as Lydia Liu reminds us, was itself a category far from stable during the 1920s, but rather an object of contestation and redefinition.[15] Indeed, within enumerative survey and diagrammatic analysis, literature can be hard to disaggregate from society or social relations, the former being epiphenomenal to the latter, thus making it conceivable that methods from social science could render useful social facts from literature—and, by a surprising inversion, that literature might lend cultural prestige to the social facts derived therein. Though marginal in their influence upon what we today take as the mainstream of this literature's history, these experiments with distant reading constituted an attempt to restructure what is knowable and perceptible about texts, thereby contributing to the period's broader debate about what modern literature could be or should do—questions which, significantly, resonated with the era's debates regarding the place of Western science in China's civilizational and spiritual development.[16]

I retain "distant reading" as shorthand for the data-driven "scientification" of literary studies but do so advisedly. To be clear, it is not my intention to establish the cases listed here as points on a historical continuum with Moretti's distant reading. Nor should the similarities be overstated. In brief, Moretti's formulation is predicated upon "close reading," to whose perceived limits the conceit of distance is offered as a supplement, with the related agenda of transcending the inherent narrowness of one canon or another. The critic Joseph North argues that in the Western academy, distant reading reflects—and furthers—literary studies' turn away from critical reading grounded in a politically conscious aesthetics toward a utilitarian and neoliberal mode of cultural historiography.[17] While I agree with this critique, it is of course possible to focus on "distance" and its stakes in 1920s China without transposing these present issues onto the past. What is useful about Moretti's distance is how economically it captures the visual logic shared by historical statistics, enumerative surveys, and diagrammatic analysis. Levering forms of pattern recognition for the study of larger and larger textual units necessarily results, we will see, in the privileging of *looking* over *reading* in the production of putatively literary knowledge. The tension between distance and reading evident in Moretti applies just as well to the older context, where it was similarly equal parts controversial and exciting: controversial because distance guts cultural, linguistic, and historical knowledge by treating literary expression as universal, just as math, chemistry, and biology are; and exciting because such universalism, together with scientific objectivity, so directly contributed to the discourse and impetus of the New Culture project. Clearly, Moretti's term is useful beyond its own context. Here it has more to teach us about modern Chinese literature and how we write its history than about the emergence or present state of the digital humanities.

The cases of distant reading explored here represent only a small part of the broader story of information graphics in China during the twentieth century. But they are exceptional thanks to a marked element of reflexivity: the produced images are discussed by their makers, rather than needing to speak for themselves. Such considerations help reveal graphic practices as a form of visual modernism—one that draws on a long-standing tradition of *biao* and *tu*, while also exceeding these older forms on account of their higher level of abstraction, where individual observations or relational schema are expressible in numerical or geometric terms.[18] Equally notable is that this visual modernism takes part in a global trend that connects a strikingly diverse range of forms and figures, from the sociological charts of Blackness by W. E. B. Du Bois to the constructivist collages of early Soviet state posters aimed at publicizing production data.[19] Ultimately, the modernism of graphics projects its own global reach through the universalizing figure of the grid—a point to which I return in the chapter's conclusion.

One final note at the outset. The aesthetic dimension of the carefully crafted images explored here provides the key to understanding their adoption and proliferation in the first place. Factors that prominently appear in other histories of information—including of distant reading—are here absent. That is to say, replacing individual reading with visual apprehension was not a strategy for coping with information overload caused by the agglutination of textual knowledge. Nor, obviously, are the *tu* and *biao* of literary abstraction legible as technologies of surveillance and biopolitical control, despite occasional convergences with them, as in the case of Liang Qichao's interest in historical population trends. Instead, these distant reading graphics represent creative solutions that were, to a degree, in search of problems. They have an ornamental role, as epitomes of the New Culture's embrace of science and democracy, that must be taken into account. For this reason, though the broader movement toward statistical graphics and the culture of the fact outlived the 1920s, the images produced by the distant reading of texts disappeared with the decline of New Culture scientific idealism and the advent of total mobilization of the war-torn 1930s.

ENUMERATIVE SURVEY: ZHANG YAOXIANG AND LITERARY PSYCHOLOGICAL DATA

The innovation of this method is tightly bound up with the rise of experimental and behavioral psychology in China during the 1920s, at the center of which was the Chinese Psychology Society (Zhonghua xinli xuehui 中華心理學會) and its primary publication venue, *Psychology* (*Xinli* 心理), where the enumerative surveyance of literature first appeared. In its nascent stage of institutionalization, the field of experimental psychology turned to textual data as an economical and credible alternative to laboratorial data. This episode is best told through the society's founding member and first president, as well as the head editor of *Psychology*, Zhang Yaoxiang 張耀祥 (1893–1964), whose influential forays into literary-psychological research inspired his contemporaries to similarly adopt datafication and enumeration in the pursuit of sociocultural analysis.

Zhang's career path typifies the influence that training abroad exerted on New Culture intellectuals. Born in one of China's concessionary port cities, Wuhan, in 1893 and educated at a missionary school, Zhang was inspired to pursue new knowledge after encountering the works of Yan Fu and Liang Qichao. In 1913 he matriculated at Tsinghua University, graduated in 1915, then continued his studies in America thanks to a Boxer scholarship (established by the U.S. government to promote Western education and values among the Chinese). Abroad, he spent a year at Amherst College before transferring to Columbia University, where he earned both his BA (1918) and MA (1919) in psychology. In New York, Zhang joined a number of compatriots at Columbia and Teachers College who would similarly play germinal roles in institutionalizing psychology and education studies as modern, scientific disciplines in China, including the future president of Peking University, Chiang Mon-lin (1886–1964), and the theologian and psychologist, Lew Ting-fang (1892–1947).[20] Originally intending to stay on and pursue a PhD, Zhang was recruited by Chen Baoquan in 1920 to return to China and take up a position at the Beijing Advanced Normal School (the future Beijing Normal University), of which Chen was then president.

At Columbia, the atmosphere of the Department of Psychology was dominated by the presence of Edward L. Thorndike (1874–1949), an enormously prolific behavioral psychologist specializing in learning and cognition in animals and a notable leader of the so-called testing movement in education.[21] By the turn of the twentieth century, in the physical sciences, the passion for precise numeric measurement and positivism had decreased significantly with the adoption of probabilistic models of the universe proposed by figures such as Josiah Willard Gibbs, Ludwig Boltzmann, and James Clerk Maxwell.[22] However, in social and cognitive sciences, the interest in bringing positivism and statistics to bear upon areas previously considered outside the realm of objective science was waxing rather than waning. "Whatever exists, exists in some amount. To measure it is simply to know its varying amounts. Man sees no less beauty in flowers now than before the day of quantitative botany. . . . If any virtue is worth seeking, we shall seek it more eagerly the more we know and measure it," declared Thorndike in a 1921 speech at Columbia. As a mentor, Thorndike was committed to "converting future educators and psychologists to numbers," a mission that was in line with the research of other Psychology Department faculty, many of whom were proponents of psychometrics. Their passion for numbers and attempts to quantify the intellectual output in scientific fields in early twentieth-century America carried eugenicist overtones that paralleled Liang Qichao's interest in measuring the distribution of intelligence in China.[23] Thorndike brought particular zeal to measurement by imagining a convergence between the roles of the psychologist and engineer in pursuit of rationalizing the study of psychic life, a dream echoed by the contemporary development of scientific management. Like followers of Frederick Winslow Taylor, "Thorndikeans" sought "precise measurements and the analytical reduction of [operations such as] brick-laying or learning to spell into all its calculable atoms of behavior.... [They] are building statistical laboratories in university departments of psychology and education . . . [and] are possessed of what can be called an obsession with quantified observation."[24]

Thorndike was particularly keen on literacy acquisition and the improvement of student performance—issues at the center of mass literacy campaigns and pedagogical reform by Chinese intellectuals of the time.[25] In his field, Thorndike's most impactful work was the massive, labor-intensive compilation of ten thousand common English words in his *Teacher's Word Book*, published in 1921 by Teachers College.[26] This project was the predecessor to the much larger program of language reform known as "Basic English," including the influential 850-word list compiled by the English philosopher Charles Kay Ogden and published in 1930. Though Ogden was critical of Thorndike's approach for being overly statistical and impractical for the specific needs of the foreign learner of English,[27] ultimately his and Thorndike's projects serve as linked touchstones within the history of vocabulary rationalization. What made Thorndike's work unprecedented was the immensity of its corpus:

> *The Teacher's Word Book* is an alphabetical list of the 10,000 words which are found to occur most widely in a count of about 625,000 words from literature for children; about 3,000,000 words from the Bible and English classics; about 300,000 words from elementary-school text books; and about 50,000 words from books about cooking, sewing, farming, the trades, and the like; about 90,000 words from the daily newspapers; and about 500,000 words from correspondence. Forty-one different sources were used.[28]

Such immensity required a significant amount of tabulation—as Thorndike alluded to in his observation that "tens of thousands of hours of further counting" would be necessary to shore up the dataset as much as he hoped.[29] But, at a total of more than 4.5 million words, this initial set of data proved sufficient to calculate word "credit-numbers," capturing both the general frequency of a word within the corpus and its range (the number of different texts across which it appears). The study's evident rigor and carefully compiled database offered a model to others looking to analyze and rationalize language pedagogy in separate contexts. As such, it comes as no surprise that Thorndike's method was introduced into China only one year after the publication of the *Word Book*, in the form of a short history of enumerative lexicography centering on Thorndike's achievement.[30] In all, Thorndike's research and teaching helped establish a blueprint for analyzing writing in a rational and systematic way, a method that defined the early work of experimental psychology in China and inspired its interest in surveyance.

For his own part, during his graduate research, Zhang Yaoxiang applied counting and statistical analysis to the study of the efficiency of reading. Zhang couched reading itself as part of the modern human condition, for, as he explains in the introduction of his master's thesis, "The man of to-day may be defined as a reading animal. When everybody reads, and some do scarcely anything else, and the amount to be read increases daily, it is highly desirable that reading should be made as easy and rapid as possible."[31] His interest in the respective impacts on reading speed of elements such as punctuation and "side-signs" (the small circles traditionally placed alongside Chinese text to denote emphasis), the horizontalization of text, and even material factors, such as page color, contributed directly to the New Culture modernization of Chinese typography detailed by Tom Mullaney.[32] Lastly, Zhang's thesis work inaugurated a career of measurement in subjective, hard-to-get-at fields like intelligence, sentiment, and sensory bias. A decade later, Zhang would sum up his Thorndikean enthusiasm for quantification with an exhortation: "Among the multitudinous affairs and things of the world, what can be known by its size, multiplicity, length, weight, strength, duration—in short, its 'proper degree' [*shidu* 適度]—without undergoing measurement?"[33]

This declaration both captures the intellectual spirit of the Chinese Psychology Society and highlights the alignment between the psychologists and the broader agenda of social reform and awakening among proponents of the New Culture movement. The Psychology Society's founding manifesto proclaims the importance of psychology beyond education and medicine, including in the discipline's scope fields as disparate as law, art, and "everyday life."[34] Their research could, Zhang and his colleagues believed, help strengthen the nation, in particular in areas such as intelligence testing, which would help improve the training of children and adults alike.[35] The foundation of the society and its journal *Psychology* (published from 1922 to 1927) signaled the establishment of experimental psychology as a legitimate scientific discipline, one that, especially in its approach to cultural knowledge, diverged significantly from other fields of psychological discourse at the time, particularly that of popular Freudian analysis.[36]

Largely trained in Western universities and employed at institutions across Beijing (including Yenching University, National University of Peking, Peking National Normal University, and Peking Women's College) and other major cities like Shanghai (Fudan University) and Tianjin (Nankai University), the society's members sought to develop an apparatus for conducting clinical work and teaching that would serve as a counterpart to the American universities in which they themselves had trained. Crucially, though, they lacked access to the significant resources needed to set up laboratories.[37] In an odd twist, this obstacle turned out to be productive, for without labs to generate data, Zhang and his colleagues were forced to devise innovative ways of collecting psychological data. What turned out to be the most fecund source was China's literary tradition, both premodern and contemporary. In the vein of Thorndike's work, society members measured character frequencies of sources ranging from older works, such as the *Thousand Character Classic*, the Kangxi Dictionary, and significant portions of traditional vernacular masterworks, such as *Journey to the West*, *Dream of the Red Chamber*, and *Water Margin*, to contemporary works, like children's literature, the May Fourth periodical *Women's Journal* (*Funü zazhi* 婦女雜誌), and the popular fiction magazine *Saturday* (*Libailiu* 禮拜六).[38] Much like Liang Qichao's "historical statistics," these experiments sought to prove that there was valuable information to be found within hills of texts—just as long as one was willing to tabulate it. What is particularly striking is the regularity with which the cohort of psychologists used forms of enumeration to produce knowledge that was specifically *literary* in nature and even to playfully use poetry to respond to their own work. By doing so, they blurred the dividing line between psychology (and the social sciences more generally) and literature—a form of transgression that would lead to a clearer distinction between the two fields by the end of the decade.

Both the appeal of textual data's at-hand nature and the impulse to versify are epitomized in a research article by Zhang on the "general psychology" of merchants in Beijing.[39] The piece opens with a note regarding the difficulty of collecting good data. As a diffuse group, Beijing's merchants cannot easily be studied by using interviews or mailed surveys, nor is it possible to derive much from their published materials, such as memoirs, of which there are too few pertinent samples. Advertisements soliciting shop owners to voluntarily send in survey data are equally unrealistic. To simplify things, Zhang shifts his focus from the human subject to that of business identity as it is symbolized in the name of the firm or shop: textual data that is easy to analyze and also (to Zhang's eye, at least) representative of a psychological disposition. But how could one collect this information? "Sending assistants into the corners of the city to walk the streets and copy down signage would not only attract suspicion from the police but also elicit the mockery of passersby. On top of that, it's uneconomical, timewise." Here the account switches to a more expressive narrative form to capture the surprise and pleasure of a discovery: "Just as I was hesitating over what to do, suddenly I saw on my desk a gray tome, about eight inches long and one inch thick: the *Beijing Telephone Bureau Customer Number Book*. I had it! Typically, among all books, this one is the least interesting, but in front of me that day, it suddenly became the most interesting of all. In my eyes it was a kind of precious treasure."[40] The reader is thus drawn into Zhang's scene of the birth of enumerative survey in "real time" thanks to this narrative—a mode of storytelling that already strains against the cool rhetoric of scientific reportage.

The survey results are important to what comes after. The total number of shops listed in the 311-page directory comes to nearly five thousand entries, a substantial sample of the general population. The entries are rendered into textual data by breaking names into individual characters and discarding characters that denote "shop" or "business" (whose tabulation would indicate little more than the distribution of shop categories). Measuring type (a unique character) against token (the number of times the character-type appears), the analysis identifies eight hundred unique characters, with token frequency ranging from one to as high as four hundred. Claiming in this preliminary (though only) article on the subject that the number of statistical tables of the final results would fill a newspaper, Zhang limits his subsequent discussion to the twenty most frequent characters. This set comprises all auspicious terms like *xing* 興 (prosper), *he* 和 (peace), and *feng* 豐 (abundance)—hardly surprising results. But in an attempt to preempt his reader's question about what, after all, is revealed by his distant reading, Zhang surveys a group of sixty-one university students, asking them to guess the results of his study. When the top answer guesses only fourteen out of the twenty characters correctly (with the average result about eight out of twenty), Zhang proclaims his project is sufficiently nonintuitive.

What *is* surprising, however, is the article's final shift from corpus analysis to a moment of play. The former borders on pop psychology in its attempt to reveal the psychological contours of business branding by studying single characters divorced from any context. But Zhang takes the results as an invitation for literary engagement. Observing various features of each of the twenty characters, he categorizes them according to classical poetic tonal categories of "flat" and "uneven." This, in turn, inspires their rearrangement into a four-line piece of regulated verse, as supplied to Zhang by his wife, Cheng Junying 程俊英 (1901–1993), a regular contributor to *Xinli* who would later become known as a scholar of Chinese classical poetry:

> According with rightness, a rich gathering is completed.
> With mutual cooperation, abundant glory endures.
> Following Heaven, splendid majesty arises.
> Tracing the origin of greatness, ascendant auspiciousness flourishes.

> 和義成豐聚，
> 公同恆裕昌，
> 順天興華泰，
> 源大盛隆祥.[41]

At first blush these lines resemble a panegyric extolling the fruits of good governance. But its woodenness and euphemizing betray an uncanny origin, a text whose source is not a living author but instead arises from human/machine collaboration. Indeed, given its basis in statistics and the deictic transcendence of an individual observer, one might ask whether this poem should be understood as a text in the first place: perhaps it is better viewed as a landscape collage, one that captures panoramically the shop signs strewn across Beijing. Though it lacks any merit by the standards of classical poetry, this poem nonetheless stands out as an original experiment, emblematic of modernism's penchant for exploring its conditions of production and mediation. Its playfulness also makes its position precarious: when Zhang reprinted his essay in a two-volume anthology of selections from the journal he omitted this poem, perhaps intending to communicate a more scientific tone.[42]

The combination of enumerative survey and poetry was not an isolated incident but, rather, appeared frequently in the pages of *Xinli*. In a profession of faith in New Culture literary ideals, namely the transparency of language for representing the inner states of the individual—and romantic—poet, Zhang and his cohort recast the classical poem as a repository of psychological data from which certain facts could be derived. On the other hand, classical poetry also bestowed to their research articles a sense of cultural legitimacy, erudition, and a perch for aesthetic reflection. For example, in a study on the cultural constructedness of "noise" (雜音 *zayin*; 噪音 *zaoyin*), in which he enumerates and categorizes noise words appearing in the canon of classical poetry, Zhang caps his discussion with some lines from the famous Song dynasty poet, Su Shi:[43]

If you say the zither's notes reside in the instrument itself,
When it is laid in its case why doesn't it still sound?
If you say the notes reside in the player's fingertips,
Why can't I hear them from your fingers themselves?[44]

若言絃上有琴聲，
放在匣中何不鳴？
若言聲在指頭上，
何不予君指上聽？

This article's conclusion is strikingly silent about how the research contributes to the advancement of psychological knowledge per se. The pivot to Su Shi instead represents a kind of tautology where the aesthetic value of poetry justifies the quasi-scientific examination that precedes it. But this move leads Zhang in the direction of cultural comparison, rather than psychological facts: "I don't believe there is a literature from any other country in the world in which one could identify more than 340 words specifically referring to noise [as in the case of China, per Zhang's enumeration]. I dare anyone to challenge this assertion!"[45] More articles soon followed: further enumeration of noise, along with analyses of various related topics like color, the sensual predilections of Du Fu, Bai Juyi, and Qu Yuan, and, in a particularly ambitious effort, the psychological profiles and "instincts" of Tang poets through a survey of more than two thousand poems.[46] Like Zhang's noise article, these pieces all close with quotations from classical poems, in effect blurring the distinctions between the author's status as a modern researcher and a more traditional literatus and gesturing to the pleasure of engaging the source canon on its own terms.

Collectively, this early work of the society merges together the psychological and educationalist mission of its members, on the one hand, and the New Culture celebration of individualism, science, and democracy, on the other. We have seen the fascination that enumeration held for Zhang and the other contributors to *Xinli*. What remains to be addressed is the particular visual experience of the *biao* that underlies the work of counting and categorizing to begin with. Zhang most explicitly addresses the effect of distance in a fascinating article titled "The Sentiment of New Poets."[47] But before turning to this article, it is necessary to contextualize it by considering the intersection between modern psychological ideas and the emergence of the free-verse poetry in which Zhang sought to intervene.

Rain, Wheat Fields, Bacteria, Bullets: Pattern Recognition at a Glance

Although by the end of the 1920s the focus of modern literature would move toward a more collectivist vision, the primary subject of the New Culture period—one shared by both writers and psychologists—was that of an individual believed to be both free-willed and expressive. In the case of prose fiction, as Lydia Liu has shown, this belief was manifest in the new modes of first-person narration and psychological interiority: "New stylistics of fiction allows Chinese writers to locate the protagonist in a new symbolic context, one in which the protagonist no longer serves as a mere element within the nexus of patriarchal kinship and/or in a transcendental, divine scheme as in most premodern Chinese fiction but dominates the text, instead, as the locus of meaning and reality in possession of psychological and moral 'truth.'"[48] Yet, while proponents of New Culture called for a rejection of classical literary style because, in their eyes, it stifled individual expression and stood as a barrier to mass literacy, they tended to underplay the expressive and potentially individualist nature of certain older genres such as lyrical poetry—precisely the tradition that the psychologists championed as a source of rich psychological data. Indeed, as we have seen, Zhang had no qualms over the construction of the traditional poet as an individual subject who, through the medium of poetry, transcended the limits of time and place to enter into the modern researcher's virtual laboratory. The facts rendered out of such a transportation could be of questionable value or application—or indeed altogether absurd, as in the curious attempt to administer an IQ test to classical poets—but, ideologically, this approach reaffirmed both the contemporary evaluation of the individual as a locus of psychological and moral truth and the status of language as a signifier of individual subjectivity.[49] (At the same time, however, the quantitative analysis of an individual also paradoxically meant that his or her subjectivity was fundamentally nonunique but rather could be notated on a shared plane with other, commensurable counterparts, as well as compared against a normative average.)

The project of inventing and exploring individual interiority is clearly discernible in the intersection between psychology (experimental or otherwise) and the concurrent rise of so-called new poetry (*xinshi*), the free-verse vernacular poetry introduced by such writers as Hu Shi 胡適 (1891–1962) and Guo Moruo 郭沫若 (1892–1978) that flourished during the 1920s. Above all, new poetry represented an exciting means of direct, oral self-expression. Such expression not only signaled new poetry's membership in the broader project of vernacularizing all writing, but also helped anchor the redefinition of modern poetic form itself. As Michelle Yeh observes, this question of definition was an urgent one, for "if modern Chinese poetry has no fixed form, classical syntax, and poetic diction, how is it to be recognized as poetry? Without the time-revered literary and structural features of classical poetry, how do modern poets justify their works as poetry?"[50] If new poetry was to be defined as the output of a modern, individual poet, the issue of its form was thus transposed to the question of what constitutes the modern individual. Here the language and knowledge of psychology proved critical as a source for articulating such a subject—indeed, it is hard to imagine such a subject in the absence of a discourse of psychology. Such discourse appears both rhetorically and conceptually in much of the early discussions of new poetry. Take, for example, "Various Psychological Views on New Poetry in Society Today" (1919) by Yu Pingbo 俞平伯 (1900–1990), a pioneer of new poetry, in which Yu bemoans the generally low quality of recent new poetry, ascribing its deficiency to the misconception that vernacular poetry is easy to compose on account of its lack of metrical rules. His call for a renewed focus on self-expression is couched in psychological terms, not only repeating words such as "brain power" (*naoli* 腦力), "mind" (*naojin* 腦筋), and particularly "genius" (*tiancai* 天才), but also employing a rhetoric of measurement by suggesting the overall output of vernacular poetry be kept lower so as to increase its "weight" (*zhongliang* 重量).[51] At the same time that he adopts the rhetoric of psychology, Yu disavows the discipline of experimental psychology as falling outside the realm of literary art: genius, he emphasizes, is immeasurable, and speech rhythms cannot be mechanically determined.

It is within this discursive nexus that Zhang's analysis of interiority in "The Sentiment of New Poets" should be understood. Zhang's focus on sentiment contributed to the valorization of affect as a central tenet of the modern—and romantic—individual subject as a "sentimental subject."[52] Like many others in *Xinli*, this article also begins with an explanation of the necessity of relying on textual data rather than lab experiments. For one thing, Zhang explains, *qingxu* 情緒 (sentiment or mood) is one of the hardest phenomena to measure objectively because of its ephemerality and the impossibility of consistently eliciting it within a laboratory setting.[53] In addition to his previous experience testing intelligence, Zhang had also experimented with measuring sentiment in youth through direct observation but judged it insufficiently objective.[54] In contrast, working with text seemed to provide a surer foundation for the objective measurement of sentiment, and modern, free-verse poetry provided especially fertile grounds for an analysis.

In order to be measured, however, literary sentiment had first to be identified in a way that could be operationalized. In the article, Zhang considers Cheng Junying's method of classifying poems according to titles but rejects it as inapplicable to the case of new poetry, for in the latter, titles are often either very simplistic or have no obvious connection to the poem's content, making them impossible to code in terms of sentiment.[55] Instead, Zhang finds an expedient means for measuring sentiment in a growingly ubiquitous typographical marker: the exclamation point (*gantan fuhao* 感嘆符號 or simply *gantan fu* 感嘆符). Historically speaking, along with other punctuation such as question marks and quotation marks, the exclamation point was a recent import from Western textual conventions, and its deployment in the early 1920s accordingly signified a kind of typographic modernism.[56] Either because he assumes it may be not wholly familiar to his readers or in the attempt to impart to his analysis an appearance of rigorous scrutiny, Zhang provides a lengthy definition of the mark, which also doubles as a statement of method:

> Amongst the new-style punctuation there is one mark, the "!," which is called the "affective sigh mark" [*gantan fu* 感嘆符], frequently used by writers of new poetry as a symbol of an affective sigh and a sentiment [*gantan qingxu* 感嘆情緒]. . . . In English, "affective sigh" [*gantan* 感嘆] is *Exclamation*; it is one noun, and [unlike the Chinese compound word *gantan*] it cannot be seen as two processes, and thus it would be a grievous mistake to argue something like "Sentiment is sentiment, sighing is sighing, [therefore] the sentimental sigh mark is used to signify sentiment, and especially used to signify a sigh." *Exclamation* can also be translated as "gasp with surprise" [*jingtan* 驚嘆], "cry out with surprise" [*jingkui* 驚嘳], "sigh with regret" [*kaitan* 慨嘆], and "cry out in sorrow" [*jietan* 嗟嘆]: all sounds emitted by a person who is frustrated. These are all clichés for expressing negativity, pessimism, and world-weariness. They are the despairing sounds of a vanquished nation. If one wants to measure the degree to which a person is disappointed, negative, pessimistic, and world-weary, one could calculate in that person's writing the phrases that are equivalent to a sentimental sigh; if one wants to calculate these, one can count up the exclamation points. This is the so-called empirical method.[57]

If one brackets both Zhang's dubious assertion that the exclamation point connotes *only* the negative—a claim that would be subsequently challenged by some of the poets whose work he analyzes—as well as his phonocentric assumption that new poetry is to be read aloud and that exclamation points actually ought to be aspirated or pronounced with an exhalation of breath, what emerges is an interesting reflection upon the translingual and affective connotations of punctuation in modern China.[58] With the entry of Western punctuation marks into Chinese texts, Zhang has discovered an elegantly simple means for distilling some dimension of sentiment. Though it is based on somewhat misguided assumptions, this method serves as a basic form of stylometry that allows the researcher to bypass the much stickier realm of semantic meaning.

Zhang's study is impressive for the breadth of its corpus. As figure 1.5 illustrates, he reports that he examined no fewer than nine anthologies of vernacular poetry, all published within the previous three years, including the most influential collections of new poetry such as Hu Shi's *Experiments* (*Changshi ji* 嘗試集, 1920) and Guo Moruo's *Goddesses* (*Nüshen* 女神, 1921).[59] His enumeration counts both the number of lines in each anthology and the number of exclamation marks in each poem. In total, the analysis covers 1,261 poems, comprising 11,339 lines of text, wherein are found 2,630 exclamation marks—an average of 1.1 exclamation marks per poem, or one exclamation mark every 4.3 lines (figure 2.1). Commenting on this frequency, Zhang humorously scolds the new poet by contrasting him with the classical counterpart: when the latter sighed, he did so only sparingly and never more than thrice in one work, in contrast to the modern youth, who sighs nonstop, such as when coming across a small island, getting into a rickshaw, or climbing a hillock. But Zhang's true target of comparison—and the grounds for establishing a normative baseline by which one can evaluate the Chinese case—is a sample of canonical Western poetry featuring selections ranging from Dante's *Paradise* to Shakespeare's *Venus and Adonis* and sonnets to Robert Browning's *The Ring and the Book*, which are laid out in another table.[60] We might well question why Zhang chose these

第　一　表

集　名	冊數	行數	！數	平均每首！數	平均每若干行有一！號
嘗試集	68	615	105	1.5	5.8
草兒	158	2,659	394	2.5	6.7
女神	238	1,517	918	3.9	1.6
冬夜	289	2,767	455	1.6	6.1
繁星	164	695	103	0.7	6.4
春水	164	700	151	0.9	4.7
浪花	67	320	41	0.7	7.8
新詩年選	123	1511	321	2.6	4.7
白話詩研究集	82	546	157	1.7	4.0
總數	1,261	11,339	2630	2.1	4.3

FIGURE 1.5 Average usage of exclamation marks in collections of new poetry. Zhang Yaoxiang, "Xinshiren zhi qingxu," *Xinli* 2, no. 3 (1924): 1-14

particular works. His baseline would look very different were he to tally the exclamations in the works of a more contemporary poet, such as Walt Whitman. But more important than Zhang's thumb on the scale is the rhetorical effect of the scale itself: the reduction of poetry into statistical variables not only gives the article's critique a patina of objectivity but also creates a striking effect of commensurability between various languages, periods, and canons. This move dovetails neatly with New Culture critics' situation of Chinese literature within a transnational frame of literary history and development, but it also shows how such universalism is paradoxically put in service of identifying national or cultural particularities—a common theme in enumerative survey more broadly, as evidenced by the previous example of claiming the top place for written Chinese regarding the range of onomatopoeia and noise words.

National concerns similarly frame the literary principles asserted in "The Sentiment of New Poetry," as John Crespi rightly observes.[61] The stakes of the former are driven home by the article's concluding quotation from the classical tradition, this time a passage from the Mao preface (*Mao xu* 毛序) of the *Shijing* 詩經 (*Classic of Odes*) regarding the tonal patterning (*wen* 文) of sentiment (*qing* 情) in poetry: "The tones of a well-managed age are at rest and happy; its government is well managed . . . the tones of a ruined state are filled with lament and brooding; its people are in difficulty."[62] Within the context of the present discussion, this article's movement from literary description to literary prescription sets it apart from the other enumerative surveys in *Xinli*, which predominantly celebrate poetry rather than critique it. Despite Zhang's ambivalence regarding new poetry sentiment, however, it would be a mistake to dismiss his criticism as a case of dilettantism—or as the attack of a classicist crank set on refuting the agenda of the New Culture movement. Zhang, as we have seen, was a devoted proponent of New Culture. And he had elsewhere written in defense of vernacular poetry as an unmediated expression of the poet's inner sentiment, arguing that vernacular was the inherent style of internal dialog.[63] In fact, his admonishment here is no more severe than the criticisms of Yu Pingbo or other contemporary writers. As such, we should read Zhang's conclusion as consciously performing the role of a literary critic who asserts his own vision of what new poetry should (not) be.

What is most striking about the article is its creatively reflexive element, which contributes to our understanding of the role and experience of data

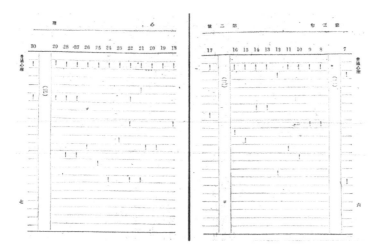

FIGURE 1.6 Guo Moruo's "Morning Peace" placed on a grid and stripped of its text. Zhang Yaoxiang,
"Xinshiren zhi qingxu," *Xinli* 2, no. 3 (1924): 1–14

visualization in the New Culture movement. To illustrate his process of tabulation, Zhang reproduces Guo Moruo's poem "Morning Peace" (*Chen'an* 晨安) as a *biao*, placing its coordinates in the traditional layout of Chinese print (top to bottom and right to left), but completely taking out all original text and punctuation marks aside from the exclamation points (figure 1.6). The result is a strange sight, where the text is emptied of all content, laying bare the frequency and placement of the exclamation points. We are in effect left with a map of the sentimental infrastructure that undergirds the original work. At the same time, the image highlights how printed text itself is distributed within the two-dimensional, discrete spaces of a grid structure, calling attention away from the linear movement of sequential reading to a more synoptic way of looking at pattern. Yet the relationship between this curious visualization and the rest of the article is not entirely clear: Zhang's method of counting is straightforward enough, so why would he devote a total of three pages to graphically illustrating it? In contrast to the article's other *biao*, and despite its clear status as a table, this one is not labeled as such. What exactly does Zhang wish to show his reader with this image?

Rather than read Zhang's image as a mere demonstration of his method—a function which would be superfluous—I submit that we read

Zhang's inclusion of this table as a kind of conceptual leap, a creative commentary that takes the *biao* not simply as a transparent instrument of organizing and communicating data, but as a meta-picture capable of considering the nature of datafication as a sort of strip-mining of text. It is also a reflection on the sensation of visualization itself. This interpretation is borne out by the text that accompanies the image, a short vernacular poem capturing Zhang's experience of gazing upon his data table:

> Seen from below, it resembles a spring rain,
> While seen from above, it looks like numerous wheat fields;
> Shrunk down, they're like numerous bacteria,
> While close-up, they appear as several rows of bullets.

> 仰看像一陣春雨,
> 俯看像數畝禾田;
> 縮小看像許多細菌,
> 放大看像幾排彈丸。

By exploring the table through economies of scale and from different perspectives, Zhang recounts a kind of visual excursion that turns the table from an ostensibly scientific instrument of parsing and tabulation into an aesthetic object of reflection about the eye's search for pattern. This visual experience effects a moment of defamiliarization, where data loses its transparency and appears instead as abstract shapes, grasped anew as a series of figurative likenesses: *like* rain, *like* wheat fields, *like* bacteria, *like* rows of bullets. The sensation of looking *at* rather than *through* is further augmented by the pictographic qualities of several of the Chinese graphs, where the small dots in the character "rain" (*yu* 雨) resemble the vertical scatter of the exclamation points, while the gridded layout of the character "field" (*tian* 田) mimics that of a basic data table. At multiple levels, the play with scale and vision recalls the microscopic/macroscopic shifts that constitute "distant reading," in which conventional text (and reading) disappears, replaced by small formal elements or larger patterned landscapes into which these pieces can be aggregated. And, like Cheng Junying's Beijing signage poem, the present piece indexes a process of recursive generation, whereby an original work (the lines of Guo Moruo's poem) has been turned into data, visualized, and re-expressed in the form of a new poem. If the addition of poetry in "The Sentiment of New Poetry" is not unique within the pages of *Xinli*, where we have seen how poetry was frequently added to reflect on the act of datafying poetry, what is distinct here is the directness and reflexivity of the engagement with the process and experience of datafication itself. The combination of image and text captures the very operation of the abstraction of datafication, giving voice to an aesthetic appreciation of both a new way of de-signing text (by excising its semantic content) and designing data (by laying out the remains upon a table).

"The Sentiment of New Poets" caused a minor stir in the burgeoning field of modern literature. Piqued by Zhang's microscopic imagery of the exclamation point as a pathogen, Lu Xun made mocking reference to Zhang in a 1925 miscellaneous essay in *Yusi* 語絲 (Threads of Talk) titled "A Reconsideration of the Collapse of Leifeng Pagoda," where he notes that China suffers from a disease, the "cross-shaped pathogenic bacteria, which have already entered into people's bloodstreams and spread to the entirety of their bodies—their force is certainly no less than the '!'-shaped bacteria of exclamatory sighs over the demise of the nation!"[64] As a former student of medicine, Lu Xun was, of course, no stranger to the power of bacteria imagery, and it has been shown that he was himself carefully thinking about the relationship between literary form and the grounds of objective, scientific knowledge at this moment in history.[65]

Others viewed Zhang's enumerative surveyance with a more sustained mix of bemusement and disdain. The most direct response of the time came from Zhang Yiping 章衣萍 (1902–1946), a protégé of Hu Shi and himself a poet, in one of the central New Culture venues, the *Chenbao fukan* 晨報副刊.[66] In a rambling and acerbic takedown, Zhang Yiping points out the irony in Zhang Yaoxiang's use of a new-style poem in his criticism of new poetry and sarcastically suggests that the government ban both new poetry and exclamation points in the interest of saving the nation. In a counterattack, Zhang Yaoxiang wryly performs an enumerative analysis of Zhang Yiping's essay, claiming that, though it is around four thousand characters in length, the piece contains no more than two hundred characters' worth of actual engagement with the original research: unassailable evidence that Yiping's writing was bloated and unserious, incapable of posing a real challenge to the objectivity of Zhang Yaoxiang's scientific method.[67] Such meddling gained Zhang Yaoxiang some lasting notoriety: in an interview in the early 1960s, one of the original editors of *Yusi*, Zhang Tingqian 章廷謙 (1901–1981),

noted that when the journal was founded in 1924 (that is, the same year that Zhang Yaoxiang's article was published), its organizers joked that Zhang Yaoxiang should not be allowed to read it for fear that he would apply his enumerative surveys there.[68]

Statistically based psychological analysis of literary texts disappeared after the mid-1920s, not only when *Xinli* stopped publication, as Zhang Yaoxiang and his colleagues turned their attention elsewhere, but also with the waning of the ethos of the New Culture movement itself. It is noteworthy today primarily as a site of discovery of Chinese literature as a corpus suitable for a form of empirical analysis that, much in the vein of Liang Qichao's invention of "historical statistics," proceeds along a scale that superseded that of the individual reader. Zhang's case asks us to consider the *biao* as more than a device for organizing information, but as a visual form whose rhetoric projects objectivism while also eliciting ocular pleasure and aesthetic engagement. The complexity of the specifically visual appeal of information graphics is further illustrated by the separate development of "diagrammatic analysis" that arose at the tail end of the enumerative survey's lifespan.

MAKING LITERATURE "INSTANTLY ACCESSIBLE": DIAGRAMMATIC ANALYSIS

By the nineteenth century, the convention of using *tu* 圖 to reproduce technical know-how was being adapted to extend to new ways of representing the human body and its interior based on the penetrating gaze of modern Western medical science.[69] This historical link to conceptions of the living body would reappear as a metaphor in the visualization of literary dynamics during 1920s and 1930s, where, as one proponent vividly put it, the diagrammatic analysis of texts could thrillingly penetrate a text without harming it, in contrast to the examiner's dissection of a still-living body for the purposes of labeling its components.[70] This relationship to the body and its systems is instructive of *tu*'s difference with *biao*. The metaphorical likeness between *tu* and the penetrating gaze of the X-ray aside, the composition of a *tu* represents a greater degree of visual abstraction than the *biao*'s on account of its ability to schematize relationships between components. In pivoting from numerical figures to abstract shapes, the *tu* compresses information to a greater degree than *biao*. Along these lines, in the context of distant reading, *tu* pictures something essential or comprehensive about its object of representation, rather than capturing relatively isolated elements such as a punctuation mark or language features, thus effecting an even greater gap between reader and the original text. For this reason, the *tu*'s elevated level of abstraction also makes it an even more expedient—and mobile—means for identifying and communicating literary patterns. Indeed, diagrammatic analysis occupied a wider section along the continuum of practices of distant reading in modern China, making its history more diffuse and sporadic than that of enumerative survey.

The breadth of *tu*-based experiments with distant reading can be illustrated by a few examples. Many new-style *tu* appeared in the translations of foreign works, such as Fu Donghua's rendition of Richard G. Moulton's literary criticism (figure 1.7), which carefully reproduced the original's elaborate charts of literary morphology.[71] The form of the morphological chart was then adapted by others to explore Chinese forms such as the Yuan drama (figure 1.8). More influential yet were the multiple introductions to Natsume Sōseki's equation of literary substance, $F + f$, such as an article by Yu Dafu 郁達夫 (1896–1945), one of the leading figures of the Creation Society group of expressionist writers. In Sōseki's formula, all literature can be expressed as some ratio of two kinds of information. F denotes a subject's focalized impression, representing the intake of sensory perception in the form of objective observations. Yu gives the example of a bank teller who mechanically counts money all day; while money might excite another person, the teller remains completely unaffected. In this vein, F is made up of "the writing that we see every day, the equations of mathematics, or the definitions in science textbooks."[72] In contrast, f designates sentiment or feeling (*ganjue* 感覺), as in the case of the *ci* 詞 poem "Searching" (*Xunxun mimi* 尋尋覓覓) by the Song dynasty poet Li Qingzhao 李清照. Given that the poet never informs her reader what stimulates the poem's expression of unhappiness in the first place, her sentiment, Yu explains, is pure and decontextualized. Educated in Japan, where he had majored in economics, and an admirer of Sōseki's, Yu was attracted to Sōseki's formula. But Yu's introduction stands out thanks to his original graph of the equation with an image of a sine wave that schematizes the dynamic oscillation between perception and stimulation that constitutes either an individual subject's experience or a literary narrative. Overall, in contrast to the discrete cells of the *biao*, the continuous nature of the lines within a *tu* makes the form

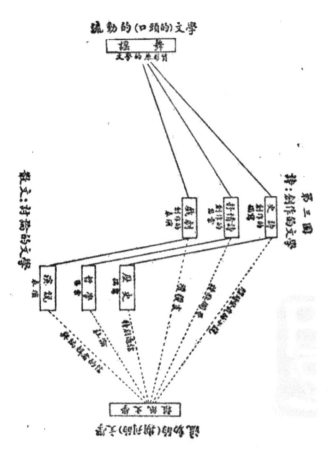

FIGURE 1.7 Chinese rendition of Moulton's literary morphology graph. Fu Donghua, "Wenxue zhi jindai yanjiu," *Xiaoshuo yuebao* 17, no. 1 (1926): 14–43

appropriate for expressing relative proportions or filiations rather than precise measurements. However, the representative capacity of *tu* is no less scientific than the numeric datafication of the modern *biao*, insofar as it accords with new subjects, like the role of energy waves in constituting perceptible reality (light, sound; see chapter 3), and new discourses, particularly that of evolution. Like the modern *biao*, a great many diagrams and graphics appeared throughout the literary and popular journals of the Republican period, including New Culture mainstays like *Fiction Monthly* and *New Youth*.

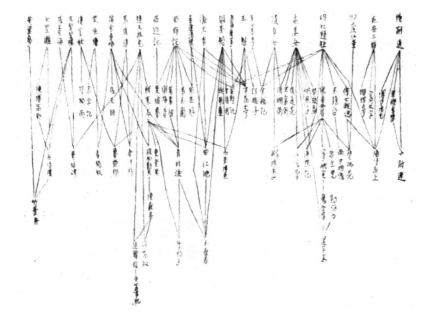

FIGURE 1.8 Genealogical diagram of Yuan drama. Zhao Jingshen, "Yuanqu shidai xianhou kao," *Xiandai* 5, no. 4 (1932): 580–92

Tu could also be put to use for analyzing the contents of narrative. Here the episode of "diagrammatic analysis" or *tujie* promoted by the leftist writer He Yubo 賀玉波 (1896–1982) deserves to be highlighted as a sustained example of distant reading. An occasional author and translator, He was far more prolific as a literary critic, churning out numerous author studies and compiling several how-to volumes for aspiring authors during the 1920s and 1930s. In a 1931 article titled "Diagrammatic Analysis of Fiction" (*Xiaoshuo de tujie* 小說的圖解), He sketched out the possibilities of using diagrams and schematics for making sense of literature. The diagram, in short, offers a new form of explicitly scientific literary criticism. The novelty of this new method requires justification and explanation, which documents the appeal of diagrams more generally. He beings his article by positing the scientific method as a general model for all knowledge production. As a pursuit of affective or subjective truth, literary knowledge is included within this purview, though it is explicitly contrasted with the objective approach to the physical world reserved for natural science.

Nonetheless, like the latter, literature evolves through the hypothesis, testing, and transmission of laws (*faze* 法则), which are manifest as diagrams showing underlying relations or principles of a given narrative and its form. As He explains of the modern *tu*:

> The *Diagram* [original in English] is frequently encountered in mathematics; it is especially common in mathematical analysis that uses arithmetic or geometry, such as when determining the value of X or Y, one hypothesizes the problem by drawing up a diagram and then solving it, thus making it instantly accessible [*yimu-liaoran* 一目了然] to others. In linguistics we also frequently encounter diagrammatic analysis, particularly of English.[73]

Tu can thus simplify and clarify an analytical principle, bringing forth some pattern of a complex system and expressing it as a fundamental fact. As a complex system in its own right, fiction is appropriate for diagrammatic analysis: "a story is often several thousand words, or tens of thousands of words, or hundreds of thousands of words in length . . . and even just its plot can be overly complex and winding, let alone elements that are even harder to understand, such as structure or its intellectual impetus."[74] Unlike the psychologists' enumerative surveys, He proposes a method of abstract analysis that is not limited to dealing with commensurable units of the same type. Instead, the diagram is to spatially express the relationality between two qualitatively different variables, such as social interactions between characters, the story's settings, plot progressions, or the passage of diegetic time. The method here is geometrical or schematic rather than arithmetical. To develop diagrammatic analysis into a mature system of literary criticism, He calls for the creation of a suite of shorthand symbols to encode the qualitative dimensions of a story. Once codified, diagrammatic analysis should resemble the historical population tables, international statistical graphs, and meteorological tables whose forms and scientific authority He covets for literary analysis.

In practice, diagrammatic analysis looks more like a logic puzzle that identifies a story's basic elements in order to test a proposition. A representative example is He's structure diagram of Mao Dun's novella *Waverings* showing alternations between characters and themes (figure 1.9).[75] Simple in its layout, the display of symmetry and order demonstrates the diagram's capacity to place distinct narrative elements onto a unified plane of relations.

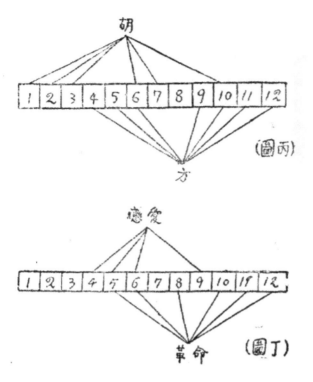

FIGURE 1.9 Structure diagram of Mao Dun's novella *Waverings*. At top is alternating emphasis by character by chapter; bottom tracks thematic emphasis on love or revolution. He Yubo, "Mao Dun chuangzuo de kaocha," *Dushu yuekan* 2, no. 1 (1931): 268

Notably, the diagram is normative rather than merely descriptive, seeing as it implies that a plot should move forward in the manner of a bildungsroman. The elementary formalism of the shapes of diagrammatic criticism, along with the dialectical tensions that they connote, anticipates the conventionalized structuration of plots in socialist realism, an emerging genre of which, as a leftist critic, He would have approved. Overall, diagrammatic analysis supplants the reader's linearly unfolding experience of a text with a more abstract encounter with the story as a two-dimensional pattern.

Three years after the publication of He's "Diagrammatic Analysis of Fiction," another critic, Wang Xipeng 汪錫鵬 (fl. 1930s), published an essay by the same name aimed at reviving He's method and giving it fuller articulation. "Diagrammatic analysis is a method of using line notation [*xiantiao de jihao* 線條的記號] to schematize [*guihua* 規劃] the contents of fiction,"

Wang states. While a general reader typically cannot explain *why* a given work is good or bad, he goes on, diagrammatic analysis expands the reader's ability to treat literature as a medium (*meijie* 媒介) and thereby analyze the *how* of its operation via its formal aspects and techniques. The scientific dimension of diagrammatic analysis helps to demystify even very profound texts, resulting in a deeper aesthetic appreciation on the reader's part. According to Wang, an author's creative process begins at an encounter with the complexity of the world, an encounter that is translated into a kind of philosophy or worldview, which is in turn recoded in the form of a literary work. The power of diagrammatic analysis lies in its ability to allow the reader to reconstitute the essence of the writer's experiences and inner state, thereby determining not only what an author meant by their work but also why they expressed these ideas or experiences in the specific terms they did. By this token, diagrammatic analysis is itself literary, for if fiction (in particular the novel) "is not a transcript of life, to be judged by its exactitude, but a simplification of some side point of life, to stand or fall by its significant simplicity," then the diagram not only unlocks literature's transcript but also mimics its mode of simplifying reality (in this case, the reality of the text) into a symbolic and essentializing distillation.[76]

Wang's description of diagrammatic analysis is filled with visual metaphors: a text can be, for example, analyzed as a work which is woven together (*bianzhi* 編織) out of a main plot strand (*zhuxian* 主線) or series, along with any number of secondary plot strands (*fuxian* 副線), each of which is knotted with "resting points" (*tingliudian* 停留點). The two primary elements of a story are its ethical development and its temporal development. Identify these two elements and their intersections, and a novel can be transformed into a diagram image or reflection (*tuying* 圖影) by connecting the various nodes (events, climaxes, digressions, dilations) that make up the basic structure of the plot. Unlike He Yubo's generalist approach, Wang builds a more coherent system that abstracts narrative into a graphical inscription. However, despite their elegant simplicity, the organization of Wang's own graphs is far from self-evident. For example, in a diagram of the triangular love relationship between characters in Zhang Ziping's short story "Taili" 苔莉 (1927), the three elements of intercharacter relations, narrative events, and plot tension are confusingly placed in the same two-dimensional space.[77] The result is too much of an information load for the X–Y axis to bear, resulting in confusion over the actual relationship between the elements. Dazzling as they may be to the eye, the graphs of diagrammatic criticism often obscure more than they explain.

THE WORLD AS/OF GRAPHICS

The trio of historical statistics, enumerative survey, and diagrammatic analysis offers a useful step toward a more encompassing history of data visualization in modern China. Such cases also suggest how the "golden age" of modern information visualization and statistical graphics that emerged in America and Europe during the second half of the nineteenth century must be understood as a more global event by the first half of the twentieth century.[78] So far I have emphasized how these projects signal a shift away from literary reading, where the sequential and one-dimensional passage through text is supplanted—if not entirely replaced—by a two-dimensional, visual representation of the text or corpus. In a process that is familiar in the age of digital media, the procedures of datafication and visualization reduce many features into one or two, trading the original for a putatively instructive abstraction. Building upon Eric Hayot's discussion of the "aesthetic world" of a work—whether historiography, poetry, or fiction—as the construction of its own totalized and self-sufficient world, the visualizations of distant reading can be seen as *maps* of a work's diegesis and/or form, guiding the reader's attention and evaluation.[79] A map does not passively represent a territory but actively reshapes its bearer's relationship to the space around them. In this vein, we might ask: Did the emergence of such mapping in turn influence the aesthetic worlds imaginable in the 1920s and 1930s? And if we treat these maps as specifically *creative* acts of worlding, what did their constructed spaces offer or make imaginable?

A full answer to the first question exceeds the bounds of the present study, but a sample of distant reading's potential for reshaping contemporary literature and its aesthetic can be drawn from the output and practice of Mao Dun, who was not only one of the period's best-known writers but also a favorite target of He Yubo's diagrammatic analysis. Before setting off on a piece, Mao Dun would himself create a "blueprint" (*lantu* 藍圖) to plot out its general structure.[80] Despite regularly falling short of his overly ambitious original outlines, his stories implicitly contain diagrams. (As we shall see in chapter 4, Shen Congwen's fiction offers an illuminating contrast as an instance of nondiagrammatic writing—He Yubo tellingly dismisses Shen's work as a "jumble, with unordered paragraphs and an unstructured storyline; it is like a painting with no lines and no coloration—just a bunch of dots.")[81] More evidence of distance as a literary device is found in Mao Dun's massive *China's One Day* (*Zhongguo de yiri* 中國的一日) project, published in 1936.[82] As a collection of reader submissions documenting their experiences of a single, randomly selected day, this work is an early experiment with mass literature. At the same time, its invocation of the masses is recognizably statistical, akin to a random sample survey. The result is a lengthy database, arguably intended to be *seen* rather than read (and certainly not engaged with in any sequential way). It was accordingly characterized as an "epitome" (*suotu* 縮圖) of everyday life.[83] Cursory as they may be, these examples reveal how information visualizations were not just passive objects of representation but, rather, active participants in the evolution of writing practices in their day.

More important to the present discussion is the matter of visualizations' status as worlding objects in their own right. After all, the epistemic claims of these visualizations—that pattern recognition uncovers latent textual truths—rests upon a gulf between text and image, making it difficult to square the experience of one with the other. What of graphics' diegetic world, if such maps can be properly said to have one? Even a fleeting glance at the images discussed here reveals a shared formal element: that of the grid, whether explicitly as lattices that make up *biao* or, in the case of *tu*, implicitly as the geometric plane or topological spaces upon which elements are laid out as schema. In her introduction to a modernist art exhibition titled *Grids: Format and Image in 20th Century Art*, art historian Rosalind Krauss describes the nonmimetic nature of the grid in a way that is relevant for thinking through their appeal for modern Chinese intellectuals:

> In the flatness that results from its coordinates, the grid is the means of crowding out the dimensions of the real and replacing them with the lateral spread of a single surface. In the overall regularity of its organization, it is the result not of imitation, but of aesthetic decree. Insofar as its order is that of pure relationship, the grid is a way of abrogating the claims of natural objects to have an order particular to themselves.[84]

Anticipating the unused cells of software spreadsheets that extend to gigantic proportions, Krauss goes on to emphasize how the grid form is endowed

with a "centrifugal" force, making a given work of art into "a mere fragment, a tiny piece arbitrarily cropped from an infinitely larger fabric" that
extends without end.[85] Krauss has in mind works of fine art, rather than
the more mundane images of statistical visualization. But these latter
images, too, express a centrifugal logic that challenges the self-enclosure
of the visualization's frame, whether it is an expressly drawn border or simply the area designated by the layout of the printed page. This modular
expandability is key to understanding the aesthetic world constructed by
modern *tu* and *biao*, namely that they are conceived as *parts of a universal
and contiguous space*. One *biao* of Zhang Yaoxiang occupies the same plane
as the next. The grid of *biao*, in turn, adjoins them to Wei Juxian's graphs and
He Yubo's diagrams. The visualizations of contemporaries like the Russian
formalist Boris Yarkho and Richard Moulton are there, too (as perhaps are
Franco Moretti's graphs, maps, and trees—maybe even *especially* so, given
Moretti's conception of distant reading as an attempt to radically expand
the reading boundaries in the field of world literature studies).[86] For the
makers of *biao* and *tu* in early twentieth-century China, this represented an
important turning point toward becoming active, self-conscious participants in a globalizing system of information aesthetics. The resulting
images offered a window onto a leveling space where, however briefly, different cultures—their languages, literatures, historical accounts—were well
and truly commensurable.

Chapter Two

PIERCING THE ROAR OF NUMBERS

Misinformation and Fictitious Capital in Mao Dun's Market-Themed Literature

A contemporary review of Mao Dun's 1936 novella *Polygonal Relations* (*Duojiao guanxi* 多角關係) observes:

> [The story's] depictions of economic impediments and entanglements form an image of the backwardness of half-industrialized society. . . . At such a time our author resembles an illustrator drawing with charcoal, using a heavy hand to work in great scribbles and erasures, with each stroke appearing pitch black with no gradation; [leaving] only a complex interlacing of forceful dots and lines [*youli de dian he xian de fuza jiaocuo* 有力的點和線的複雜交錯] that forms multiple shifting points of view.[1]

This characterization aptly fits much of Mao's prodigious output from the preceding five years, including, besides *Polygonal Relations*, a collection of short stories, numerous essays, and his magnum opus, *Midnight* (*Ziye* 子夜, 1933), which all focus on economic topics such as the buying and selling of commodities, issues of debt and credit and liquidity, and the motif of economic calculation, in effect forming a body of market-themed work that offers an extended ethnography of the vagaries of modernization in China at the time.[2] But what makes this review's imagined scene notable are the visual terms by which it depicts Mao Dun's writing. If this bit of ekphrasis bids us to look, what do we see? In its construction of basic elements of dots and lines, the story-become-picture departs from the chiaroscuro and per-spectivism of realism in favor of an unexpectedly spare formalism. Though the visual register is of extreme proximity, its effect is one of distance. Not unlike a cubist painting or network scheme, the image effects different per-spectives or subject positions. These refer to the spectrum of socioeco-nomic viewpoints represented in Mao Dun's fiction—the elite banker and stock speculator, the factory manager, the pawnshop owner, the factory worker, the rural silk producer. Above all, then, the picture offers a kind of "systems aesthetics" whose abstraction into dots and lines shifts away from the mimetic reproduction of a perceptible environment to instead repre-sent a set of socioeconomic relations or structure.[3]

This short passage speaks to the diagrammatic quality of Mao Dun's lit-erary practice that we noted in the preceding chapter. More important, the notional image alerts us to the subjects of abstraction and visuality arising from Mao's decisive encounter with the stock price board during his visit to the China Merchants Stock Exchange in 1931. How his subsequent market-themed work—particularly *Midnight* and *Polygonal Relations*—takes up the task of revealing China's economic structure and the inequities of finan-cial capitalism while also exploring how to *see* such a structure are the subjects of this present chapter. Such efforts resulted in an extended and unprecedented literary investigation into the information order of the day, an experiment that stands as a landmark in modern Chinese history. A careful reading of this market literature demonstrates its author's ongoing attempt to see through abstraction. As a key part of his Marxist agenda of undoing reification, Mao Dun's description of abstraction had important implications both for his specific positioning of literary realism and his con-ception of individual subjectivity within a changing information order.

THE GAME OF SPECULATION

Reading Mao Dun's market-themed literature today reveals the striking extent to which the hustle and bustle of 1930s Shanghai, characterized in *Midnight* as a "time of speculation" when anyone with a bit of cash bet on the market,[4] anticipated the fantasies of enrichment in postreform China of the 1990s, where the stock market has once again emerged as an engine of national economic development. As the crown jewel of this set of works, *Midnight* at once both details and dramatizes the spread of speculation through the schemes of its principal character, the industrial capitalist Wu Sunfu, as he struggles to maintain control over his factories, his household, and even his body amid the ups and downs of the stock and bond market. When Sunfu and his clique of industrialist magnates attempt to corner the market for silk, he is defeated at the hands of his rival, Zhao Botao, who is backed by even more powerful foreign capitalists. In staging such a conflict, *Midnight* introduces the world of high finance while also touching upon pressing forms of class struggle, from worker strikes at Sunfu's silk factories to the rapid takeover of the surrounding countryside by Communist "bandits." The result: a grand panorama of an unstable historical moment, where the necessary collapse of capitalism portends the hopeful—but far from certain—arrival of a socialist "dawn."

Midnight represents a turning point in Mao Dun's literary career that has long attracted the interest of readers. The novel demonstrates Mao's growing embrace of a Marxist-Leninist worldview but also shows an eagerness to draw lessons that go beyond questions of political economy, strictly speaking. Indeed, the novel's primary message—that national industrial capitalism is ultimately overpowered by transnational finance capital—balances uneasily with its choice of protagonist and its tight focus on speculation. Why did Mao Dun take up the gilded realm of Shanghai's industrial tycoons and wealthy financiers rather than the proletarian masses, who are ostensibly the "true" subject of revolutionary history? This choice has largely been attributed to historical accident: in the early 1930s Mao Dun suffered severe troubles with his eyes, which temporarily forced him to give up writing but freed him to mingle with Shanghai's elite through the auspices of a wealthy uncle, exposing him to a world of smoke-filled back rooms of restaurants, hotel penthouses, and the quintessential playgrounds of modern capitalism, the city's stock exchanges. As we have already seen, the Shanghai China Merchants Stock Exchange, the largest such institution in the country at the time of his visit, left a deep impression on Mao, who subsequently took the opportunity to introduce this enigmatic space to his readers.[5] "Enigmatic" because entry had become restricted to licensed brokers, traders, and their associates, so that by the early 1930s exchanges were largely occluded from the general public, as evidenced by the relative paucity of pictures of exchanges in contemporaneous film and other visual media—for instance, in his foreword to a set of woodcut illustrations for *Midnight*, the artist Liu Xian 劉峴 explains that he could not depict the exchange because he has no images or personal experience to work from—not to mention an absence of the subject of stock trading and speculation in New Culture–inspired literature outside of Mao Dun's.[6]

But on its own this special access does not fully explain Mao's prolonged fascination with the subjects of speculation and calculation in his market-themed literature—an interest which some critics have viewed as *Midnight*'s biggest flaw, labeling the novel's lengthy descriptions of the ins and outs of stock trading excessive and dry. In his field-setting historical survey of modern Chinese fiction, C. T. Hsia, for example, declares *Midnight* "a work of tremendous research, impeccable in documentation, larded with allusion to topical figures, and crammed with political and economic facts," which the reader finds "often irritating and boring."[7] Another influential voice, Joseph Lau, concurs: "Page after page of unrelieved boredom when the Bulls and the Bears in the novel start to talk shop, when Mao Dun the novelist is carried away by Mao Dun the amateur stock broker."[8] By accusing *Midnight* of a didacticism that doesn't square with the genre of fiction, such evaluations inadvertently reproduce the literature/information opposition inherent to the formation of modern literature in China and elsewhere. In his masterful reading of the novel, David Wang analyzes this division head-on by identifying the text's amplitude of details—manifest as inventories of facts, psychological data, and references to current events—as a matter of literary style adopted by Mao Dun in an attempt both to borrow authority from historiography and to surpass its limited accessibility.[9] For Wang, information is relayed as part of the novel's suite of techniques of literary realism, where superfluous but precise-looking financial data creates an effect of verisimilitude.[10] While I agree with Wang's perceptive reading, we must go further in centering the thematization and formal experiments with information in Mao Dun's market-themed literature. By engaging with the details of speculation, *Midnight* is not just full of information; it is also *about* information, a subject that fuels Mao's economic imagination and conceptualization of literary realism rather than being subjugated to them.

To see this, let us return to Mao Dun's formative encounter at the stock exchange. In his autobiography, Mao recounts how his former colleague from the Commercial Press brought him to an exchange.[11] He notes his ability to expediently understand the operation of financial speculation thanks to his childhood in a sericultural region of China, where he witnessed firsthand the buying and selling of commodity futures in the form of mulberry leaves in the run-up to each silkworm growing season:

> For others, perhaps [the trading in stocks or futures] would be difficult to grasp quickly. But for me it was different. This was because of the similarities between buying and selling on the stock market and the annual mulberry leaf market in my home region [of Wuzhen]. There, just as soon as the spring silkworms would begin to emerge, a few people would establish a leaf trade—but in actuality they had no mulberry leaves in their possession. About three or four months before the high point of the silkworm season, those in the leaf business made different guesses about and assessments of the outcome of the silkworm crop. Those who thought the silkworm crop would be poor would sell [in advance] several bales of leaves to familiar townsfolk; they resemble the bears at the stock exchange. Those who guessed that the silkworms would mature well would make an advance purchase of several bales of leaves from landlords who owned mulberry plots but didn't raise silkworms, located in their own village or a neighboring one; they are like the bulls of the stock exchange. Because they were *sold and bought in advance*, the price of every bale of leaves was usually quite low, [so] during the busy part of the silkworm season, if the silkworms flourished, the leaf price rose, and those who had sold in advance [i.e., the bears] had no recourse but to buy [actual leaves] at three or four times [the earlier price] in order to fill the peasants' orders. In this way, they not only lost their operating costs, but even faced bankruptcy. In contrast, those who had purchased in advance could profit greatly. . . . *The leaf market concludes after three months, but the stock exchange [runs continuously so it] has a monthly settlement. This is the only point of difference between the two.*[12]

This description immediately brings to mind another of Mao's most famous works, his short story "Spring Silkworms" (1933), which he wrote alongside *Midnight*, and the parallels it draws between the transnational, bank-backed world of high finance on the one hand and, on the other hand, the rural economy of his home region. In both the short story and the quoted autobiographical passage, Mao Dun identifies a temporal logic where value can be "produced" through betting on price differentials over time, thus creating a bidirectional potential for gain (a bull profits through a rise in the commodity's price, a bear through its drop).[13] By this logic, speculation requires no ownership or exchanges of the physical commodity: one merely bets on the gap between opening prices and closing prices.

Crucially, the autobiographical passage next observes how the leaf market, and by extension the stock exchange, is not simply a matter of testing an individual's prognostication abilities against a neutral market where commodity prices are the natural product of the balance between supply and demand. Instead, competing speculators would actively manipulate the value of the leaves by

> widely circulating misinformation [*hongchuan jiaxiaoxi* 哄传假消息] to make the price of leaves rise or fall. This misinformation typically regarded the great success or utter failure of the silkworm crop in such-and-such village in the neighboring region. If one said the neighboring village was enjoying a bumper crop of silkworms, it meant [their] leaf supply would be insufficient, and that [buyers] would come to this village to purchase several bales, thus causing a rise in leaf prices. Conversely, if the misinformation suggested the neighboring village had a disastrous silkworm crop, then [that unfortunate] village had an excess of leaves and would sell them to this village [cheaply], thus causing the leaf price to drop.[14]

As a form of anticipation about future events or conditions, speculative success is contingent upon teasing out true information from the misinformation or disinformation spread by competitors. By the same token, what makes a stock market a market is its atmosphere of dynamic uncertainty, where information asymmetries in the form of insider knowledge or rumor-mongering determine who exploits whom. The critical value of information is further indirectly reinforced throughout *Midnight* and its related shorter works, where the ills of the Chinese economy in the early 1930s are predominantly diagnosed not as a problem of production—Mao Dun's farmers enjoy good crops, his factories feature strong output—but rather one of miscalculation and maldistribution. One cannot miss the lesson: that the economic livelihood of an individual, enterprise, or community turns upon the ability to distinguish good information from bad.[15]

Returning to Mao's sketch of the Shanghai China Merchants Stock Exchange, we can see how this insight particularly attunes him to the multivalent ways in which information flows through the building. Traders who are directly involved in buying and selling are not exclusively oriented toward the exchange's "stage" at the front of the pit. Instead, they turn toward one another, forming a "heterarchical" network with no fixed center, making it impossible to discern which individual or what interaction causes which effect.[16] The relative lack of focal point is further highlighted by the other modalities of communication crisscrossing the space—including telephones, courier deliveries, and scribbled notes. As Mao observes, some messages trail off, others cascade throughout the crowd. Information dominates the scene, constituting for participants a deep-seated source of anxiety and pleasure alike, where "a baseless rumor blown into the stock exchange can excite large waves of rises and falls in bonds and stocks. These people fantasize within the rumors, are excited or rendered spiritless by them. *No one is more sensitive than these people. But, if they didn't have such sensitivity towards rumor, the bond market wouldn't become a market.*"[17] This observation is tongue in cheek, but, coupled with his autobiography's explanation of the mulberry leaf trade, it nonetheless carries what for Mao is a basic truth: information is a crucial element of any speculative market, and, more important, its value can be decoupled from the truth of the situation that it is about, as demonstrated in the preceding examples by the circulation of rumors or fake news.

In sum, Mao Dun's visit to the floor of the stock exchange results in two insights about information in relation to forms of fictitiousness. The first, as we have observed in the introduction, regards the hyper-abstractive nature of modern financial instruments, as emblematized by the spectacle of the red-lit numbers floating above the crowd of traders in the pit, and which made capital more mobile and extendable. But there is a second realization of fictitiousness at stake, one that departs from Karl Marx's concept of it (capital symbolically abstracted as financial instruments) to instead highlight a distinction between information and true knowledge, where the circulation of the former does not necessarily result in an increase of the latter—and indeed may even be deleterious to it. Speculation is, in other words, a matter of distinguishing signal from noise (a metaphor drawn from radio and that was central to the information discourse of the 1930s, the subject of the following chapter). The distinction and relation between these two forms of fictitiousness return us to the dual function of information as both a medium itself (here, the stocks and bonds that come to supersede physical commodities) and an index of communication (the mobility of symbolic forms of capital along with numeric figures more generally, as well as tidbits of news and orders to buy and sell). They are collectively manifested in *Midnight* as the flood of economic data scattered throughout the story, on the one hand, and, on the other hand, the frenetic circulation of information that Marston Anderson, in his reading of the novel, places alongside money and sex as symptomatic of capitalistic society's broader "fetishization of the transmissible object."[18]

What remains to be understood in the wake of this set of cues is how these two sides of information intersect in Mao Dun's writing. The impressions articulated in the "Sketch" signal that the exchange and, by extension, his writing about the market generally play a different role for Mao Dun than simply a target of caricature of the elite. Instead, the prolonged theater metaphor, the captivation with the virtual nature of the floating red numbers, and the keen observations of the myriad ways in which messages circulate collectively invite key questions regarding Mao's fiction: What is the significance of information (whether true or false) not just to the generation of fictitious capital and its agents, but to modern subjectivity and epistemology more generally? Is there a relationship between the virtuality of speculative capital and Mao Dun's project of literary realism? Let us take up these questions as they are staged in *Midnight* and Mao's other related 1930s works about the market.

HUNTING AND GATHERING

How does information appear within *Midnight*? Besides the many details, economic facts, and exchanges of messages between characters, information is articulated explicitly as an object when it circulates as *xiaoxi*, making the novel an active participant in the larger discourse of information of its day. As glossed in the introduction, *xiaoxi* is a deictic marker whose semantic value is determined by its specific context, akin to "today," "they," or the term "information" itself. Such linguistic emptiness makes *xiaoxi* easy to overlook as a relatively empty signifier but also imparts it with a metadiscursive property that reveals (and makes possible) the tokenization of a bit of knowledge removed from its original context. By paying attention to the term's appearance within a text, one can trace the movement of *xiaoxi*/ information to reveal larger structures of relations that make up the encompassing information order. Indeed, *xiaoxi* runs through *Midnight* like an iodinated contrast dye, foregrounding communication pathways between characters across various media such as telephone and newspaper. As such, its percolation reveals the novel's understanding of the stock exchange as a processor of information, along with the economic, political, and even epistemic stakes of this apparatus.

The movement of *xiaoxi* and characters' unequal access to it thus provide a protocol for understanding the social world of *Midnight*. If successful speculation depends on the abilities to collect and distinguish what market intelligence is valuable, from rumors to insider tips, and on manipulating information to one's advantage, *Midnight* accordingly offers a gallery of information managers whose internecine struggles over *xiaoxi* help steer the novel's plotline. These information managers extend well beyond the novel's core of industrial capitalists and financiers to include the constellation of minor speculators, government bureaucrats, company administrators, landlords, and socialites that make up Shanghai's upper crust: men (primarily) who see themselves as the "heroic knights and 'princes' of the twentieth century's industrial age, who, unlike their predecessors who were skilled in fencing and riding horses, [now] make calculations and drive cars" (91, 77–78). What makes each one of these characters a manager of information/*xiaoxi* is not their job or social position, but rather the more generalized activity of projecting control onto their environments. Put differently, the issue of managerial control—"twin activities of information processing and reciprocal communication," to use James Beniger's description from his information-centered history of the Industrial Revolution—serves as a measure of each character's identity as an agentive subject.[19]

As the novel's central character, Wu Sunfu also offers the most detailed portrait of information management in action. Throughout the story, he attends to his business affairs using telecommunications such as the telephone and the telegraph, as well as a network of subalterns who collect or transmit *xiaoxi* on his behalf. The subject of control is dramatized when Sunfu runs up against a series of challenges in his attempts to corner the silk market. Chief among these are the many failures of the telecommunication infrastructure, which create a sense of contingency in speculation and show the importance of synchronicity between Sunfu and the objects of his managerial reach. When he is on occasion stripped of his technological support systems, he is made impotent by a fog of war; indeed, disruptions of the regular order open spaces for moments of heightened consciousness such as midway through the story, where Sunfu, suspecting he has been betrayed by his coconspirators in their latest scheme, anxiously awaits the arrival of news from both his broker and his factory agent. Upon discovering that his telephone line has gone down in the just-passed thunderstorm, he rushes off in his car to check in on his factory. In the back of the moving vehicle, removed from the stable, wired space of his office, Sunfu experiences a fleeting moment of self-awareness about his condition as an information manager:

> He glanced out of the windows, breathing heavily. Suddenly an unusual sensation came over him: he was one of the captains of industry, ruthless and go-ahead at every moment, but half-suspended before him were nothing more than absurd and empty mirages! And what were the people around him but so many blurred, misshapen figures? His progress in industry was just like his present journey—an aimless rush through a blinding mist! (197, 166)

Evoking a sense of embodiment (breath, kinesthesia) as a contrast to the forces of abstraction that underlie advanced capitalism, this passage calls attention to the extent to which Sunfu has naturalized the virtual experience of his normal communicational milieu. Only now do Sunfu's associates and subordinates become "blurry, misshapen figures," suggesting that typically he manages to keep them in sharp relief. But their blurriness and ephemerality are their true nature rather than the product of confusion: the empty mirages are the very symbol of fictitious capital.

A similar breakdown occurs at the novel's climax, nixing Sunfu's final rally of his team of speculators at the exchange. While Sunfu is holding out hope of a victory, his confidence is temporarily buoyed by a telegram he receives from an ally who has gone off to solicit credit for their industrial trust fund:

> The telegram was from Tang Yunshan in Hong Kong and contained thirty or fifty characters, not yet decoded. Wu Sunfu opened his telegram code book and translated seven or eight characters . . . the telegram was full of good news [xiaoxi]. . . . But even if Tang Yunshan had struck lucky this time, Wu Sunfu was still displeased with the man's muddle-headedness. Hadn't he sent Tang telegram after telegram urging him to wire money back the moment he laid hands on any? But this was yet another worthless telegram! And what did he mean by "coming back to Shanghai immediately?" Anyone

would think Hong Kong was still living in the eighteenth century and using bulky silver ingots that could only be brought back to Shanghai by Tang Yunshan in person! (571–72, 527–28)

This infrastructural failure is operative rather than physical: the telegraph line has not come up short per se, but for the purpose of Wu Sunfu's endeavor it may as well have, given Tang's insistence on carrying back physical cash from Hong Kong rather than wiring funds directly. What Sunfu and his allies need in this critical moment is the *immediate* infusion of money, wired as a message between account holders. Indeed, only the medium that carries Tang Yunshan's message from Hong Kong can "put out a fire with water a league away" (571, 527). Tang's failure betrays a mistaken attachment to the materiality of the money medium (as silver), a belief that has become outmoded in a modern context where value can circulate as abstract information.

As crucial as telecommunication failures are to the novel's investigation of control, noise poses an even greater threat to the livelihoods of *Midnight*'s characters. Noise, as the ethnomusicologist David Novak reminds us, is fundamentally the product of cultural or individual perception rather than an objectively definable sonic phenomenon. Its constructedness and semantic range make it a potent symbolic counterpart for a variety of categories, from culture and human expression to rationality, control, and information transmission.[20] In *Midnight* noise is an essential feature of the stock exchange: as the din of pit trading, of course, but also more metaphorically as impedance to knowledge about market conditions, both as rumors or misinformation (where noise presents opportunities for arbitrage, as we have already seen in Mao's memoir), as well as in the form of the uninterpretable, random movement of stock prices.[21] Throughout the story, noise plays a key role in the development of characters' fortunes and misfortunes, giving further play to the novel's imagination and politics of information.

At nearly every major juncture in the plot, noise jams Wu Sunfu's and others' ability to communicate effectively. At the opening of chapter seven, a pivotal section where the collaboration between industrial and finance capitalists begins to unravel, Sunfu is shown sitting in his study "like a commander-in-chief planning an offensive," taking in messages from his network of representatives at the exchange, his factory managers, and agents from his hometown in the countryside (190–91, 160). A thunderstorm erupts just as his brother-in-law, Du Zhuzhai, arrives with news:

Wu Sunfu and Du Zhuzhai began talking about the day's events at the Exchange. Lightning flashes, thunderclaps, and the roar of rain filled the room so that the conversation was barely audible. But by watching Du Zhuzhai's lip movements, Wu Sunfu managed to get the gist of what he was saying. When the lips stopped for a moment, Wu Sunfu laughed bitterly and shouted, "You say there are still new bears turning up? They must be mad!" (192, 161–62)

They realize they have been betrayed by the financier Zhao Botao—a surprise they failed to anticipate earlier on account of the "noise and stuffiness on the floor of the Exchange" (192, 161–62). The thunderstorm itself metaphorically intimates that the madness of the bears' position in the market will soon spill over into Sunfu's office. Altogether, the melodramatic symbolism of bad weather is so recurrent and closely tied to the novel's speculation-related scenes that one could track the narrative's climaxes through the storms alone—a pattern so obvious that it threatens to disrupt the realism of the novel, as one contemporary critic noted.[22]

As a form of informatic excess, noise also features in moments of imbalance and miscommunication. It is especially prominent in moments when a proper signal must be teased from a background of irrelevant or actively harmful ones. The connection between chaotic noise and misinformation is borne out in the novel's descriptions of the exchange floor. In one dramatic passage, the character Liu Yuying, a consort and herself a minor speculator in stocks, visits the floor during a period of frenzied trading caused by the approaching settlement day:

The floor of the exchange was even noisier [*caoza* 嘈雜] than a food market. . . . Up on the platform the announcer and the telephonists were all red in the face as they gesticulated and shouted, but it was impossible to hear a word they were saying. Seventy or eighty brokers, together with their hundred-odd assistants and innumerable speculators, produced such a thunderous roar of numbers that no ear could have made anything of it. (333, 294–95)

In a space where information is too condensed, communication breaks down amid a digital static that makes it difficult to recognize exactly which pattern or development anticipates the movement of the market. Chaos ensues, and even conversation becomes impossible.

FIGURE 2.1 Schematic illustration of communication in *Midnight*. Liu Xian, *Ziye zhi tu* (Shanghai: Weiming muke she, 1937)

Here it is instructive to draw a contrast with a contemporaneous woodcut illustration of *Midnight*, in which the artist, Liu Xian, portrays the circulation of *xiaoxi* among investors behind the scenes of the exchange and its spectacle (figure 2.1). The image shows information's movement among a discreet network of the truly elite speculators. What stands out is the picture's understated sonic quality, which suggests that valuable information—the true signal of the market's movement—is transmitted quietly, from lips to ear, worthy of eavesdropping. Whether in the novel or its illustration, noise looms as a kind of subject in its own right, acting upon characters even as they contribute further to it through their machinations.

Much like the men depicted in the woodcut, Liu Yuying is not swept up in the noise at the exchange. Due to her unique social access as a consort to rival speculators, she has obtained insider knowledge about their tactics and knows who is primarily responsible for the market's ups and downs. If the fluctuations of stock prices at the exchange appear to many brokers and minor speculators as inscrutable, quasi-random responses to the chaos of the crowd at hand, to Yuying's knowing ear they sound off a deeper meaning as signs of a hidden struggle:

> How comical it all was, she thought: here in the exchange was the "market," while somewhere outside away from it all Zhao Botao and Wu Sunfu were lounging on their sofas with their cigars and pulling the strings that made these puppets dance! As for herself, she now held the secrets of the two string-pullers in the palm of her hand. All these men here were fighting in the dark, and she alone knew what was going on. (333, 295)[23]

When she runs into a group of small-timers frantically trying to make sense of the situation, Yuying "saw and heard clearly all that passed between them [and] could not help smiling again" (335, 297). And when she flirts with revealing her secret to one of them, the landlord-cum-speculator Feng Yunqing, the latter is so distracted by his own schemes and the surrounding noise that he misses her veiled suggestion that she harbors critical knowledge about which way the wind blows. Marston Anderson rightly points out how this scene represents the novel's sustained play between forms of transmission, where sex, money, and information are fully interchangeable.[24] But what further makes this moment important is what *doesn't* occur. We see how Yuying is positioned as a hub in the network of speculators. Given the stock market's sensitivity to rumor and information, her secret could sway the entire stock market and completely disrupt the struggle between Wu Sunfu and Zhao Botao. Feng Yunqing's failure to understand her underscores the contingent nature of speculation in a market where the psychosocial dynamic of pleasure and anxiety overwhelms the individual's capacity for sound decision-making. This point is redoubled in the following scene between the Feng and his daughter, whom he has assigned the unsavory task of finding out the very market intelligence that Yuying has just teased him with. After arriving home—and with the pandemonium of the exchange floor still ringing in his ears—Feng probes his daughter for any information she has managed to pick up. Having failed to obtain any real news, his daughter simply fabricates an answer that readers recognize as incorrect. But Feng decides to believe her answer when he hears the sound of wind outside the window, which he misinterprets as a good omen (345, 306). Noise has sealed his fate.

Whether phenomenally or figuratively, noise thus is an essential feature of *Midnight*'s interrogation of speculation and finance capitalism more generally. But the novel introduces another form of noise that jeopardizes the game altogether: the roar of the laboring masses. Here, too, the threatening potential of noise plays out in informatic terms. In chapter 9, for example, the passionate roar of an anti-imperialist street demonstration is juxtaposed against both the confused discussion of current events among the effete cohort of youths that hang around the Wu household and the perilous attempt of the economics professor Li Yuding to backchannel a reconciliation between Zhao Botao and Wu Sunfu. The power of the protestors' roar intervenes in the supposed "rationality" of the elite speculators and evinces a positively coded, liberating energy, a politics of sound that appeared often in leftist literature, film, and art of the period and contributed to the broader interpellation of the masses as both a subject and object of history.[25] As an embodied emanation, this collective noise contributes to the narrative's acoustic realism while highlighting the supposed solidity of the working class.

And yet *Midnight*'s linkage of communication and class politics does not follow a simplistic equation between mass noise and the power of the laboring class. Instead, mass consciousness amongst factory works is portrayed as another matter of information management. In chapter 13 the narrative turns from Wu Sunfu and his family to the community of women workers employed at Wu's silk filature who are trying to mobilize an industry-wide strike. These workers depend on a network of organizers forced underground by the constant threat of Sunfu's informers, spies, and rumormongers. This labor network is spatialized in the labyrinthine layout of the factory's residence slums. Groups of workers move from node to node to spread news and consult one another, all the while attempting to avoid the attention of patrolling thugs dispatched by factory management. Unlike at a noise-filled rally, here information percolates along an extended kinship-like structure of labor relations. Through the extended passage the narrative traces this series of relays by shifting character viewpoint from the factory workers Zhu Guiying to Chen Yue'e and finally to the Communist intellectuals Cai Zhen and Ma Jin.

The chapter not only effects a multivalent flow of information but also demonstrates how, like speculators, the Communist organizers are themselves information managers taking in reports, brokering relations between groups from different factories, and working to collectivize labor into a concerted political force. These women face a sly opponent in the factory headman, Du Weiyue, himself a capable manipulator of information whose skill is evidenced earlier in the novel, after Sunfu cuts wages at the factory, when although again the "buzz of [the laborers'] voices began to swell into a tide, this time it *flowed through a channel which had been engineered* by Du," thereby diffusing the workers' rage (208, 176; my emphasis). In chapter 13, however, the women unintentionally sabotage their own efforts to organize when their mobilizing slogans and jargon (*shuyu* 術語) end up reducing their communication to the compulsive recitation of formulas. For example, when Chen Yue'e reports on factory conditions:

> Her diction was of the simplest, but she larded it freely with some of the jargon she had lately picked up—the women's "spirit of struggle" was running high; given "leadership," there was no question of their not being "mobilized" immediately. . . . [Meanwhile, the Communist organizer] Ma Jin made no comment, but still watched Chen Yue'e with an intense stare, as if trying to detect any exaggerations the latter might be making in her "report." She had the feeling that there were some complicated problems involved in the "report," yet, not being a swift thinker, she could not for the moment make an accurate analysis of what these problems were—she just had a vague sense of uneasiness. (397–98, 356–57)

Because they were clear and "rational"-sounding (*heli* 合理), these slogans "had been firmly memorized by Chen Yue'e and through her instilled into the minds of [her coworkers] Zhang Axin and He Xiumei, whose simple minds and warm hearts were just the right sort of fertile soil for such 'formulas'" (398, 357). But in this bitingly sarcastic portrayal of the two leftist intellectuals, the Communist "formulas" (*gongshi* 公式) risk obscuring the true situation by collapsing complexity into meaningless (but highly mobile) phrases. Their redundancy reduces valuable descriptive information, which is made evident in the ensuing debate between Ma Jin and Cai Zhen when the argument devolves into a verbiage-filled duel of slogans. Repeated ad nauseum with little reference to reality, such signifiers lose their meaning to become instead a form of white noise—not dissimilar to the roar of price quotes at the exchange. Indeed, the various recurrence of forms of noise in the animation of class consciousness reveal in the novel a deep-seated ambivalence about the masses themselves, who at times appear all too similar to the shortsighted brokers at the exchange.

Midnight thus explores the dyad of communication and control through two interrelated motifs: breakdowns of infrastructure and the phenomenology and symbolism of noise. Swinging between bouts of frustrating scarcity and confusing overabundance, the novel's depictions of information asymmetry reveal the inner workings of speculation that drive the apparatus of the market, while also emphasizing this mechanism's many irrationalities and contingencies. But, as the episode involving the labor organizers demonstrates, correct information management is a concern that extends beyond the financial elite to the very masses that they oppress. In this sense, speculation at the stock exchange serves as an allegory about the broader social and political significance of information in modern China. The words of one character, the provincial landlord Zeng Zanghai, to his craven son read like an admonishment directed to the reader: "If you're going to do your job properly, you must get to know about local conditions. You should go around and try to find out about this and that. Information [*xiaoxi*] won't come and knock at your door" (106, 90). Coupled with this less-than-subtle bit of reported speech, Mao Dun's thematization of information asymmetry stages a lesson that's hard to miss: to survive in a rapidly changing world, the reader must themselves become a skilled hunter and gatherer of information.

But there are limits to this prototype's ability to navigate this world. *Midnight* raises a question regarding information's relationship to knowledge: Does collecting information necessarily lead to meaningful insight? The category of "knowledge" may seldom appear in the novel in an explicit manner, but it nonetheless hovers at the periphery of story's interest in information. Here let me briefly pivot from *Midnight* to the short story "Mr. Zhao Can't Fathom It" ("Zhao xiansheng xiangbutong" 趙先生想不通), one of the key works in the satellite system of Mao Dun's market fiction. The story caricaturizes an experienced broker who is very much drawn from the elite circles of *Midnight*. Mr. Zhao appears supernaturally equipped to handle the roar of numbers at the exchange, for he has eyes like a hawk. No matter how many hands were wildly signaling bids, no matter how many fingers were being held up on each hand, he could take them all in at a glance. At once he could calculate the total number of fingers; he could fill in on his mental chart how many hands were raised palm up, how many palm down. Nine cases out of ten, he could even guess the brokers to whom the hands belonged. His ears were first rate too. From the babble of numbers he could pick out a quietly mentioned figure—for instance, three dollars and sixty cents. "Ah, a new quote!" he would immediately say to himself.[26]

Despite his elevated sensitivities, Zhao's intractable pessimism about the movement of bond prices makes him always look for a fall in the market (*kandi* 看低). He is stuck at the level of information, a reactive cog who cannot tease out (*xiangbutong* 想不通) the deeper significance of stock movements or overcome his own psychological biases. Put differently, Mr. Zhao and others like him can hunt and gather information, but they can't process, or cook, it. This short story not only stakes out a gap between information and knowledge in Mr. Zhao but also asserts the narrative's privileged position relative to the character, for it knows (and shows to the reader) the character's limitations to a degree inaccessible to the character himself. Such establishment of (literary) knowledge relative to (financial) information is not incidental. Rather, it is a sustained opposition in Mao Dun's market-themed literature and fuels his practice of literary realism in *Midnight* and after. Such realism, in Mao Dun's hands, offers the direct antidote to the excessive abstraction of fictitious capital.

COOKING

The importance of information to Mao Dun's long-standing interest in realism is captured by a crucial passage at the beginning of *Midnight*'s eighth chapter. Here the narrative meanders away from the main plotline to develop the character Feng Yunqing, the predator landlord who has moved to Shanghai from the countryside to escape bandits and appease his demanding concubine. Feng has now put his fortune into speculation at the exchange. After a good run, his luck has run out amidst the throes of the market caused by the struggle between Wu Sunfu and Zhao Botao. Here we find him working in his study:

Sunlight was streaming through the bamboo blinds and throwing a criss-cross pattern of light and shade over part of the room. At the slightest breeze the blinds gently swayed, and a filigree of shadows would ripple over the chairs and tables, conjuring up strange black and white patterns. Sitting at a square mahogany table under the window, Feng Yunqing was turning the pages of his account book with his right hand while holding a cigarette in his left. As the shadows wavered across the pages of his book, the figures in the ledger seemed to dance with them. Suddenly irate, Feng Yunqing brought his palm down on the book with an impatient thwack . . ."It's just my bad luck!" (221, 188)

Anxiously focused on his accounting calculations, Feng isn't directly aware of the shadowed patterns that dance on the book's surface; they signal his fate to us readers, but for the character, they remain at the level of subconsciousness. If this suggestion of psychological depth, coupled with the detailed description, is typical of literary realism, it is one whose effect of verisimilitude is put into service as a direct contrast to the ledger book that appears in the scene. For if the latter serves as a meeting point between Feng's desires and the social reality of his debts, it also juxtaposes competing kinds of representation, where the cinematic play of shadows upon the ledger's surface offers up a reality no less strange and immaterial than the numbers filling up the page. The narrative asserts itself as the privileged source of critical knowledge by encompassing both shadow and numeric figures—and seeing through both.

More than the difference between diegetic and extradiegetic dimensions of the novel's world, this focus on the ledger book is significant as part of a larger trope in Mao Dun's market-themed work, where characters regularly obsess over profits and losses. Whether as mental calculations or in the appearance of characters' account books, the trope underscores the logic of exchange value that mediates so many of the social relations in *Midnight* and its related texts. But read alongside the "Sketch," the ledger trope shows the specific significance of abstraction to financial capital, where transactions are decoupled from actual exchanges of commodities or money and instead operate as inscriptions of information. (Indeed, at its most extreme, this abstract quality of the ledger's numeric figures makes them "float," as Mao Dun remarks of the price ticker's numbers at the exchange.) In this sense, the ledger constitutes a system of writing that, as such, can be set in relation with other genres, in particular narrative fiction.[27] As such, the ledger trope operates as a reflexive literary device in Mao Dun's market fiction along with his literary criticism. Its proliferation in Mao's work invites what Lydia Liu calls a "figural reading"—"a kind of coded reading bodied forth or *represented* within the text itself."[28] For if ledgers frequently help Mao expose the wealthy's techniques of exploitation, they also pose a productive comparison with literary realism as a different (and mutually constitutive) system of writing. Ledgers do not simply demonstrate how fictitious capital results from the cooking of books—they also offer a rather clearer understanding of how literature can "cook" raw information into a more refined—and more palatable—form of knowledge.

Before turning to further instances of the trope in Mao Dun's work, let us first consider its invocation in several pieces of criticism that bookend either side of *Midnight*. The most significant of these appeared in 1941, as the first entry of a series titled "Small Solutions to Large Problems" (*Da ti xiao jie* 大題小解).[29] In the essay, Mao Dun bemoans the dearth of Chinese novels about the wartime economy, thus obliquely offering a self-commentary on *Midnight* and the relationship between realism and fictitious capital. He beings with an observation regarding government financial figures appearing in newspapers and how they ought to be understood:

> Recently, the papers have frequently spoken of the severe condition of our economy. Nearly all the discussion relating to this has appropriated the method of what literary authors call "figuration" [*xingxianghua* 形象化], so the entire page is covered with descriptions of the circulation of material goods, capital inflows, the stabilization of commodity prices, and so on, without touching upon the fundamental problem. At present, there is no literary work that comprehensively and fundamentally explains and describes the various phenomena of the several years since the beginning of the War of Resistance. . . .
>
> If one wished to write such [a piece], then, first and foremost, regarding the mindset of those who yesterday advocated resistance [against the Japanese] but today no longer do, or those who originally weren't passionate about resistance but now, on the contrary, hope that the "stalemate period" ends, one must research their "wealth profit and loss" account books to understand how the war years have affected the vicissitudes of their wallets . . . otherwise, I'm afraid it would be difficult to write [such a work].[30]

The point of the piece is not merely to chastise writers for failing to produce an updated sequel to *Midnight* capable of documenting the political
economy of the War of Resistance Against Japanese Aggression (1937–1945).
Mao Dun's immediate thrust, clearly, is that materialism explains ideology
and that the question of why some Chinese are mobilized and others are
not boils down to economic motivations rather than national consciousness or patriotic duty. But to understand the oscillations of the economic
figures listed in the newspaper, one needs to get at the individual accounts
that in aggregate make up the larger economic trends. Here Mao Dun calls
for a specifically *literary* intervention, not only because fiction can fabri-
cate individual accounts and perform an unmasking of the motivations
behind them, but also because of literature's own capacity for "figuring" or
"visualizing" (*xingxianghua* 形象化) the economy in a vivid and moving
fashion.[31] In its placement of literature directly alongside economic figures
as compatible and competing genres (and sources) of economic truth, this
essay echoes the previously cited passage from *Midnight* showing Feng
Yunqing in his study. With the aid of this retrospective criticism, Mao Dun's
earlier literary practice should be understood as an engagement with statistics and figures that is as formal as it is thematic.

The convergence of the ledger and narrative writing also appears in a
semi-autobiographical essay from 1935 titled "Old Accounts" ("Jiu zhangbu"
舊賬簿), a full translation of which joins the "Sketch of the Stock Exchange"
in the appendix.[32] Here, Mao Dun reflects on the ledger as raw material
for writing history along with its role in his own passage to becoming a lover
of literature. The piece opens with a question about representation: How
should one go about compiling a gazetteer (*zhi* 誌) of local history? Printed
compendia of local knowledge and events, gazetteers had been popularized
in the Song Dynasty and were crucial to local self-identity inasmuch as they
served as a potential battleground over social status and property interests.[33]
In the essay, a wealthy old-timer from the narrator's hometown has recently
decided to revive the local gazetteer. He consults friends and associates,
including a fellow from the neighboring village who recently completed a
gazetteer and recommends the inclusion of a record of taxation and a price
index of common goods. Compiling such an index, however, requires access
to the old ledgers of the town's merchant families as primary source material. In what is likely a reflection on Mao Dun's own experience, the narrator pauses to recount his material relationship to account books:

After that, I often thought of the wooden chest full of old annual accounts that was stored in the attic in the back of my family home during my child-hood. I don't know why, but these old accounts were kept around, and as a ten-year-old I frequently would flip through them, ripping out blank pages at the back to use as scrap paper for arithmetic exercises. By now, I am sure, that chest full of old annual accounts is long gone. Whether it was incinerated or traded for sweets, I can't clearly recall. At any rate, twenty years ago, [the books'] fate had already come to an end. And I had long forgotten about my family's collection of such worthless "antiques."

Now, upon hearing the words of this Old Mister Jin, I recalled not only how each heavy volume of the old accounts had provided me with scrap paper for calculations, but also how I had moved them back and forth to serve as a stepping stone for when I wanted to locate some old woodblock-printed novel on top of the cabinet; in those times, it never occurred to me that these old "stepping stones" were a part of the historical record of my family—no, I should rather say a resource for the "town gazetteer."

In truth, if we want to know how our grandfathers' grandfathers lived, among the [resources] that can tell us the most authentic information [xiaoxi],[34] I'm afraid nothing surpasses these old account books!

We know that our history is also but a type of "old annual account." It is lamentable, however, that there are so many "fake" [xuzhang 虛賬] and "embellished" [huazhang 花帳] accounts![35]

We ought to recall that, before pursuing a career in literary criticism, a young Shen Yanbing (prior to his adoption of the pen name Mao Dun) had been pushed by his father to study accounting (suanxue 算學) as a field of new knowledge, a course of training that would lead to a promising career at a modern institution such as a bank, textile mill, or railway.[36] To an adolescent, the dreary financial records filling these tomes merely provided the scratch paper for math practice or—tellingly—as a boost up to the shelf containing classical literature. In the narrative present, however, the accounts reappear as critical source for an authentic history—one that is recursively depicted as itself a kind of accounting, which the narrator declares requires its own inter-pretive "method of reading" (dufa 讀法) much like the specialized notation of a financial account. Indeed, the final lines emphasize the fluidity of the boundaries between the ledger and narrative history, where the distortions in the latter are likened to inappropriate techniques of accounting.

One final example of the ledger trope, this time from Mao's early career before becoming an author, appears in a 1922 essay that later became part of the canon of New Culture criticism. Titled "Naturalism and Chinese Modern Literature,"[37] this piece calls for the renovation of Chinese narrative fiction by the adoption of Western realist and naturalist literary techniques. Mao Dun makes his case by attacking older Chinese fiction using a string of accounting metaphors that pejoratively characterize the descriptive techniques of traditional serial novels (*zhanghui xiaoshuo* 章回小說) as rote and listlike. Traditional Chinese novels approach the description of a new character's face, physique, dress, demeanor, and so on as a sort of "incidental expense account" (*lingyong zhang* 零用帳), a series where, like "the merchant's method of 'four-column accounting' [*sizhu zhang* 四株帳],[38] every stroke of the [author's] brush, from start to end, narrates everything in an artless way." The ledger metaphor scales up from the level of description to the structural elements of a story, such as character development and plot, for, "what's more, [readers used to] find commendable [a writer's] ability to clearly 'give an accounting of' [*jiaodai* 交代] the 'ending' (*jieju* 結局) of all the characters in the book [note: all the characters!], praising them for 'without a careless stroke, not leaving out a single thread' [*yi bi bu gou, yi si bu lou* 一筆不苟, 一絲不露]."[39] As the metaphor gains momentum, Mao Dun further builds out the likeness between literary representation and financial accounting:

> [Serial novels] like to narrate every action of every event in great detail; for example, in describing an individual getting out of bed, it's usually something like "so-and-so opened their eyes and looked out the window, seeing that the day was well underway, they hastily pushed back the pillow and cast aside the quilt, sitting up, they draped on a cotton-padded jacket, followed by white silk stockings, and then pants, cinched the pant legs, and only then got out of bed, proceeding to the side of the bed to put on a pair of slippers..." The whole paragraph directly records continuous action but contains no description. When we read this type of "ledgeristic" [*jizhangshi* 記賬式] narration, we only feel that before us is a wooden person, not a living one, nothing but a thoughtless automaton lacking a brain or the ability to think; if they were a living person, then throughout the course of their actions their entire body would express some amount of feeling, and from

such expression we could indirectly spy the movements of their inner heart. . . . It is a rule that a piece of literature should emphasize description, not recording, and especially not "ledgeristic" recording. The human brain can associate and understand suggestion. Regarding many aspects of daily life, it can hear A and associate it with B without waiting for a "ledgeristic" description that spares no detail. Only [indirect description] will be felt to be intimate and interesting. Contemporary serial novels fundamentally mistake the suggestive and associative human brain as nothing more than an abacus to be moved this way and that.[40]

When narrative elements like an event or a character's face are broken down into a long series of discrete observations, one risks excess at the expense of a suggestive indirectness. One need look no further than Erich Auerbach's classical comparison of mimetic modes of description in Homer and the Old Testament to recognize how reductive is Mao Dun's claim that the tradition of Western realism exclusively avoids detailed and listlike description.[41] More important, however, is how the inability to write in such a way that the reader "hears A and associates it with B" describes the problem in terms of information, where the ledger's wealth of financial facts leaves no space for the play of imagination or discovery—the processing of data into knowledge, in other words. It is no surprise that an agent of fictitious capital like Mr. Zhao, as we saw at the end of the previous section, suffers from the inability to think inferentially. By processing information selectively, the techniques of realism are proffered as a higher state of consciousness that can mitigate the ledger's (and traditional narrative's) tendency to overload its reader with explanatory information—a point that ironically anticipates Hsia's and Lau's very criticisms of Mao Dun when it comes to *Midnight*.

Bookending either side of Mao's period of writing about markets and speculation in the early 1930s, these three essays show both the duration of the ledger trope in his work and its significance as an Other to modern literature. For Mao Dun, the formal aspects of an account book—its lines of "raw" financial data, the rhetorical effect of numbers—serve as more than a metaphor for moral indebtedness and instead inspire him to imagine literary realism as a counterbalancing mode of representation. Juxtaposing realist literature with the ledger also places fiction within a broader information order that encompasses both forms. By this token, literature itself is also a mode of information management, one whose capacity to make invisible processes and patterns sensible, to plumb psychological depth, and to capture social reality at scale must be at least partly understood in terms of processing data to produce and communicate knowledge.

Nowhere does the juxtaposition between literature and the ledger play out more clearly than in Mao Dun's 1936 experimental novella *Polygonal Relations*, the de facto sequel to *Midnight*.[42] Praised by contemporaries as the culmination of Mao's market-themed literature and his most carefully structured piece of fiction,[43] the story is rife with images and rhetoric of accounting, so imbued with a kind of calculative consciousness that the entire story can be read as an extended ledger in its own right. It represents both Mao Dun's most direct attack on fictitious capital and the apotheosis of his attempt to work through the relationship between information and realism through the figure of the ledger.

Polygonal Relations draws its name from the unstable web of credit and debit that manifested in a countrywide financial crisis between 1934 and 1935.[44] This historical episode has been attributed by scholars in large part to an effect of the ongoing global depression, delayed in China because of the Nationalist government's adherence to a silver standard.[45] In 1934, thanks in large part to a new U.S. program to buy up silver at artificially high prices, the weight of silver became worth more than the face value of Chinese coinage, prompting the Nationalist government to abandon the silver standard in favor of fiat paper money. This policy was put into practice in autumn of 1934 but was publicly announced only in the autumn of the following year, a delay that compounded growing economic uncertainty. The sudden shift to a new monetary standard and subsequent deflation across China collectively serve as the novella's backdrop and help explain both the pervasive anxieties in the story toward a shortage of circulating silver and the subsequent crisis in trust between parties.

Polygonal Relations keeps a tight focus on economic ties rather than on character development. The emphasis on socioeconomic structure is furthered by the narrative's synchronic temporality in which the overall time frame spans only a single day but traverses between many perspectives, thus recreating the feel of a complex network from an elevated, bird's-eye perspective. Nearly every character is preoccupied with two related crises. On one hand, they desperately try to collect money from debtors in order to pay their own debts. Everyone both owes and is owed, but, thanks to the credit crisis and a severe lack of liquidity, there is not enough cash to support the circuitry of economic obligation, leading to the collapse of the local economic system. On the other hand, each character strains to collect relevant information about everyone else's circumstances in order to maintain their own assets and credit. The tangle and reach of this economic network, coupled with the difficulty each character faces in determining their own position within it, is encapsulated neatly in an early passage where a minor character, Zhu Runshen, considers his situation while awaiting the powerful Tang Zijia at the latter's manor:

> [Zhu] knew that Tang's [other] visitor in the front room was doubtlessly here regarding a credit connection. But he wasn't very clear on whether this "connection" [*guanxi* 關係] was one in which Tang owed the other, or the other owed Tang. Nor did he want to know. [Zhu Runshen] had always been of a very casual temperament. In his life he had encountered countless credit disputes [*jiufen* 糾紛, lit. "entanglements"], but he had always taken care of them in an offhanded way. This was because for three generations his family had served as "managers," while at the same time maintaining some of their own "services," making his positional relationships [*diwei guanxi* 地位關係] very complicated. When even a slightly serious credit dispute occurred, in his "professional" capacity he would perhaps represent the creditor, but in his "private" capacity he might directly or indirectly count as the "debtor." This caused him great difficulty, and he could never tease out his own position. After a long time, this attitude of "incomprehension" [*bu nongqing* 不弄清] became his modus operandi.[46]

Much like the characters Feng Yunqing and Mr. Zhao before him, Zhu's confusion is emblematic of the moral turpitude of the managerial, landlord class. He primarily serves as a foil for the novella's project of tracing the financial complications of the wealthy Tang family. The issue of disputes or entanglement (*jiufen* and *jiuge* 糾葛) joins the ledger as another trope, and appears so frequently that the roles of complexity and scale emerge as major themes in the novella's investigation of fictitious capital. Entanglement in turn is carefully organized and analyzed through the figure of the ledger, where records of debt and credit structure the plot and illuminate the depth of local corruption. To this end, the narrative shifts between the

Tang manor and family affiliates, producing a study more compactly organized than *Midnight*, but also more sustained and systematic than stand-
alone snapshots of economic imagination in Mao Dun's contemporaneous
short stories such as "Spring Silkworms" or "The Lin Family Store."

The patron of the Tang family, Tang Zijia, is a wealthy landowner and
would-be industrial capitalist who also dabbles in Shanghai real estate and
stock speculation. The story opens with his lecherous son, Tang Shenqing,
making advances on his mistress. But just when Shenqing promises to take
her to Shanghai or Hangzhou to celebrate the upcoming lunar new year (a
period when debts are traditionally settled), he recalls that he is short on
cash. Shenqing must approach his father for money, whereupon the narrative turns to address the elder Tang's much larger crisis. Rather than suggest
the Tang household's economic situation through the flow of the story, the
narrative interrupts itself to directly "reproduce" a summary account of
the family's financial holdings. This is an original moment in Chinese fiction, where the ledger is appropriated directly as a narrative device to
serve as a kind of direct evidence, bolstering the feeling of verisimilitude.
As the narrator explains beforehand: "[These figures] haven't undergone
an accountant's formal audit (*zhengshi hesuan* 正式核算) or been published
officially, but some busybodies who enjoy playing the part by estimating
[people's] worth have come up with the following table." The ledger lists
the household's assets in three categories: *income* (including rice from tenant farmers, rent from Shanghai property, and uncollected loans); *debits*
(security for loans, money owed on bearish positions on stock futures,
money owed to stockbrokers, money tied up in the family's pawnshop, in
addition to the matured bonds issued by the Tang family's Huaguang silk
factory, as well as the factory's mortgage, loan deposit money, and owed
worker wages); and *capital holdings* (farmland, personal and commercial
real estate both in the village and in Shanghai, Huaguang's machinery and
raw goods, the family's cars, antiques, and cash). Beyond offering a striking example of literary realism's capacity to assimilate different forms and
genres (after all, what could feel more realistic than such a transparent and
seemingly objective account?), the passage provides a basis for assessing the
"polygonal relations" of local society that the story subsequently lays out.[47]

Arriving home, Shenqing finds his father and the family accountant, Old
Hu, poring over a thick ledger, examining the same details of the family

account that the novel's reader has just encountered. Now replaced back into the story's diegetic world, the ledger becomes a central point of attention over the next several chapters. The narrative repeatedly cuts to Old Hu's gaze upon Tang Zijia's finger as it roams across the lines of the account. Hu's social position as an outsider who is nonetheless privy to the reality of the Tangs' circumstances serves as another entry point into the complexity of Tang Zijia's situation. His position highlights the tension between master and servant: "As Second Master's [Tang Zijia] fat finger slowly moved across the page of the account book, a ray of sunlight shot in through the wooden X-latticed window, giving a red gloss to the Master's digit, making it look like an expensive sausage. In the middle of this 'sausage' sat a golden ring with a dazzling gem the size of a pea, gleaming so brightly that it set Old Hu's eyelids aflutter." But the calculation of Tang's assets is not a pleasurable exercise for the master, either. Soon his general quandary becomes evident to Tang himself as he realizes his precarious position: he cannot pay his debts because his own debtors are unable to pay him. He bitterly rebukes his profligate son's request for an allowance: "Money? It's all in this account book. I can't collect any rent from my farmland, nor any rent from my city properties! And yet you and your mother only press me for more money; you must think it grows from my body!"[48] The inability to convert credits and contracts into liquid assets, coupled with diminished production at the factory, threatens to strip Tang's land deeds, rental contracts, and stocks of their symbolic value and expose their fictitious nature by transforming them into mere paper.

And yet, for a short time, Tang and the other characters are able to keep things going without cash by creatively employing various sorts of promissory notes (*yinpiao* 引票). These instruments proliferate in a narrative where, despite the frequency of economic transactions, cash only appears several times, most prominently—and ironically—when the sickly Mrs. Tang pays her Buddhist soothsayer silver in exchange for karmic credit, and the nun replies in supplication: "A bit of good karma for a single coin!" (*yi fen shanyuan yi fen yin* 一分善緣一分銀). In the absence of cash, other media of exchange appear in addition to promissory notes: land deeds, restaurant bills, and even bolts of silk. But such media are of limited value. For example, when another character, the laborer Huang Axiang, having received his wages from the Huagang Silk Factory in silk (offered to him as a sort of "foreign money" [*yangqian* 洋錢]), offers the silk as security on his outstanding rent debt, he is told by his landlord, Tang Zijia, that only cash is acceptable. Huang only later figures out that "Landlord Tang" and "Factory Owner Tang" are one and the same, and furiously seeks out Tang Zijia to settle accounts (*suanzhang* 算賬).[49] On his way to confront Tang, Huang encounters a group of fellow workers who have similarly come to demand back wages, and together they lay siege to the Tang manor. While the violent clash that ensues serves as the novella's putative climax, the cathartic release of open class conflict is preempted by Tang Zijia's escape from the scene and departure for Shanghai. In the meantime, the fall of the Tang household quickly sets off a chain reaction of local business foreclosures and bankruptcies as the news of the incident spreads.

The novella's actual climax arguably comes in the wake of the collapse of the town's credit network, narrated over several late chapters from the standpoint of a shop owner, Li Huikang, and his own ledger book of customer accounts. Li is bound to the Tangs financially as a minor shareholder in Tang Zijia's local pawnshop, as well as through his daughter, Li Guiying, who has been impregnated and abandoned by Tang Shenqing. Insofar as he is an honest vendor, more a victim of fate than of business foolhardiness or personal immorality, Li Huikang's plight is similar to that of the sympathetic shopkeeper described in Mao Dun's story, "The Lin Family Store." On paper, Li's income apparently outpaces his debts. But, like everyone else in town, he has been paid by his debtors using invoices (*zhangdan* 賬單), while in turn his creditors demand payment in cash or similarly secure assets. When Tang's pawnshop is foreclosed upon, Li is personally dragged asunder as an investor. Next, his business becomes hopelessly insolvent, and his creditors converge upon his shop to divvy his remaining assets. Finding himself turned out onto the street, Li mechanically wanders about, slowly coming to terms with his fate. Then he reaches an epiphany, as

the street in front of him suddenly brightened. He instinctively turned to where it was lighter and began walking. He seemed to be himself again: those shadow images were no longer before him, and instead in his mind was now spread out an enormous abacus, with an incredibly complex account above it: he owed others, others owed him, he had been forced out of business—all of it melded into a big ball. But the last "column" transformed into an iron rod. He instinctively took another breath. He unconsciously stood on the street corner, then laboriously opened his eyes, as if trying to calculate what he should ultimately do.[50]

Li's confusion about his financial position, and the diffusion of his consciousness across the mental ledger and his physical surroundings, is representative of the larger panic sweeping across the village. He suddenly hears from across the way a multitude of voices excitedly exchanging *xiaoxi* about the series of bankruptcies. As they interrupt one another, the voices capture the fall of dominoes in real time. Their irruption into Li's consciousness makes him understand the true nature of the credit crisis:

> Among the series of shop names that flew into Li's ears most were quite familiar. His whole body began to tremble, and in his outer pocket his hand tightly grasped upon a stack of something—a stack of paper, a stack of invoices! He felt as if he had seized in his hand the majority of small shops that had been "toppled" [*daitan* 帶坍]—those very shops on this street that owed him money. He understood that the number owed to him was not insignificant. But now they had truly become merely numbers on paper [*zhi mianshang de shumu* 紙面上的數目]![51]

The invoice is momentarily denaturalized as its now-suspended function as a symbolic medium of exchange is forced into the background by its immediate material presence. Whatever the inscriptions on the surface of the paper, they are now meaningless: digits are digits, and an iron rod is an iron rod—the revolutionary symbolism is impossible to miss.

Here lies the complexity of the ledger trope in Mao Dun's work. On the one hand, the novel employs the figure of the ledger as a key device for producing the effect of verisimilitude by lending the narrative a strongly factual quality.[52] In *Polygonal Relations*, this authority is further augmented by a prevalent rhetoric of numbers. Phrases that allude to counting and numbers proliferate across the text: the nun's exclamation of the Buddha's "knowing the number" (*youshu* 有數), that is, knowing definitely how things stand; Zhu Runsheng's sharp, on-the-dot recollection (*rushu huixiang* 如數回想); as well as idiomatic formulations that contain numbers, such as "considered as the first or second [in quality]" (*shuyi-shu'er* 數一數二), "various affairs" [lit. "grasping sevens and eights"] (*jiaqi-jiaba*

夾七夾八), and "five organs and six tracts" (*wuzangliufu* 五臟六腑),[53] and so on. All of which adds up to a socioeconomic account that caps off Mao Dun's market-themed literature as a whole. With its multiple perspectives, *Polygonal Relations* documents the forces of economic integration between local, regional, and even transnational levels, making visible the way that macroeconomic forces such as stock prices or the adoption of fiat currency impacts the fates of those well beyond the world of high finance. As a narrative account, the novella also places the reader in the position of moral bookkeeper who identifies and tracks the injustices embedded in the structure of credit relations. In this sense, *Polygonal Relations* both reintroduces the dispensation of praise and blame that is characteristic of traditional fiction, and at the same time serves as a stepping stone to the revolutionary discourse of the Maoist era, where the establishment of a new social order dominated by the working class was turned upon a rhetoric of judicious and full clearing of historical accounts (*qingsuan* 清算; *suanqing* 算清) between tenant laborers and landowners.[54] In all, the ledger's demonstrated capacity for expediently revealing economic relations make it an enduring lever for the critical investigation of Chinese socioeconomic structure in the 1930s and beyond.

At the same time, the novella also repudiates the ledger as a system of representation that is as much responsible for the rise and maintenance of fictitious capital as it is a literary means for reproducing it in fiction. For Mao Dun, the opposition between literary realism and the abstractions of financial or fictitious capital is a dialectical one. The "real" of literary realism is, as Marston Anderson shows, often located in narrative elements that gesture to something internally subjective or otherwise difficult to represent with language: hunger, violence, disease, sexual desire, death.[55] It is invoked by Mao Dun in his market-themed literature, for example the appearance of noise and the breakdown of communications in *Midnight* that precipitate very real-feeling bodily experiences. But such a construction of the real must equally be understood in terms of an opposition with and intervention into the virtuality of information. In the preceding passages from *Polygonal Relations*, the transmutations effected by the iron bar and the reversion of financial instruments to "merely numbers on paper" plainly demonstrate realism's ability to expose both fictitious capital and information alike by unwinding its abstractions using metaphor and defamiliarization. Mao Dun's didactic project thus revolves around experimentation assimilating the information-rich form of the account book into realist narrative, dramatizing the encounter between ledger and fiction as one between capitalist and revolutionary forms of knowledge production. Ultimately, it takes literary realism to judge finance capital's fictitiousness in its own fictionality.

Chapter Three

RIPPLE EFFECTS

Ether and the Information Order During the Propaganda Era

In the introduction I briefly considered how Liang Qichao's novel *A Future Record of New China* leverages the media ecology of the late Qing by framing the narrative itself as information delivered to the reader. The story's opening contains a minor but significant detail regarding the novel's mode of address and its potential to propagate its message of political reform. Recall that the words of Mr. Kong's lecture that make up the novel's main chapters purportedly reach readers in near "real time" thanks to the speed of telegraphy and spread of industrial print. But the brief description of the circumstances of Kong's speech—perhaps the first portrayal of a mass oral address in Chinese literature, and an emerging practice that was as modern as the technical media that send it abroad—includes a detail that calls into question the realism of the scene.[1] The in-person audience for Kong's lecture at the Shanghai exposition is specified as twenty thousand Chinese, along with an additional twelve hundred foreigners who have learned Chinese. Setting aside issues of language (What dialect of Chinese does Kong speak in? Would all in the audience understand it?), this scene begs an even more basic question: Given the stadium-sized audience, could the majority of the listeners have even *heard* the speech? Electrical amplification and the public address system would only come out a decade later in the West, prior to which public rallies were hampered by the limited reach of megaphones. The (necessary) absence from the scene of microphone and speakers reveals how Liang, for all his attention to the speed and breadth of the dissemination of the lecture, nonetheless imagines this oral address in primarily textual terms. China during the early twentieth century, as Tie Xiao has recently illuminated, saw the notion of the masslike crowd (*qun* 群) emerge as a specific object of sociological and psychological discussion.[2] But in the present scene there's no there, there. The listening audience is, without doubt, a stand-in for a public of readers.

This lack of concern regarding the audibility of Kong's voice stakes out a unique and paradoxical possibility: large-scale mass address without the physical capacity for it.[3] The apparent muteness of this episode stands in contrast to the political speechmaking of the generation that followed, when amplification and mass media began to appear as integral elements of the act. Consider, for example, Xiaobing Tang and Michel Hockx's account of Guo Moruo 郭沫若 (1892–1978), the leading voice of expressionist poetry during the New Culture movement and an ardent leftist, standing in front of an audience of nearly 200,000 rallygoers in 1927:

> Guo found himself holding a microphone and repeating after [the leader of the Nationalist Party] Chiang Kai-shek, who was delivering a speech to a huge crowd gathered in the recently conquered city of Nanchang to commemorate the second anniversary of Sun Yat-sen's death. "[Chiang] would speak a sentence, and I would then broadcast it. Halfway through, his speech was filled with a counterrevolutionary rhetoric." Increasingly offended, Guo Moruo had the urge to knock Chiang off with the bullhorn, but had no choice, under the circumstances, but to finish serving as his mouthpiece.[4]

Unlike the spectacle hinted at in *Future Record of New China*, this one includes sound. Besides the presence of the microphone (*chuanhuatong* 傳話筒), what stands out is Guo's acute self-awareness of mass address as such, marked by his use of "broadcast" (*chuanda* 傳達) to describe his amplified speech, mixed with an ambivalence at finding himself caught in the role of the ventriloquized puppet who serves both as a passive receiver and as a complicit speaker, a position that briefly earned him the derogatory nickname of "mouthpiece" (*chuihao* 吹好) in leftist circles.[5] In between the twenty-five years spanning these respective episodes, thanks to the introduction of broadcast media ranging from PA systems to radio, a truly modern mass of listeners had emerged.

The arc between these two accounts of mass mediation and audience also tracks a paradigmatic shift in political communication that occurred under the aegis of an old term that, like *xiaoxi*, was finding a new life during the decades of the Republican period: "propaganda" (*xuanchuan* 宣傳). The propagation of messages was, of course, hardly new to China in the twentieth century. The word *xuanchuan* (which is neutral in connotation, in contrast to the negative tone of *propaganda*) dates to around the first century BCE to refer to promulgating policies and laws, spreading customs and values, and disseminating information.[6] From the early imperial period to the 1920s, *xuanchuan* was primarily conceived as form of moral suasion along the lines of the Confucian notion of *jiaohua* 教化, to enlighten by education. This understanding of indoctrination is illustrated by the opening lines of Liang Qichao's essay "On the Relationship Between Fiction and the Government of the People" ("Lun xiaoshuo yu qunzhi zhi guanxi" 論小說與群治之關係, 1902), wherein he lays out the impetus for deploying fiction as a matter of popular enlightenment, aimed at renovating the people of a nation by improving their morality and learning, and, even more elementally, reshaping "the human mind and remolding its character" by staging salutary ideals and behavioral models.[7]

The domain of *xuanchuan*/propaganda broadened significantly in the early twentieth century when it became an integral part of modernized governance. In 1920, Sun Yat-sen and his Nationalist Party (Guomindang 國民黨, hereafter GMD) created a propaganda bureau (*xuanchuan bu* 宣傳部) at the party headquarters in Shanghai, followed by branch establishments in Guangdong in 1921 and Guilin in 1922. Conceiving of propaganda as far more than moral education, these organs pursued a range of goals that collectively elaborated a systematic approach to managing information on multiple fronts. Specifically, this modern propaganda apparatus aimed to attract financial support from overseas Chinese, to "drill" (*caolian* 操練) Sun's basic Three Principles of the People into the population under Nationalist governance in the south, as well as to mount "psychological attacks" (*gongxin* 攻心) to win over all Chinese to the cause of the GMD and to delegitimize the competing Beijing government.[8] This list captures the emergence of a more cynical attitude toward propaganda as information management and ideological manipulation. It marks the arrival of a new

era of propagation, one characterized by the pursuit of sociopolitical con-
sensus using ideological messaging and countermessaging. It also signals
the emergence of propaganda as a distinct field of social-scientific knowledge
and instrumentalized practice. Guo Moruo's account is again instructive:
serving as Chiang Kai-shek's microphone despite his distaste for Chiang's
politics, he positions himself as a mere relay within this modern apparatus of propagandistic messaging.

The history of propaganda and its deep impact on the literary field in
China has received ample attention. But this history must be revisited as
an integral part of the modern information discourse traced out in this
book. This is due, in part, to the appearance of "information" as a key category in discussions and plans for propaganda. Indeed, when the nascent
Chinese Communist Party proposed the organization of an Education and
Propaganda Committee in 1923, it explicitly called for an "Information
Bureau" (original in English) to manage issuing and responding to news.[9]
(Here the CCP was taking its cue from the United States and Britain, where
state propaganda institutions were established in the early twentieth century as "Information Bureaus.") More important, modern propaganda was
directly linked to information thanks to its association with mass media,
communications infrastructures, and information management. Both the
practice and the *imagination* of propaganda were inherently supported by
a notional vision of an information order.

This and the following chapter examine the nexus between propaganda
and information as it was represented within—and historically reshaped—
modern fiction and woodcut art. The reformation of literature into a tool
for propagandization and debates about culture's independence from politics have been well documented by scholars.[10] The plotline of this trend runs
from the inauguration of political novels by Liang Qichao, to the expansion of social reform fiction under the New Culture movement, and on to
the increasing domination of literature by partisan politics during the Nanjing Decade (1927–1937), its near-total engulfment as part of mobilization
campaigns of the War of Resistance against Japanese Aggression (1937–1945),
and, finally, the propagandization of all creative expression under Mao
Zedong that culminated in the Cultural Revolution (1966–1976). What
remains to be investigated is the acute reflexivity of many of the early works
of propaganda, particularly those that emerged during the fecund and pivotal decade of the 1930s. As I show, the representation of propaganda and

mass mobilization in the outwardly leftist works developed by one of the vanguards of the mass literature movement, Ding Ling 丁玲 (1904–1986), offers a significant case in point. So, too, do the illustrations of propaganda in woodcut prints by a coterie of young artists such as Huang Xinbo 黃新波 (1915–1980), Luo Qingzhen 羅清楨 (1905–1942), and Zhang Hui 張慧 (1909–1900).

These literary and pictorial works about propaganda reveal a dialectic of signal and noise that unfolds across different media and spaces and whose visible ripple effects trace the contours of China's modern information order. Much like Mao Dun's appropriation of literary realism to capture and interrogate the symbolic abstraction of financial capitalism, these works do not merely thematize information but rather situate themselves directly within the information order as they imagine it. After exploring the historical emergence of this dynamic in the present chapter, I pivot in the next to the work of Shen Congwen and his last (and unfinished) novel-length project, *Long River* 長河, the only work in modern Chinese literature to mount a sustained interrogation of the propaganda era and its fantasies regarding broadcast communication.

Before turning to Ding Ling and woodcut art, it is necessary to detail the mutually constitutive relationship between propaganda, broadcast communication, and the information discourse of Republican China. The following section revisits the formation of propaganda as a prevailing field of knowledge about information management during the 1920s and 1930s. Let me preface this discussion by observing that the field of propaganda science and practice was predicated on two interrelated notions: First, that propaganda resembles a form of signal engineering whose aim is to outdo competing signals of enemy propagandists, which are recast as impedance or noise. In this paradigm, propaganda is *like* an electrical pulse or wave transmitted from a central broadcast tower to dispersed receivers. By this token, an underlying logic of Manichean opposition between signal/noise both justified and historically precipitated a feedback cycle wherein one must continuously maintain an active propaganda apparatus in order to outmaneuver enemy counterpropaganda (*fanxuanchuan* 反宣傳). Second, both signal and noise were imagined to occupy a shared communicational field that was spatially figured as "ether" (*yitai* 以太). By envisioning the rippling expansion of propaganda signals across this imagined medium, writers and artists made visible the information order in unprecedented and urgent ways.

SIGNAL AND COUNTERSIGNAL: PROPAGANDA AS COMMUNICATIONS WARFARE

The year 1927 marked the beginning of a new phase in the history of propaganda following Chiang Kai-shek's violent purge of the GMD's leftist elements, many of whom were concurrently members of the Chinese Communist Party, by creating a new ideological front that became a fertile ground for the redefinition of propaganda as an indispensable weapon of symbolic warfare. In Wuhan, for example, right-wing and left-wing partisans published in rapid succession articles in the struggle to frame the unfolding schism. The result was, Mao Dun would later declare, the outbreak of China's first "information war" or "news war" (*xiaoxi zhan* 消息戰).[11] Forced underground, Communists and their supporters came to resort to a more targeted set of agitational techniques aimed at attracting groups such as students, farmers, intellectuals, and women. For its own part, the GMD wielded an expanding suite of "integration" propaganda, aimed at habituating people to Nationalist rule and values through sustained messaging.[12] Both sides shared a similar view of propaganda as an essential means for self-preservation. Propaganda precipitated counterpropaganda, initiating a feedback cycle which demanded ever greater resources and more refined techniques.

The emerging concern over the threat of counterpropaganda (along with rumor, a separate but related "other" of propaganda) is evident in the discussions of both leftists and rightists after the 1927 GMD-Communist split. A 1926 article introducing propaganda as an instrument of national enlightenment still imagines it as an apparatus that operates within a kind of vacuum, a matter of messaging to an audience rendered as, if not entirely tabula rasa, at worst benightedly clinging to traditional ideas: "Spirits [of a nation] are united by the intellectual tide of the times, and what spreads this current of thought is *'propaganda'* [English in the original], without which people are scattered across different places; lacking a thing that can integrate their hearts by targeting their spirit, they can only group together through mere coincidence, just like a plate of loose sand."[13]

But the target of propaganda shifted in 1927, replacing the plate of loose sand (or another trope, a blank sheet of paper), with that of counterpropaganda. For example, in his famous "Report on an Investigation of the Peasant Movement in Hunan" (1927), Mao Zedong discusses the efficacy of Communist propaganda and messaging as a problem of outflanking counterrevolutionary propaganda.[14] Similarly, in a resolution on propaganda policy issued by the CCP in 1929, viewed by scholars as the party's first truly comprehensive document on the subject, reactionary propaganda and its influence on the masses take center stage: now Communist propaganda must strive to rapidly respond to GMD messaging on Sun Yat-sen's Three Principles of the People (*Sanminzhuyi* 三民主義) and reformism (*gailiangzhuyi* 改良主義).[15] Settling in to govern a broadly unified China and administer itself as a "highly disciplined, pedagogical state," the GMD government in Nanjing, too, sought to counter the CCP and its promotion of class politics and instead assert itself as the rightful bearer of revolutionary national consciousness.[16] As the party in power, the GMD coupled its propaganda operations with an increasingly effective censorship apparatus.[17]

Reconstituted as a form of competition, propaganda became a matter of channeling messages through a field of oppositional noise.[18] Such a paradigm refigured propagation as a form of signal engineering. By calling it this, I want to highlight how propaganda was at once understood as a generalized form of communication (i.e., medium agnostic) but also envisioned in specific terms that borrowed heavily from one of the most impressive broadcast media of the day: the radio. Successful political communication required an expert—or engineer—in order to design and implement an effective signaling apparatus. This specialized knowledge was frequently expressed in multidisciplinary terms. As one scholar observed in a 1931 study titled *Propaganda Technique and Mass Movements* (*Xuanchuanshu yu qunzhong yundong* 宣傳術與群眾運動), the new discipline cobbled together aspects of social science including psychology, sociology, economics, and political science and further combined them with "expressive sciences" (*fabiao kexue* 發表科學) such as rhetoric, logic, literature, art, and music.[19] In establish propaganda as a standalone science, this text and many others like in China both drew from and paralleled contemporaneous developments in Europe and North America, where significant public and private resources had been directed toward scientizing propaganda since the Great War (1914–1918).[20] The numerous articles and book-length studies of this new science not only document a new era of propaganda, but also constitute a rich trove of writing about information as a reified object of propagandistic knowledge production.[21]

Within this burgeoning body of works the most formative text was *Propaganda War* (*Xuanchuan zhan* 宣傳戰), published in 1931 by a high-level adviser to the Nationalist army named Chen Yuxin 陳裕新 (fl. 1930s).[22] A manual for military and government operatives, the text undertakes an exposition of the *form* of propaganda rather than its content or ideology. Its focus and political neutrality make it representative of the broader discourse and theorization of propaganda-as-signal engineering shared by both the Nationalists and the Communists from the 1930s onward, as evidenced by its frequent citation in subsequent studies. As such, Chen's study deserves our attention as the earliest extended articulation of propaganda science in Chinese.

Propaganda War begins with a discussion of how this new discipline arises from techniques developed in the West along with those of China's native tradition of military administration, diplomacy, and statecraft that are documented in classical texts like the *Sunzi*, the *Analects*, and later accounts of the Warring States period (475–221 BCE).[23] This premodern genealogy is brought into the twentieth century with the consolidation of propaganda as an institutionalized practice and, on the other hand, as a discourse entangling technology, mass social communication, and information management. Chen in particular exalts the British model and celebrates the figure of Lord Northcliffe, Britain's director for propaganda during the Great War who was, as one historian has since put it, the advocate of "an empire of information at least as extensive as the British Empire itself."[24] Observing the emergence of a set of standardized techniques that have resulted from propaganda's scientization, professionalization (*zhuanyehua* 專業化), and "systemic centralization" (*zhidu zhongxinhua* 制度中心化), Chen argues that present-day China must embrace this science for the sake of consolidating internal unity as a nation and improving its position in the international order (22). To that end, *Propaganda War* sets out to define propaganda and illustrate its potentials.

The definition of the propaganda proposed by Chen takes basic form as message transmission: "to advance [something] and cause it to be known" (*jin er shi qi zhi zhi* 進而使其知之) (31).[25] Chen elaborates with the image of a bow and arrow. Here I quote at some length to give a sense of Chen's

semiclassical style and technical rhetoric, one that is appropriate for a treatise aimed at uniting Chinese and Western traditions:

> If one wishes to sum up the arduous and complex matter of propaganda sim-
> ply and without leaving anything out, it is naturally quite difficult. But if
> we see its methods, observe its cause, check its whereabouts, and apprehend
> its general nature, then certainly it's not impossible. I think if one wants to
> give propaganda a clear and appropriate definition, then we ought to first
> recognize its various constitutive components. Propaganda is like shooting
> an arrow: there must be a target, there must be an arrow, there must be a
> cause for shooting the arrow, and there must be something lasting after the
> target is hit. . . . Propaganda's audience is like the target; its material is the
> arrow; its motive the cause for shooting the arrow; and the objective is
> the lasting effect of striking the target. If these four elements are present,
> then propaganda is accomplished. (33)[26]

Following Chen's analogy, we might expect the arrows to be messages only.
But he clarifies that the arrow is not just information but medium too. By
this token, there are many kinds of arrows: newspapers, lectures, telegraph,
telephone, news agencies, slogans, and literature, along with some surprising
items such as hot air balloons, carrier pigeons, and even dogs (presumably
employed as couriers).[27] Encompassing these—and by extension all
other—media, propaganda flattens out the differences between them by
placing them within a shared sphere of communication. But the aegis of
propaganda does not only bring these media together conceptually—it also
combines them materially to effect a total and unending stream of messaging. In the zero-sum struggle over people's spirits, the propaganda signal
must be so ubiquitous that it becomes naturalized and unnoticeable.
"Because the mindset of the propaganda enterprise is propaganda for the
sake of propagation . . . all institutions or personnel involved in propagation, and even all media for communicating propaganda, should be kept
as veiled [*yinhui* 隱晦] as possible" (43). Propaganda should thus not be legible as such, but rather a more subliminal form of messaging, "as unfailing
as a mountain call's valley echo [*shanming guying* 山鳴谷應], and as constant as the movement of the wind and sounds of waves [*fengdong boxiang*
風動波響] . . . so that even the smart will fall unawares under its spell. Only
then will there be hope of winning the propaganda war" (43).

With this rhetoric, Chen's description shifts the practice of propaganda into a sociophysical register that is as abstract as it is atmospheric. This shift suggests the second important feature of modern propaganda: that the general medium of its signal is the air itself, conceived in the form of ether. Appearing in China at the end of the Qing dynasty in the work of Confucian intellectuals such as Tan Sitong 譚嗣同 (1865–1898) who sought to articulate the interconnectedness between peoples based on the conductive power of this invisible substance,[28] by the 1920s the notion of ether had been scientifically superseded, but still carried popular purchase as an imagined medium for the radio wave. For some later scholars of propaganda such as Peng Leshan 彭樂善 (fl. 1940s), ether constituted an actual, physical substance, saturated with broadcasts of information, music, and lectures.[29] In *Propaganda War*, by contrast, ether is a more hypothetical medium or discursive construct whose spiritualist essence is appropriate for a war over spirits. But in all cases, propaganda made ether imaginable and vice versa.

In her examination of the link between cinema and propaganda theory in China during the War Against Japanese Aggression, Weihong Bao richly demonstrates how the concept of ether was given new life in theories and practices of propaganda. The "ether medium," she deftly observes, departs from conventional media insofar as it is paradoxically at once both immaterial (making it invisible and everywhere) and material (embodied by specific media technologies): "In contrast to a linear model of the medium as a directional transmission of message, the affective [or ether] medium is encompassing and pervasive and resists the clear division between sender, receiver, and conduit; nor does the affective medium fit neatly either with a model of an immersive environment or with a mediating intermediary. Instead, the affective medium conjoins both models as a *mediating environment*."[30] The both/and quality of such a mediating environment helps us to square Chen's coupling of an arrow analogy (transmissive media) with his view of propaganda as an immersive blanketing of the landscape with signals. Ether is, Bao continues, a kind of ur-medium that combines a broad range of other media (including all sound and light media), thus transcending its own ontology as a medium. Here again Chen's work is instructive, since it brings together all media into the fold of propaganda, blurring the boundary between medium and communication. As a mediating environment, ether offers a conceptual and imaginative "para-space" through which signals pass or fail to get through.[31] Bao's elucidation of the complexity of ether as mediating environment sheds light on modern propaganda's imagination of an information order, for if ether is the grounds for affective communication (Bao's focus), it is at the same time a crucial means for mass pedagogy, broadcast news, and the collection and transmission of intelligence, and thus the key ground for struggle over "communications sovereignty," as two of Chen's contemporaries put it.[32] In its abstractness, ether is a primary medium for making information perceptible. In turn, the imagination of ether during the Nanjing Decade is most evident in the representation of broadcast radio, a technology that was, along with film, celebrated as a mass medium par excellence.[33] Discussions and depictions of radio broadcast not only highlight ether's role as a mediating environment but also reveal the political stakes of the information order at large.

In his recent monograph, *Seeking News, Making China*, John Alekna recounts how broadcast radio arrived in China in 1923 in the semicolonial space of Shanghai and then in the Manchurian cities of Shenyang and Harbin, before spreading rapidly in the early 1930s as part of the GMD's efforts to promote its use. What made broadcasting so appealing to Nationalist and other state builders was its capacity to reach the provincial and county seats in the hinterland, where receivers were installed in public places and equipped with loudspeakers. From there, broadcast information could be remediated into writing on blackboards and wall papers, or in local newspapers. Collectively, Alekna argues, the radio brought with it a mass-media "information revolution" whose impact and reach were greater even than that of industrial printing and the newspaper.[34] Radio's specific potential for propagandization was a major inspiration for the GMD that culminated in the establishment of a new and unprecedently powerful broadcasting station in Nanjing in 1932.[35]

Alongside the advent of the radio age, imaginations of ether space proliferated. Nowhere was this more prominent than in the so-called New Life Movement (Xin shenghuo yundong 新生活運動; hereafter, NLM) initiated by the GMD in 1934, a broad campaign aimed at promoting neo-Confucian morality and fealty to the Nationalist government (and which takes center stage in Shen Congwen's *Long River*, as we will see in the next chapter). Signaling a major expansion of the state's program to mobilize—and keep permanently mobilized—the populace, the NLM was a pivotal event in the history of propaganda. At its very core, the movement was conceived in terms that resonated with Chen's articulation of a contemporary "spirit war."[36] Indeed, Chiang Kai-shek announced the project's aim as a total invigoration and mobilization of a people that had become "lacking in spirit" (*meiyou jingshen* 沒有精神).[37] In terms of practice, the NLM led to efforts to expand the reach of radio broadcasting into rural areas by nearly doubling the number of official public radio receivers in provincial and county centers.[38] In representational terms, meanwhile, China was reimagined as an ethereal space filled with waves, where radio could achieve a synchronized national body by leapfrogging older and more expensive—and increasingly decrepit—communications infrastructure such as roads and telegraph wires.[39] Imaginations of a unified China under centralized governance were still something of a fantasy—in reality, the Nationalist government had only limited influence across much of the country, and the effects of the NLM were unevenly distributed in different parts of the country[40]—but it was an incredibly potent dream that elevated the role of mass media and propagation in the first place. In representing its communicational dispensation, propaganda from the campaign visualized ether and information order alike.

We can see the matrix between propaganda and ether as it was neatly illustrated by the publication of *Broadcast Weekly* (*Guangbo zhoubao* 廣播週報, 1934–1949), an essential venue for NLM propaganda. Established at the beginning of the NLM, *Broadcast Weekly* was to be the central (and long-lasting) print supplement to the GMD's radio programming.[41] The journal reprinted radio lectures, articles on NLM priorities such as ethics and hygiene reform, photos of the GMD's radio facilities, and the weekly program schedule for the central broadcast station in Nanjing operating under the call sign of XGOA. The journal also served as an important venue for the promotion of amateur science, regularly including articles on the mechanics of the transistor radio, batteries, and electrical engineering. Besides propagating the central tenets of the NLM, then, *Broadcast Weekly* also propagated the radio itself as the apex of modern technology, entertainment-based consumerism, and cultural citizenship. The journal's prominent iconography of the radio's role in Chinese nationalism is particularly striking, as figures 3.1 and 3.2 reveal. In the first image, the standard cover for the journal, radio's reach is shown linking China to the globe.[42] In this style of representing the globe (termed azimuthal equidistant projection, a common mode for the geography of radio signal, where all points on the map are at proportionally correct distance from the

報週播廣

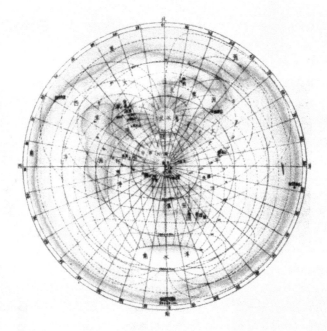

期 六 第

版出處理管台電線無播廣央中

六期星日十二月十　　中華民國二十三年

FIGURE 3.1 Cover image of *Broadcast Weekly* (*Guangbo zhoubao*), 1934.

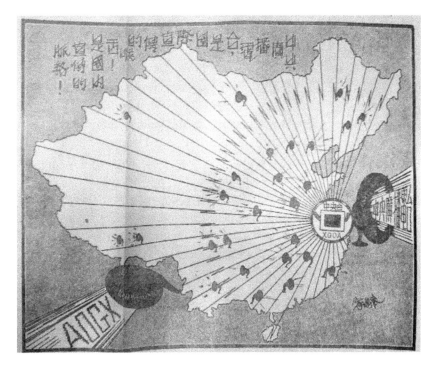

FIGURE 3.2 Foldout showing radio's nationwide reach, from *Broadcast Weekly* (*Guangbo zhoubao*), 1934.

center), the flattening of a three-dimensional space into two dimensions heavily distorts the appearance of the map near the poles. Nanjing occupies a primary pole, while on the other side of the world sits South America, stretched across the entire horizon. Such a restaging of the globe as an abstracted space of signal flows, coupled with the lines showing the reach of GMD radio broadcast, constructs an ether space that is crosshatched with broadcast energy waves.

While the journal's cover image demonstrates the transnational reach of radio, figure 3.2 shows another kind of integrated space of flows. The image, which appeared as an inset in the sixth issue of *Broadcast Weekly*, shows radio waves emanating from the central station in Nanjing to fill up a national space while also extending outward to international space. The caption above announces: "The Central Broadcasting Station is a mouthpiece for international propaganda, and an artery of domestic propaganda!" What is interesting about this image is how it makes radio signal visible, whereby a broadcast array, figured in modernist jagged lines indicating electric energy, stretches across an ether space to reach receivers in provincial centers across China. The outward-facing transmitters, meanwhile, emit signals labeled as XGOA and "Central Broadcasting Station" (Zhongyang guangbo diantai 中央廣播電台), whose concentrated energy is depicted by dark lines.

Insofar as propaganda was inspired by the mass medium of broadcast radio, these images illustrate how the former could be conceived as operating in/as the environmental medium of ether. Leftist literature and woodcut art during the 1930s similarly took up the subject of propaganda by thematizing broadcast signal. By contributing an iconography of ether, these works sought to elevate propaganda as an exciting and modern practice befitting the masses while at the same time seeking to challenge the exclusivity of Nationalist power over the information order.

CONTESTING THE ETHER: DING LING'S EARLY PROPAGANDA LITERATURE

Paralleling Britain, where authors such as Ford Madox Ford and Joseph Conrad participated in British propaganda activities during the Great War,[43] many of China's better-known New Culture authors participated in institutionalized propaganda during the 1920s prior to the rightist purge of Communist Party flank within the Nationalist Party. This list includes Guo Moruo, as we have already seen, as well as Yu Dafu and Mao Dun (who, like Guo, briefly worked in the GMD propaganda service prior to Chiang Kai-shek's purge of Communist members from the government).[44] Following the intensification of the GMD's mobilization campaigns after 1927, leftist writers came to see modern propaganda as an existential condition of everyday life and politics. Similar to GMD propagandists such as Chen Yuxin and his elevation of propaganda as a modern *techne* of communication, leftists embraced propaganda as an expedient and necessary means of ideological awakening. Accordingly, they pursued the reorganization of cultural production around the needs of propagandistic signal management, which, again, would play out over the shared field of ether, forging a discursive connection between broadcast media, communication, and the formation of the masses.

In the wake of Liang Qichao's unfinished *Future Record of the New China*, literature explicitly *about* propaganda took off a generation later, beginning in 1927 with Jiang Guangci's 蔣光慈 (1901–1931) amateurish novella *Sans-culottes* (*Duankudang* 短褲黨), which describes the agitation and propaganda activities of a group of underground Communist organizers in Shanghai. The first literary work to be formally banned by the Nanjing government, the novella was immediately celebrated by the left, including Qian Xingcun 錢杏村 (1900–1977), who directly declared it to be China's first work of *propaganda* (original in English).[45] *Sans-culottes* was soon joined by other works on the subject of propagation, including Mao Dun's *Vacillation* (1928) and Ye Shengtao's influential novel *Ni Huanzhi* 倪煥之 (1928). The latter, as Mao Dun notes in his famous essay on the piece, explores the arc "from education to mass movement, and from liberalism to collectivism" through the life of its eponymous character.[46] Set in the present day, this arc reflects the historical shift of propaganda to the more active form of mobilization and ideological inculcation that I have traced. While the story's ambivalent portrayal of crowds as being easily manipulated led Mao Dun and others to call for a more optimistic representation of the masses in literature,[47] the novel and critical response to it helped to establish propaganda as a literary subject for the decade afterward.

Fiction about propaganda especially flourished between 1930 and 1932, a short but intense period bookended by the formation of the League of Left-wing Writers (Zuolian 左聯) in 1930 and popular protests in the aftermath of the Japanese bombing of Shanghai in early 1932.[48] Literature of this period, Marston Anderson observes, evolved away from the individuated subject set forth by the May Fourth and New Culture movements, to instead feature a new kind of protagonist, "a special kind of crowd, *abstractly conceived yet possessed of an overwhelming physical immediacy*."[49] The tension between abstraction and physical presence is closely related to the imagination of an ether space, as authors and artists alike innovated ways of visualizing propaganda and mass mobilization and their ripple effects across the atmosphere.

Among the authors who took up the subject, the most prominent was Ding Ling. Following the GMD's arrest and execution of her husband, Hu Yepin 胡也頻 (1903–1931), for being a Communist, Ding took an increasingly active role in the League of Left-wing Writers. By the end of 1931 she had abandoned her explorations of individual interiority, the ennui of urban life, and alienation in such works as *Miss Sophia's Diary* (*Shafei nüshi de riji* 莎菲女士的日記).[50] Now fully committed to the League's mission of fomenting mass revolution and opposing Nationalist rule, Ding Ling led the way in the wholesale adoption of literature as a propaganda tool by developing a new mode of proletarian literature.

Ding Ling's conversion to leftist politics and adoption of literary propaganda are well known,[51] but it remains to be noted how closely her literature tracks the historical rise of propaganda as a facet of everyday life. Many of her stories from this period feature propagandists as characters, such as we see in her two-part novella *Shanghai, Spring 1930* (*1930 chun Shanghai* 1930 春上海). The novella's first part follows the evolution of a young man, Ruoquan, from an author into a propagandist engaged in speech-making at factories and other organizational work. The story's central female character, the impressionable Meilin, abandons her long-term relationship with a bookish man to join Ruoquan. The novella's second part features the conversion of a student named Wangwei into a propagandist who now busies himself translating newspapers from Chinese into English and vice versa, delivering documents, and holding underground meetings (141). As a professional propagandist, he maintains a daily regimen of newspaper reading, such that "quite a bit of information (*xiaoxi*) would accumulate in his brain" (151).[52] In turn, he "sought to summarize these materials relating to the world economy. Moreover, he would gather [*souluo* 搜羅] reports on the development of revolution in China and collect images of the daily weakening of the ruling class" (151) to pass on to his fellow organizers and propagandists. With his revolutionary ardor, Wangwei's commitment to propagandizing ultimately subsumes his sexual desire for his beautiful but apolitical girlfriend, Mary, who disdains his work—"You don't need to use your propaganda on me," she rebukes him at one point (156)—and ends up leaving him. Now on his own, Wangwei finds a libidinal outlet in his propaganda work. In the final chapter, Wangwei prepares to give a public speech: "He felt an excitement that he couldn't suppress, as if he were seeing a surge of roaring waves toppling the mountains and churning up the seas.... It was possible that [an uprising] might happen immediately, since so many people were ready for it! And he, he would accelerate the great storm" (169). Once the demonstration gets underway, the chaos of the masses erupts and bodies of protestors surge forth, as "many clamorous shouts occupied [*zhanling* 佔領] the atmosphere" (169), their "quivering soundwaves [*yinbo* 音波] resounding in the air" after police violently disperse the crowd and haul Wangwei off as an instigator (170). The convergence of sublimated sexual energy and revolutionary politics results in an acoustic imagination that reimagines the air as full of soundwaves, attesting to the figural influence of radio and ether to propaganda.

The novella's closing image of mass action anticipates Ding's turn to a more experimental phase the following year. The year 1931 was a fitful one for the nation. The summer saw deadly flooding in the Central Plain that left millions displaced. In the fall Japanese forces occupied Manchuria in the northeast and then conducted aerial bombing of Shanghai's Zhabei district in early spring of the following year. It would be difficult to overestimate the impact of these events on leftist writers, dramatists, artists, and filmmakers, whose tightening embrace of politicized art was given a fresh injection of urgent subject matter. Their works attracted new audiences as outrage spread over Chiang Kai-shek's and the GMD's perceived inability to deal with domestic and international catastrophes.[53]

The same year, the League of Left-wing Writers Central Committee invited Ding Ling to become chief editor of its new flagship journal of revolutionary fiction and criticism, *Big Dipper* (*Beidou* 北斗), seeking to leverage her reputation to that point as a relatively apolitical writer in order to help the journal sidestep the attention of government censors.[54] Ding Ling would end up publishing two of her most prominent propaganda-themed stories in *Big Dipper*, "The Flood" ("Shui" 水, 1932) and "Eventful Autumn" ("Duo shi zhi qiu" 多事之秋, 1932). Both stories were immediately hailed in leftist journals as a major advancement of the emerging field of class-conscious literature. As one leading critic, Feng Xuefeng 馮雪峰 (1903–1976), commented in an essay titled "Concerning the Birth of a New Fiction" ("Guanyu xin de xiaoshuo de dansheng" 關於新的小說的誕生),[55] Ding Ling's stories were new both on account of their engagement with class struggle and the idea of dialectical materialism, but also because of her innovative attempts to rework the masses into a coherent protagonist subject for literature. Regarding the latter, Feng writes, Ding's recent fiction "does not have only one or two protagonists, but rather a grouped mass; it does not analyze individual psychology, but rather collective action and expansion [*kaizhan* 開展]; its characters are not individuated and stable, but rather, part of a whole, mutually influencing and developing."[56] If Ding's stories portray the masses in a newly dynamic way, it is by tracing how propaganda mediates collective subjectivity through the circulation of information.

"The Flood" appeared in serialized form across the first three issues of *Big Dipper* in 1932.[57] In the story a community of peasants struggles for survival in the wake of a massive flood. Working in the dark of night to shore up the local system of protective dikes, they are acutely attuned to changes in the situation in a way that plays out over the novella's soundscape. Sound, in turn, forms the conditions for the spontaneous emergence of a collective consciousness. At the start of the story, women, elderly, and refugees from neighboring villages are discussing the threat of the dikes' collapse when they hear the toll of the alarm gong signaling the impending deluge:

> The *dong, dong* rolled across the fields from the direction of the dikes, a confused and clamorous note shaking people out of their houses, rousing all the animals and fowls, and even startling roosting birds. The whole village burst into life. The universe itself seemed to have been strung on a line, ready to break at this touch of sound. . . . [Soon] the dogs yelped maddeningly, cocks crowed, and the wind rushing through the crowd twisted the mingled sounds with the voices it carried of the excited men and the rising waters they fought.[58]

The imagery of floodwater dispossessing the peasants of their land is soon repurposed to describe the wave of peasant refugees as they march on the walled city to demand relief from the well-off (and among whom hide the absentee landlords from the countryside). After much stalling on the part of the city's representatives, who refuse to open the reserve granaries and instead only promise to circulate a call for volunteer donations, the hungry peasants rally around a particularly loud member of the group. Having climbed a tree to speak from a height, the agitator is able to drown out other voices and becomes the de facto leader of the masses, who exhort him to continue speaking. In this position, he quite figuratively becomes a broadcast tower:

> Carrying within it an abundant force, this hoarse and bitter sound radiated from near to far, in the process stirring quite a few hungry hearts. His every sentence awoke them, for it put into words what they had already intuited

but for which they had not yet found appropriate language. In this moment, the peasants willingly listened to his directions, they were of one mind to pass on this command to the greater group, and their hearts were filled with a limitless light.[59]

The center-to-periphery, one-to-many model of propaganda is on clear display. And the receivers of the message will help spread it by disseminating it further outward in an ever-expanding ripple of sentiment. With their newfound collective consciousness, the peasants have rebalanced the local information order in their favor and will no longer be individually exploitable by the landlord class.

Published between late January and July 1932 (overlapping the Japanese bombing of Shanghai the same spring), "Eventful Autumn" exploits the imagination of propaganda even further. The story has gone relatively understudied despite its status as Ding's first attempt at a more full-length novel (she originally planned it to be about ten thousand characters long)[60] and its distinction as the culmination of what Feng had styled as "New Fiction." Like "The Flood," "Eventful Autumn" was serialized in the pages of *Big Dipper* and features a narrative voice that is intermixed with and dispersed by the reported speech of the anonymous masses.[61] "Eventful Autumn," too, offers a mythopoetic account of the emergence of revolutionary mass consciousness precipitated by waves of energy that sweep across gathered crowds. In contrast to "The Flood," however, the novel is set in an urban Shanghai and deals directly with the topics of government propaganda and the materiality of communication. By exploring propaganda, signal and noise, and the mediating environment of ether at length, "Eventful Autumn" is the quintessential literary emblem of the propaganda era.

Building on the panoramic mode she explored in "Daylight" (*Ri* 日, 1929), Ding Ling's "Eventful Autumn" expands its scope to the bustling streets of Shanghai, shifting from the interiority of individual characters to a broad canvas of the masses in motion. The narrative weaves together a public consciousness out of largely anonymous voices, exploring communication between various groups, including students, workers, and government representatives, and the resultant catalysis of mass consciousness and action. Across six sections, the story depicts first the spread of news/information (rendered as both *xinwen* and *xiaoxi*) regarding the so-called

September 18th Incident (*Jiuyiba* 九一八) of 1931 in which Japan, using a false-flag bomb attack to destroy a train line in Shenyang as a pretext, significantly escalated its imperialist claims over China's northeast territory of Manchuria. Outrage over the GMD's weakly diplomatic response spread in Shanghai, leading to mass demonstrations that were in turn brutally suppressed by police. Like the politics of sound in "The Flood," "Eventful Autumn" imagines the force of the masses sonically as waves of noise that overcome the much weaker sound signal of GMD propaganda. The constitutive role of sound is established in the opening lines of the narrative:

> The rumble and roll [*honglong-honglong* 轟隆轟隆] of the tram car, the screeching sounds [*zhiya-zhiya* 吱呀吱呀] of steel wheels running over steel tracks, as well as the ceaseless peeling of bells, the clamoring city [*xuannao de shi* 喧鬧的市] sounds move from Jing'an Temple to Ka'de Road, to the racetrack, and settle in an even noisier [*caoza* 嘈雜] spot, where a million kinds of noises [*naosheng* 鬧聲] converge together in one place: the broad road in front of the gates of the Shi Company.... Here the flapping of countless flags accompanies the ear-splitting sounds of the automobiles, and the various cacophonies [*xiaonao* 囂鬧] of all the people, machines, iron, and wood distant and near pool into one giant, taut tide of sound [*coucheng yi ge juda de jinzhang de shengyin de langchao* 湊成一個巨大的緊張的聲音的浪潮]. (1:25)

Through the rhetoric of excess where sound piles on top of sound, the description evokes a sensation of rising energy, setting the tone for the rest of the story and its theme of noise. Indeed, the novel positions itself as a kind of recording device that captures the city's tense soundscape. In doing so, the story participates in a form of what Linda Henderson terms "vibratory modernism," whereby fiction of the period makes visible soundwaves and their transmission.[62] Shanghai is thereby transformed into an etherscape filled with propaganda and counterpropaganda, signal and noise, news and misinformation. But in its rich depiction of the saturation of propaganda across Shanghai, the text also places *itself* within the very same information order that it depicts. In the only scholarly treatment of the text in English, Charles Laughlin analyzes "Eventful Autumn" as an early example of the genre of "reportage literature" (*baogao wenxue* 報告文學) developed by leftist writers in the wake of the September 18th Incident of

1931.[63] As a piece of reportage, the story speaks to a leftist and proletarian readership in a way that runs counter to the bourgeois biases of contemporary newspaper reporting. As such, it describes the existing order while concurrently seeking to construct a new one.

As the protesters gather, the tide of sound in the opening scene becomes an outflow of communication when special edition newspapers and other pamphlets get passed out. These "fly into the hands of some bystanders, and then again fly off into other places. . . . In thousands and tens of thousands, the papers are opened in countless hands" (1:25–26), disseminating updates about developments in Manchuria. The effect is, again, aural: "amidst all the cacophony, the information [*xiaoxi*] drums up an even larger sound wave, this shocking news [*xinwen*] spreads in all four directions along with the reactions [*fanxiang* 反響, lit. 'repercussions'] it elicits" (1:26). This wave of information, sentiment, and sound takes further form as a string of representative anonymous exchanges that stands in for the totality of communication amidst the thronging population of Shanghai: "information [*xiaoxi*] was transmitted from street to adjoining street, transmitted to all of the indigent areas, the working-class areas," and then on to neighboring cities (1:26–27). The media of transmission include conversation, lectures, and pamphlets, which mutually supplement each other and effect larger chain reactions. More than anything, the shape of mass communication follows along the center-to-periphery radial structure modeled on broadcast or amplified speech. Indeed, the narrative directly adopts this comparison when, at the beginning of chapter 6, it exclaims that news about the killing of several protestors "was immediately transmitted across all of Shanghai at a speed even more rapid than radio broadcast" (3–4:527). Although the control of communications infrastructure in the semicolonial space of Shanghai is predominantly shared by Nationalist and foreign governments, along with private enterprises, Ding's story takes pain to demonstrate that their institutions do not have a monopoly over the information order. Grassroots transmission or spontaneous gatherings, too, can fill the ether with signal and reshape the information order from below.

The visualization of the ether space as a stand-in for the general space of the information order is on fullest display in the opening of chapter 3, which details the flurry of communication that happens alongside (and in reaction to) student-organized propagandizing:

The staff at the telegraph office went into overtime but were still unable to keep up. Several dozen provinces, several thousands of counties, several tens of thousands of groups all seemed to compete in sending telegrams and declarations that were unsparing in length. *Electric currents filled the air* [*dianliu man kongzhong fei* 電流滿空中飛]. The wireless communications [*wuxian jiaotong* 無線交通] of various consulates and dignitaries were left no time to rest. Then there were the newspapers and their reporters, who blindly rushed off in all directions. The typesetters had even less time to sleep. The price of paper suddenly spiked, half on account of the great increase in newspapers, journals, manifestos, and pamphlets, and half on account of the boycotts. All of the students in China came out to give lectures, and across the country the calls to boycott Japanese goods arose like a tidal wave. (1:30–31; my emphasis)

Here, Ding's attention to the materiality and labor of communication (paper, typesetting, etc.) further enhances her description of an urban atmosphere shaped by the hypermediated frenzy of collecting, transmitting, and consuming information. On the whole, the crisis precipitated by unfolding events disrupts the normal operation of the information order, as workers and students assert themselves as active participants in shaping public opinion.

But this signal of current news and patriotic sentiment is not uncontested, as the GMD attempts to issue counterpropaganda to defuse public sentiment. In contrast to the explosion of popular communication, the government responses are represented as clipped and ineffectual. The weakness of the GMD's propaganda signal is quite literal, as we see in a key scene where officials attempt to organize a mass rally in support of the Nationalist government. Hungry for an explanation about what the government plans to do, a crowd of three hundred thousand gathers. "They fill the entirety of the public grounds, as well as the surrounding streets, even the nearby walls and rooftops. More people squeezed in among the sea of gatherers. Banners and flags flew from poles, and voices shouted out among the tide of sound" (1:31). The contrast with Liang's absence of concern about sound amplitude in the opening of *Future Record* is again telling of the historical and perceptual differences between his era and Ding's eras:

The sounds [of impatience cries] carried off, and shouts arose from afar: "Begin the meeting! Begin the meeting!"

A fat man with a yellow face, wearing a Sun Yat-sen jacket, grabbed a megaphone [*chuanyintong* 傳音筒] and strode to the front edge of the platform. He loudly proclaimed:

"Please quiet down everyone, we are beginning the meeting! Would the chairman please step forward . . ."

But people on all four sides couldn't hear clearly and asked those in their vicinity:

"What's he saying?"

"Quiet down, listen to them!" (1:32)

The shortfall of sound augurs an inauspicious beginning to the event. Expecting an agitational meeting in the vein of student propagandists' rallies, the gathered people can't make sense of the officious speeches that follow. The government's failure to communicate continues to be described as a weakness of amplitude, for when the chairperson does begin speaking, his voice is unable to reach the majority of the listeners:

The wind scattered [*chuiduan* 吹斷, lit. "blew apart"] his speech, sending discontinuous words in all directions:

"Japan . . .

"Fellow countrymen . . .

"Great meeting of citizens . . .

"Government . . .

"League of Nations . . .

"Request that you express your opinions . . ."

Thereupon he retreated, and another tall, thin man stepped forward.

"What's he saying? I still can't hear!"

"These officials, what are they showing to us? What have they come to do, that they're so fancily dressed?"

"We will organize!"

"We don't trust the League of Nations! . . ."

"We want the government to immediately dispatch troops! . . . " (1:32–33)

The "ear" that here shuttles from the speech of the government representatives to the audience reactions performs two functions: In the first half, by breaking up the oration into a string of fragmented utterances, the narrative performs the ineffectuality of the GMD propaganda signal. This is followed by a contrasted response—typical of Ding's experimental New Fiction—whereby the utterances of the anonymous masses are strung together into a coherent and swelling reaction. Their sequencing forms a kind of relay system that adds up to a shared stream of consciousness, resulting in a mass voice of protest that rivals the riptide of the Qiantang River in its roar (1:33).[64] Soon student activists displace the officials from the stage and begin their propaganda speeches; unlike the government's, their slogans are clearly received and rapidly fold the listeners into a "unified body" (*dajia yizhi* 大家一致, 1:35). The play of signal/countersignal in this scene is reenacted elsewhere in the story as the GMD's attempts to placate the public are repeatedly rebuffed by popular counterpropaganda (3–4:520, 527–28).

The vibratory modernism of "Eventful Autumn" echoes Chen Yuxin's Manichean formulation of the propaganda/counterpropaganda feedback loop. Above all, this cycle poses propagation as a kind of *pharmakon*: both a poison (the false consciousness of government information) and a cure (the enlightenment of student and leftist propaganda).[65] Within the narrative, the importance of signal engineering establishes a mediological analogy between the channels of propaganda and the frequency bands of the ether. Either because the Nationalist government shuttered the offices of *Big Dipper* or because she found it too difficult to sustain the narrative's rhetoric of excess, Ding Ling abandoned "Eventful Autumn" after two installments. Nonetheless, more than any of Ding's other works, the story responds to the impetus for literary propaganda that was just then emerging, stoking fantasies about a captive and engaged audience hungry for leftist signals. Whereas "The Flood" portrays the emergence of the masses as an essentially self-organizing process, in "Eventful Autumn" popular sentiment is shaped through the efforts of students and journalists. The lesson is impossible to miss: dedicated propagandists play a leading role in awakening the people.

Overall, Ding Ling's imagination of Shanghai as an ethereal space filled with propaganda waves invites us to reconsider the masses as a narrative subject. Without the proper communication practice, the masses must remain unbound and scattered. They cohere through a kinetics of information exchange effected by propaganda. Here one more piece in Ding's oeuvre of early propaganda fiction is worth noting. Published in the summer of 1932 (just as "Eventful Autumn" was approaching its second installment), this short story is titled "Xiaoxi."[66] It offers a more focused view of information's role in social mobilization, and as such it deserves to be read as a companion piece to "Eventful Autumn." "Xiaoxi" inverts the latter's ecstatic bursts of information by instead depicting the clandestine work of organizing within one of Shanghai's lower-class households; it also adds a distinctly gendered and domestic perspective largely absent in Ding's other propaganda fiction. This story's central character is an aging woman who lives with her adult son, his wife, and their small child. The son frequently invites his friends from the factory over for group meetings. During these gatherings, the elderly woman is banished to a tiny side room. From here, despite noise from the street and her incomprehension of certain terms, she overhears enough of the workers' conversation to catch the gist of what they're up to. Inspired by their revolutionary spirit, she desires to contribute to their cause in some way. Finally, she goes to the neighboring household to talk idly with Old Woman Wang, where their gossip attracts other neighbors. This exchange helps the women piece together an awareness of the larger force behind the worker strikes (i.e., the Communist Party). The women wish to send the organizers a telegram sharing their understanding and wishing them good will. As part of a collection drive they embroider a piece of cloth with red flowers. The next time her son gathers with his coworkers, the elderly mother shyly presents the piece on behalf of the fourteen neighborhood women, stating that she knows what he's up to and urging him to accept their token of support. She bashfully asks one of the men if "that association" could use old women like her; amused, the young man says they do. The story ends with her earnestly telling him that she and twenty or thirty of her friends are at the service of the organizers. The story thus explores how information both moves on its own accord (the woman's eavesdropping) and promotes the idea that even a relatively lowly figure can become an organizer sharing information judiciously. Through it, Ding Ling again underscores the importance of communication (eavesdropping, gossip, sending messages) to the formation of class consciousness, while zooming in on the dispensation of the information order at the bottom rungs of society. The contiguous space of the ether thus extends into even the most marginalized spaces of the city.

LINES OF FORCE: SIGNAL AND ETHER IN WOODCUT ART

As Ding Ling was thematizing propaganda and information in her writing, the nascent field of modern woodcut art also grew into the propaganda era by exploring new ways of visualizing signal and noise. The histories of leftist literature and woodcut are closely related: in print, woodcut images were featured in nearly all the leftist literary journals of the period,[67] and the artists themselves shared social circles with writers. In their survey of the modern Chinese woodcut, Julia Andrews and Kuiyi Shen split its early history into two periods: the first spans from 1928 to the outbreak of the War of Resistance in 1937, while the second covers 1937 to the establishment of the People's Republic of China in 1949. In the second phase, woodcut art served as a widespread tool of political mobilization oriented toward national salvation, becoming the "de facto 'official art'" of the Communist forces' base in Yan'an.[68] By contrast, during its first phase, woodcut art's primary aim was to raise class consciousness through social realism. During this initial period, the most prominent promoter of leftist woodcut art in China and a significant arbiter of its trends and aesthetics was Lu Xun, who began publishing foreign woodcut art from his personal collection in a series of compilations as early as 1929 and until his death in 1936 served as a financial patron and intellectual muse for a coterie of young artists.[69] In contrast to traditional Chinese woodcut images, which were produced anonymously, the woodblock art that emerged in Shanghai and Guangzhou in the 1930s was produced by youths who identified themselves as individual artists, rather than craftspeople; they carved their own blocks, printed and exhibited their own works, and counted themselves part of a broadly internationalist art movement. During the 1930s they worked to develop their own modernist, cosmopolitan aesthetic variously influenced by the cubism, expressionism, and realism of a range of foreign counterparts such as Kathe Kollwitz, Lynd Hunt, and Frans Masereel.[70]

Although it was by no means the earliest modern form of visual propaganda,[71] because the woodcut evolved directly alongside the onset of the propaganda era, it serves as the latter's richest mode of visual expression. Indeed, departing from the decorative function of traditional woodblock printing and the mix of education and entertainment found in lithographic pictorial journals such as the *Dianshizhai huabao* (點石齋畫報, published

1884–1898), 1930s woodcut art took agitation and propagation as its basic mission: only a few months after the League of Left-wing Writers formed in March 1930, the smaller League of Left-wing Artists (Zhongguo Zuoyi Yishujia Lianmeng 中國左翼藝術家聯盟) was organized under the auspices of the Communist Party's Central Bureau of Propaganda.[72] Just as Japan's annexation of Manchuria in 1931 and bombing of Shanghai in early 1932 precipitated the development of New Fiction and reportage literature, so too did these events spur a rapid propagandistic turn in woodcut art, as artists abandoned a liberal and humanist approach to their subjects in favor of fanning popular outrage and mass politics.

This compulsion to propagandize is epitomized by an early piece by Hu Yichuan 胡一川 (1910–2000), *To the Front!* (*Dao qianxian qu* 到前線去), an image first displayed at an exhibition in 1932, and which became iconic of the burgeoning woodcut art movement's political turn (figure 3.3). The same month as the exhibit, Hu's group, the Spring Earth Society, issued its manifesto: "Modern art must follow a new road, must serve a new society, must become a powerful tool for educating the masses, informing the masses, and organizing the masses. The new art must accept this mission as it moves forward."[73] Paralleling Ding Ling's literary intervention into the

FIGURE 3.3 Hu Yichuan, *To the Front!* Reprinted in *Banhua jicheng: Lu Xun cang Zhongguo xiandai muke quanji* (Shanghai: Lu Xun jinian guan; Nanjing: Jiangsu guji, 1991), 4:1455

information order of the day, Hu and his associates sought to "establish an interpretive frame on [the sense of] overwhelming crisis . . . [and offer] impassioned visual commentary on contemporary history."[74]

What is most striking about Hu Yichuan's *To the Front!* is the powerful aural quality exuded by its subject: a yelling man exhorting his fellows to follow him forward. Analyzing this image and others like it, Xiaobing Tang remarks an "aural turn" in woodcut art beginning in 1932, when the form enters a "new phase in an acoustic reality, namely [by representing] the experience of overwhelming and unnatural sounds and noises . . . [in] a search for or recognition of the human voice." Tracing the visual leitmotif of shouting bodies, Tang argues that this aural turn speaks to a shared "wish to project a resonating voice, whether it was the voice of a larger-than-life individual or that of a unified collective. The consequent aspiration to picture an invisible object so as to inspire passion and action was a challenge that would ultimately entail an imaginative transgression of the boundary between the visual and the aural."[75]

The aural turn of woodcut art is generally consonant with a phonocentrism already put in motion by spoken drama and vernacularization of literature during the New Culture movement.[76] Besides foregrounding the sounded voice, woodcut art also took up the subject of communication as a way of reflecting upon the propaganda era within which it arose. This is manifest in the proliferation of images that represent information exchange in innovative ways, particularly instances where the woodcut print remediates other media, including oral transmission and mass media such as the newspaper or radio. In addition to the work *Xiaoxi* that I considered in the book's introduction, we may turn to another print of the same title. Produced in 1935 by Tang Yingwei 唐英偉 (figure 3.4), this *Xiaoxi* depicts three urban workers reading a newspaper against a factory backdrop, carved in a deliberately crude style to heighten the effect of social realism. What I find significant here is how the woodblock medium depicts another print medium, the newspaper, to comment on the latter's place among the proletariat: even the poorer classes are keen readers to stay current. The later *Xiaoxi* (see figure 0.2 in the introduction), whose original English title is *A Bit of News*, similarly thematizes information by representing an intimate oral exchange between two men. While neither piece exactly qualifies as the search for a voice that Tang identifies in modern woodcut art, both nonetheless exude a strongly aural quality: discussions of news, whispered

FIGURE 3.4 *Xiaoxi*, by Tang Yingwei. Reprinted in *Banhua jicheng*, 3:779

rumors—one hears these scenes upon seeing them. These images further-more demonstrate a strong interest in the formation of mass conscious-ness. In doing so, each piece both acts as a propaganda vehicle that inter-polates the viewer to share in the spread of (leftist) revolutionary consciousness among the working class, while also reflecting on the act of propagation itself: *this* is how information spreads among vectors of soci-ety and binds the masses together. If an impulse "to explore and present the essential nature of its own medium" is characteristic of modernist art more generally,[77] these woodcuts go a step further by exploring the broader media ecology and information order within which they are embedded. As we will see, here, too, this environment is visualized through the evocation of a contiguous and contested ether space, offering a pictorial form of the kind of vibratory modernism that is the hallmark of Ding Ling's writing from the same period.

In line with such a vibratory modernism, even the names of the early woodcut artist associations—which tended to form and dissolve quickly in the highly censored and suppressive environment of Shanghai—suggest currents of sound and energy: Empty Wave Painting Society (1933), Wild Wind Painting Association (Yefeng huahui 野風畫會, 1932), Wooden Bell Society (Muling muke yanjiuhui 木鈴木刻研究會, 1932), and Rapid Torrent Woodcut Research Society (Jiliu muke yanjiuhui 激流木刻研究會).[78] Here we will focus on the propagandistic works of several of leading figures in the field of woodcut art before the outbreak of war in 1937: Luo Qingzhen, an influential Cantonese artist and one of Lu Xun's favorite artists; Huang Xinbo, who had studied at the Shanghai School of Fine Arts and in 1933 cofounded the influential Unnamed Woodcut Society (Weimingshe 未名社); and Zhang Hui, another Cantonese member of the avant-garde woodcut art movement. All three were associates whose works frequently appeared in the same journals, collections, and exhibitions. And they share an impulse to remediate ether in their woodcuts. Ether's synesthetic essence as a medium that carries both sound and light in turn makes visible a general, abstract space of communications that propaganda seeks to territorialize. And, equally important, the evocation of ether attests to the formative influence of the very medium that made it imaginable: broadcast radio. The general interplay between ether and broadcast signal appears in these works in three interconnected forms: the foregrounding of air/ether filled with waves of light and sound, the specific representation of the latter as an electrified (and electrifying) extension of the human voice, and the adoption of a centralized focal point with an attendant "array" layout that parallels the form of a one-to-many broadcast. In all, these features made a significant contribution to transforming information into an object of perception during the first half of the twentieth century.

The first example of early woodcut art's engagement propaganda is the 1936 piece, *The Masses Rise Up* (*Dazhong qilai* 大眾起來), also titled *The Voice of the Masses* (*Dazhong husheng* 大眾呼聲]), by Luo Qingzhen (figure 3.5).[79] In this powerful image, a man in the foreground is backed by a roaring crowd of protestors. As the title indicates, the piece presents the

FIGURE 3.5 *The Masses Rise Up*, by Luo Qingzhen. Reprinted in *Banhua jicheng*, 4:1372

emergence of the masses as a unified subject. Such an image may as well have served as an illustration for Ding Ling's "Eventful Autumn" and its concurrent representations of this new subject of history. But what I want to call particular attention to is the activity at the horizon, above the crowd, where the sense of sound emitted by the human figures is augmented by stylized and dynamic lines that fill the register. Though the diagonal strokes suggest the immense energy of a violent storm, clearly this is no natural weather event. Reminiscent of the "force lines" of futurist painters such as Umberto Boccioni,[80] the horizon is a primary site of the modernism of the piece, creating a sense of auditory amplitude, whereby sound reaches beyond the border to tele-cast the power of the collective voice of the masses.

Broadly speaking, the horizon constitutes an important zone of graphic experimentation during the 1930s. The filling of space with rays of energy or light was unprecedented within the history of visual art in China, where, despite a long tradition of woodcut printing, horizons were left blank. The representation of sound/light waves with dynamic lines clearly shows the influence of Western woodcuts, particularly the modernist style of Frans Masereel. To be clear, the representations of waves at the horizon is not limited to propaganda-themed scenes of the urban masses. For example, in Zhang Hui's *Glow of the Evening Sun in the Countryside* (*Nongcun xizhao* 農村夕照, 1935), the rays of the sun occupy a significant area of the image, serving as a focal point and showcasing the artist's command of the medium (figure 3.6).[81] However, urban-themed images showing propagandizing make a point of repurposing the horizon as a field of signals and noise. Besides *The Masses Rise Up*, this is illustrated by Luo's *Roar* (*Paoxiao* 咆哮, onomatopoeic for the sound of crashing waves, 1937; figure 3.7), where the depiction of a throng of protestors combines the woodcutter's study in light with the subject of mobilization.[82] In this new representational practice, the air is not just a negative space or vacuum, but rather serves as an ethereal mediating environment that carries energy in the form of light waves or sound vibration. Similar to the pictorial imagery of radio broadcast, the horizon becomes a space of ideological contestation and revolutionary sentiment.

Woodcut artists' addition of light rays to their images is joined by another unprecedented experimentation with depicting sound waves. Viewing Huang Xinbo's 1935 commemorative portrait (figure 3.8) of the leftist composer Nie Er 聶耳 (1912–1935),[83] one is struck by the variety of techniques used to ring the foregrounded figure with an aural register: the wave motifs above Nie Er's shoulders, the sonar-like lines that bring into relief the distant bodies of soldiers and laborers, and the scribble-like line in the upper left corner all denote the emanation of sound. This piece is particularly poignant because Huang produced it the same year that Nie Er made his biggest contribution to modern China's sonic history when he

FIGURE 3.6 Zhang Hui, *Glow of the Setting Sun in the Countryside*. Reprinted in *Zhang Hui mukehua di er ji*
(Shanghai: Kaiming shudian; Beiping: Lijian shuju, 1935), 7

composed the score for "March of the Volunteer Army" (*Yiyongjun jin-xingqu* 義勇軍進行曲), the future national anthem of the People's Republic, which appeared that year in one of the earliest sound films of leftist cinema, *Young People of a Stormy Age* (*Fengyun ernü* 風雲兒女; dir. Xu Xing-zhi 許幸之, 1935).[84] Here the amplification of sound figures Nie's revolutionary and patriotic passion.

The aural quality foregrounded in these images (as well as many more presented by Xiaobing Tang in his study) is not just a matter of filling the air with sound waves. Specifically, these waves are *amplified*—particularly via electricity, another form of energy wave carried by ether. Such amplification is on display in Huang Xinbo's *Bellow* (*Nuhou* 怒吼), published in 1934 (figure 3.9).[85] In this image a man is shown letting out a roar while shaking his fist at the sky. On the left is laid out a pastiche of miniature

FIGURE 3.7 Luo Qingzhen, *Crashing Waves*. *Luo Qingzhen muke zuopin xuanji* (Shanghai: Renmin meishu chubanshe, 1958), 327

FIGURE 3.8 Huang Xinbo, *Portrait of Nie Er.* Reprinted in *Xinbo banhua ji* (Beijing: Renmin meishu chubanshe, 1978), 10

scenes of disasters then besetting China: droughts, floods, and aerial bombing. A jagged line suggests the electrification of the man's voice, while his looming shadow—whose source of light is the radial sun in the scene of drought—suggests the extension of his anger. Notably, both the foregrounded figure and the people in the miniatures gaze upward, calling attention to the sky as a menacing space: perhaps the man's defiant roar will fill the ether and call the nation to action, or perhaps it can supplant the parching sun and shatter the enemy planes. Whatever the case, *Bellow* and these other examples collectively dramatize the presence of amplitude while also suggesting that, so extended, the human voice will mobilize the masses as such.

The sense of electrified amplification as well as the centeredness of the human figure in *Bellow* further calls attention to the third characteristic of many of the propaganda woodcuts of the period: their highly

FIGURE 3.9 Huang Xinbo, *Bellow*. Reprinted in *Banhua Jicheng*, 4:1241

centralized and arrayed composition, which, coupled with the theme of propagation and communication in many of these pieces, forms a formal analogy to broadcast's one-to-many communication. This type of centralized focalization is exemplified in figure 3.10, *News* (*Xinwen* 新聞, 1935) by Zhang Hui,[86] an image that evokes a broadcast aesthetic and yet again remediates the newspaper. In the foreground a newsboy hawks a paper whose sensationalist contents are presented via the surrounding collage of scenes: a suicidal leap from a skyscraper, a marching infantryman, a naked woman, a prostrate body, and refugees fleeing disaster. The space above

FIGURE 3.10 *News*, by Zhang Hui. Reprinted in *Banhua jicheng*, 3:986

the newspaper is conspicuously filled by the sun and its rays. These radial lines not only illuminate the national space-time produced by the newspaper; they are also suggestive of broadcast transmission from a central source to multiple receivers. Such centered composition is typical of Zhang Hui's work, as the subsequent example of *Street* (*Jietou* 街頭) shows (figure 3.11). Created in the same year as *News*, this image also evokes the dynamism of a busy street.[87] But even as the image refracts by showing

FIGURE 3.11 Zhang Hui, *Street*. Reprinted in *Banhua jicheng*, 3:984

disparate experiences within the same frame, it is also tightly organized around an offset center point, which, not coincidentally, is the diegetic source of light and energy. On its face, a picture like *Street* is neither a depiction of propaganda nor propagandistic in nature; it nonetheless captures the feeling of sensory overload caused by the city. In this way, *Street* offers a different look at an existential condition of the modern individual, namely, a state of paralyzing confusion brought on by the growing complexity of the world—one of the problems which modern propaganda aims to solve through simplification.

To end the chapter, let us consider one final woodcut image that takes communication as its subject (figure 3.12): Zhang Hui's carefully composed *Xiaoxi* (1935)—the third work with such a title that I have come across.[88] This print is particularly notable for how it both affirms and challenges the

FIGURE 3.12 Zhang Hui, *Xiaoxi*. Reprinted in *Banhua jicheng*, 3:992

tendencies of woodcut art to configure ether and broadcast communication that I have outlined here. Zhang sets a number of leisurely figures on a bridge, backed by a city landscape replete with factories, smokestacks, and a water tower. One person appears to be reading a newspaper, another standing and gazing outward, while two others sit, all involved in a casual exchange. In contrast to the many contemporary works that suggest an amplification and amplitude of sound, this image evokes a feeling of silence or inaudibility, contemplation, and even a tinge of mystery (despite its mundaneness) by positioning the viewer at a distance from the scene. This foursome could hardly be taken for a mass. The muted feel of the scene is further enhanced by the depiction of the airspace above the city, which occupies fully half of the overall image. This aerial register is entirely filled with diagonal and horizontal lines that suggest ominous weather, and, on the other hand, amorphous black patches of factory smoke. *Xiaoxi* inverts the conventional proportions of figure and ground, emphasizing the smallness of the human figures in contrast to the expansiveness of the sky above. In doing so, the picture exudes a distinctly sublime feeling.

However, similar to Ding Ling's short story "Xiaoxi," there is a productive gap between title and content: Where, or what, is the *xiaoxi* suggested by the title? What is the "point" of the image? Clearly the title partially rises out of the four figures who, in their repose, exchange some bit of news. But the broadcast aesthetics that we have identified here should lead us to see a second dimension of *xiaoxi* in the image, namely in the peculiar atmospherics and their reflection or extension of the figures laid out below. Neither unidirectional nor arrayed, the lines at the horizon do not show a singular broadcast or a unified source of waves. Instead, their angular incidence parallels the human figures' multivalent postures, suggesting a multitude of signals filling the air.[89] The fullness and dynamism of this etherscape thus serves as a visual metaphor for the circulation of information among the people below. As the other woodcut images show, the techne of propaganda is the amplification and channeling of a communication signal to broaden its social impact. By reflecting on the subject of information itself, rather than on propaganda or broadcast per se, this *Xiaoxi* appears to be markedly apolitical and nonpropagandistic. All the same, by visibilizing the environmental medium of the ether as it envelops city and society, this subtle image offers the most paradigmatic example of an emerging, reflexive aesthetic of the propaganda era—one that renders the modern information order not as content, but as climate.

Chapter Four

NARRATING NETWORKS

Shen Congwen's Literary Craft and the Social
Life of Information

In 1935, the prolific regionalist author Shen Congwen (1902–1988) published a short story about the telephone.[1] Titled "Unemployed" (*Shiye* 失業; see appendix for a complete translation), the piece has been curiously over-looked in scholarship on Shen.[2] The story deserves attention not only on account of its status as the first work in Chinese literature to so prominently feature a telephone switchboard as a narrative device, but also because it captures Shen's longstanding interest in social networks. "Unemployed" portrays a small-town youth named Daren who has assumed the post of switchboard operator at the new office of the growing long-distance telephone network. An inexperienced and somewhat naïve high school graduate, Daren is a quintessential May Fourth idealist who dreams of contributing to the mission of social reform through his literature. To this end, his current position seemingly offers an incomparable opportunity, for, "When you think about it, who has more experience than the long-distance telephone operator and his ear? This is a central exchange hub (*jiaohuan zong jiguan* 交換總機關) for the corrupt souls of the region. What vulgar language would fool the operator? What novel and strange affairs does he not know?" (*SCQJ*, 8:313). Instead of helping launch his writing career, how-ever, Daren's job increasingly bewilders him when the network reveals a complex and deep-seated web of corruption among local elites and the regional military. Thus exposed to their profiteering and mutual back scratching, Daren comes to feel increasingly disillusioned and becomes paralyzed before the monumental task of making China modern. As a switchboard operator he is both an insider and outsider to others' conversations, a position that is mirrored by his standing in the village, where he is a passive witness to corruption and abuse. Unable to cope with daily incidents of corruption and his role as enabler, Daren decides to pursue a different career. The story concludes with his rejoining the ranks of the unemployed.

Beyond its use of the telephone as a strategy for painting a picture of local corruption, the narrative of "Unemployed" engages with a critical formal problem that Shen Congwen was himself grappling with during the period. Besides infrastructural and social networks, the story features a third, interrelated web: literary writing. Daren diligently records the fragments of conversations that he overhears at his post. Though the disembodied voices of telephone customers give him access to insider knowledge, they also profoundly fluster his attempts to organize them into a coherent order. His diary is "filled with fragments of confused language" (*yi pian hutu de yanyu* 一片糊塗的言語): "After writing a bit, he'd read it over to himself and get really angry, abandoning the unfinished writing, and smoothly flipping [*fan* 翻] back to and reading over previous days' entries" (*SCQJ*, 8:311). In their refusal to develop linearly, the entries fail to add up to a narrative and provide instead a kind of stream-of-consciousness recording of abuses hurled at Daren by his callers. Contrary to his idealism regarding the leverage such a position might provide for an author, this tangle of fragments instead reflects the complexity and intractability of a network of corruption. His deepening realization of his inability to tease out causality between events is ironically highlighted by the arrogant confidence of the local toughs, who frequently extort villagers by threatening to "get to the bottom of things" if they don't comply. If one wants to write a story exposing the network of corruption, where does one begin or end? Daren is trapped within the labyrinth of calls.

The use of the telephone in "Unemployed" as a narrative device to emphasize the relation between ear and voice is not incidental and instead parallels Shen's adoption of a dialogic and oral style in longer and better-known works such as *Border Town* (*Biancheng* 邊城, 1934) and *Random Sketches on a Trip to Hunan* (*Xiang xing sanji* 湘行散記, 1936). But "Unemployed" best exemplifies—and problematizes—the role of heteroglossia in Shen's work. In "Discourse in the Novel" (1934), Mikhail Bakhtin conceptualizes heteroglossia as the "multiplicity of social voices and [the] wide variety of their links and interrelationships" that appear within and indeed constitute a novel, imparting the text with an inherent social tension. Along these lines, Bakhtin continues, heteroglossia carries significant political stakes, for it "gives expression to forces working [against] concrete verbal and ideological unification and centralization, which develop in vital connection with the processes of sociopolitical and cultural centralization."[3] A similar significance emerges in Shen's heteroglossic style and his identity as a regionalist focused primarily on the voices and practices of western Hunan, far from urban centers like Beijing and Shanghai.

What calls for further investigation is not so much Shen's uses of locally colored language and manifold voices in his work—interesting as they may be—but the specific *form* that such heteroglossia takes in his literature during the height of his writing career, between the early 1930s and 1945.[4] In what manner does Shen's literature weave together the "thousands of living dialogic threads" in order to produce their heteroglossic effect?[5] How does the multiplicity of voices in his works contribute to Shen's unique vision of society as a communications network? While Daren, the protagonist of "Unemployed," ultimately abandons the network of telephony, thus leaving his career as a writer in doubt, by the mid-1930s, Shen Congwen himself was only just getting started with networks, which appear repeatedly in different aspects of his literary work and criticism, including his distinctive brand of literary formalism, the materiality of his writing, and, most urgently, his interest in China's modern information order.

The cultural and political backdrop to this period was, as described in the previous chapter, the emergence of a new era of propaganda, counterpropaganda, and broadcast communication. Shen had sympathy for leftist politics at the outset of his writing career in the mid-1920s, but unlike his close friend Ding Ling, he shied away from Communist political activity and declined membership in the League of Left-wing Writers. He became even more politically reticent after several of his friends in the CCP were executed following the Nationalist Party's purge of its left wing in 1927. But this does not mean that his work was apolitical or that he didn't have a great deal to say about propaganda itself. In exploring Shen's work on western Hunan (Xiangxi 湘西) and his formative influence on the genre of modern "native soil" literature, critics have tended to position Shen outside the political milieu or interpret his works as only obliquely engaging with the political debates that raged among fellow writers.[6] While Shen's prolific output spans across many genres, styles, and themes and thus defies any attempt at neat categorization,[7] a story such as "Unemployed" gestures to important questions that Shen would raise during the 1930s regarding the political import of information, media, and literary practice: How did the circulation of information contribute to communality? What role did different media play in such circulation? And could such media be effectively harnessed for large-scale propaganda? To explore these issues, Shen experimented extensively with different forms of networks in order to plumb the complexity and contingency of social systems in a way that his character, Daren, could not in "Unemployed."

The network form is a lens for exploring what I call the "social life of information" in Shen's literature and criticism between 1930 and the mid-1940s, when his literary career tapered off. "Social life of information" refers to how news and gossip moves through a locality by way of different media and how such movement both reshapes information and society alike.[8] Shen's interest in the subject of information and the sociopolitics of communication culminated in his last novel-length literary project, *Long River* (*Changhe* 長河, 1945).[9] The first and only sustained work in modern Chinese literature written in direct opposition to the propaganda era, *Long River* explores the communications network of a region far upstream from the capital city of Nanjing. In doing so, the novel presents the reader with critical insight into the social life of information and the informatic life of society.

Shen's interest in the social dimension of information in works such as "Unemployed" and *Long River* stands as a unique case in the encounter between modern Chinese literature and information. In chapter 2, we saw how the contemporaneous work of Mao Dun thematizes *xiaoxi* to investigate the abstraction of knowledge. In *Long River*, the word *xiaoxi* also appears again as a kind of master term, but almost exclusively as the object of oral exchanges between fellow villagers, unlike in Shanghai where it circulates via media like telegraph, newspapers, and radio.[10] Such person-to-person interactions highlight *xiaoxi*'s function as a token of social exchange while also effectively deemphasizing the actual content of any particular message. In his consideration of the social dimension of meaning-making in language, the anthropologist Bronislaw Malinowski might as well have been glossing Shen's version of *xiaoxi* when he coined the term "phatic communion," the gossip and everyday exchanges ("How are you?") whose function is first and foremost to affirm bonds between social actors.[11] Taken compositely in *Long River*, across time and space, the largely phatic circulation of *xiaoxi* reveals a dynamic network of social relationality. This network, along with Shen's interest in oral communication generally, presents an information order that is vastly different from the one imagined by the propaganda apparatus. Indeed, the social life of *xiaoxi* traced in *Long River* calls to account the fantasies about the immersive reach of propaganda (inspired by radio and ether), on the one hand, and, on the other hand, the "hypodermic needle" conception of mass communication's efficacy (along the lines of Chen Yuxin's bow and arrow) in which a propaganda signal need but reach the target population to mobilize it.[12]

Shen explores information and network in earlier literature and criticism before *Long River*. This includes Shen's own forays into propaganda literature during the early 1930s, when he wrote avant-garde pieces that are strikingly reminiscent of the contemporary treatment of propagation in Ding Ling's literature and in woodcut art discussed in the previous chapter. While such experimentation was to prove short-lived (and markedly cynical in tone), it marks the beginning of Shen's budding imagination of an information order, which would in turn provide critical lever for his reassessment of the legacy of the New Culture and May Fourth movements' idealism toward modernizing society through modern literature. Observing the growing dominance of propaganda on cultural production in the 1930s, Shen consequently developed an oppositional aesthetics around the idea of "technique," an approach to literary writing that centers on the material arrangement of words and envisions itself as a form of craftwork. This aesthetic presages Shen's withdrawal from fiction writing after 1949 when, finding himself unable to write the kind of propagandistic literature demanded by the socialist state, Shen subtly pivoted his energy toward the realm of China's history of material culture. In doing so, he sublimated his conception of literature-as-handicraft into reading actual handicrafts as literature, in effect carving out an alternative space of creativity set apart from a cultural sphere dominated by propaganda.

THE CRAFT OF WRITING: SMALL NARRATIVES IN A GRAND AGE

The late 1920s were a time of transition for Shen Congwen: he was gaining prominence as a writer and journal editor, and in 1929 he relocated to Shanghai from Beijing, where he cofounded with Ding Ling a new journal, *Red and Black* (*Honghei* 紅黑). At the same time, Shen also began experimenting with portraying the masses and leftist politics—precisely the sort of work that would eventually be termed by Xue Feng as New Fiction (see chapter 3). Shen's works in this vein have largely gone overlooked by scholars, perhaps on account of their falling so far outside of conventional understandings of him as a regionalist author or as politically liberal. They are worth examining because they suggest Shen's participation in an emerging leftist imagination of an information order that I discussed in the preceding chapter. But they are also important because they help us chart first Shen's embrace of the underlying "grand narrative" of socialist politics— the necessity for and inevitable victory of proletarian revolution (manifest in Shen's work through themes such as factory labor and mass protests)[13]— followed by his decisive turn away from leftist politics and propagandistic writing later in the mid-1930s.

One such early story, "A Trifling Incident in a Big City" ("Da cheng zhong de xiao shiqing" 大城中的小事情, 1929),[14] features naturalistic depictions of workers at a small steel mill located on the Yangzi River. The story describes how a rumor arises among the laborers that the Communist Party is organizing a citywide revolution. The mill's boss, whose means are not significantly above those of his workers, becomes increasingly suspicious of the laborers thanks in part to his daily reading of newspaper reports. When the city's steelworkers move to unionize, however, the boss co-opts a seat on the labor representative committee, from where he is able to comfortably maintain the status quo by misrepresenting the interests of the workers at his mill, the fact of which his employees remain ignorant. The story places special emphasis on this latter point by showing how critical information either fails to reach the workers or is misinterpreted by them entirely. The story ends on a pessimistic note: despite the laborers' penchant for modish revolutionary terms such as "down with . . .!" (*dadao* 打到), the boss no longer worries that they poses any real risk of radically overturning relations at his factory (*SCQJ*, 5:430).

"After the War Reached a Certain City" ("Zhanzheng dao mou shi yihou" 戰爭到某市以後, 1932) offers another example of Shen's early interest in information.[15] Shen wrote the piece amid the uproar over the GMD's tepid response to the Japanese bombing of Shanghai in January of that year. Set in an unnamed city outside Shanghai, the story describes the social turbulence in the wake of news of Japanese incursions into China, focusing on the dissemination of messages across urban space and the manipulation of news by authorities. Both in its acerbic tone and in its construction of the masses as a literary subject, "After the War" largely reads as if it were written by the Ding Ling of *Eventful Autumn*. The narrative opens with a description of the city's information order by charting the noise and broadcast waves that ripple across it, evoking a tense atmosphere:

> Just as thunder shakes the human body, war shakes the human soul. . . . In XX City, telegraph dispatches [*dianxun* 電訊] of the sounds of steel and flight, the sounds of cries and massacre, the scenes of utter destruction by fire, were [all] put into a type of unregulated, unrhymed, unordered account, then printed into innumerable special editions, whereby they were distributed at various points along the city streets; the people at XX's main street gathered along the street corners, all harboring feelings of anxiety mixed with a little feeling of unexpected luck, hoping for some bit of unexpected news [*xiaoxi*]. (*SCQJ*, 4:476)

Devoid of individual character development, the first half of the story continues in a panoramic vein, exploring public discourse through the lens of the stream of news headlines as they travel across the city. The information garnered from domestic and foreign newspapers takes on a social life, as "these good city folk, walking off in different directions, gathered together with strangers and acquaintances in threes and fives, and, with keen interest, discuss everything with each other" (*SCQJ*, 4:477). Narrative description is punctuated with anonymous pronouncements and utterances—the murmurs of public sentiment. As information spreads outward from the main street, discontent with the government grows, causing people to take to the streets. Crowds form, and several speakers step forward to agitate. The narrative rhetorically marks the transition from a (news) public into a *mass* of people by shifting from the word "urbanites" or "city folk" (*shimin* 市民) to "masses" (*dazhong* 大眾) to describe the groups (*SCQJ*, 4:479, 482).

Indignant over the government's paralysis during crisis, the masses organize to call a general strike and collect relief resources to send off to the front.

Initially, the political threat posed to the local government by the masses is met with force as police officers violently disperse the crowds and haul off several of the speech-giving agitators. In drawing a dramatic contrast between the masses and the authorities, the narrative adopts the conventions of leftist social realism: on one side stands the local government, joined by those elites whose fate is most closely tied to that of the state, such as the local merchants and bankers. On the other side are the masses, united by their collective oppression (*SCQJ*, 4:479). As an ostensible work of leftist mass literature, the story seems steered toward some moral affirmation of the very crowds it hails. But in contrast to Ding's madding crowds' eruption into pure revolutionary energy, Shen's are susceptible to mollification and manipulation: after the authorities release all but one of the accused instigators, the workers lift the strike. "Only a river with water can flow, only a mind with understanding [*zhihui* 智慧] can think deeply [*sisuo* 思索]; the people of XX City were so frighteningly sincere that they were beguiled and fooled, and ended up resuming work. Thus the disturbance [lit., 'wind-wave,' *fengbo* 風波] passed" (*SCQJ*, 4:481). Advancing its skepticism regarding the political will of the masses and their limited capacity to "think deeply," the narrative goes on to detail the formative role of information management:

A few days afterward, in the special edition of XX's newspapers, official news [*xiaoxi*] about victories in battles outpaced the information [*xiaoxi*] obtainable from other sources; at the same time, more information appeared regarding some city's volunteer army setting off or the central government's transfer of forces to the front. Every day were published various kinds of news [*xiaoxi*] that appeared to be produced specially on behalf of the people of XX, shamelessly exaggerating their significance, deceiving the city populace, and easing their cold enmity toward the authorities. (*SCQJ*, 4:479–80)

Thus, alongside the cycle of social disruption and suppression, authorities use information as a means of keeping the citizens docile, uncomprehending, and "asleep" (*SCQJ*, 4:482), even while the Nationalist government prepares for a civil war that will place XX City along the front line.

The narrative here elliptically pivots to the second half of the story, which focuses on a particularly disturbing episode involving information management. While his car is stuck in traffic along the main street, XX's mayor is set upon by an assassin. The mayor's bodyguards open fire and immediately kill the attacker. The government puts the city under martial law, causing rumors of the mayor's death to circulate. Meanwhile, the police's secret investigation internally reveals that the assassin was nothing more than a local medicine shop owner patriotically seeking to petition the mayor to issue a circular telegram encouraging the central government to save the nation. Publicly, however, the government insists that the shop owner had a weapon, and the mayor's lackeys duly produce a gun to back up the falsified account of the "attack." This evidence is then passed to the press, making the government's version of the event uncontestable. The story's conclusion describes the newspaper headlines and their effect:

> "A plot! An obvious assassination attempt! If the guards aboard the mayor's car hadn't acted first to bravely kill the bandit, then XX City would have been thrown into unimaginable chaos!" That very night, the city's people silently read such news reports in the papers. After three or four days, papers in Tianjin and Shanghai carried similar stories, this time also publishing photographs of the assassin's dead body and his weapon; when they read such news, far-off friends of XX's mayor invariably shed sweat. But did the people of XX City bear any suspicion toward the truth of the situation? They did not. (*SCQJ*, 4:485)

Like "A Trifling Incident in a Big City," "After the War" also concludes pessimistically. Whereas propaganda in Ding's narrative is central to the self-awakening and mobilization of the masses, in Shen's version, propaganda is a tool of social manipulation by those in power (though in this case both authors would agree that, whether for good or ill, propaganda and mass media have a powerful public effect).

Shen's literary experimentations involving the masses were short-lived: "After the War" was his final piece resembling New Fiction. The story's despairing conclusion dramatizes Shen's contemporaneous political split with Ding Ling, who had already taken a leading role in the propaganda turn of leftist literature.[16] The cynicism on display in Shen's two stories shows that he chafed against the (perhaps inevitable) shift from May Fourth and New Culture ideals of literary social reform toward a more politicized form of mass literature. The period of the early 1930s was also a period of personal crisis for both Shen and Ding, individually. Ding was captured and for a time put under house arrest by GMD operatives in 1933.[17] Shortly afterward, in 1934, Shen's first trip home to Hunan in well over a decade left him with unsettling impressions of the deteriorating conditions in the countryside, along with a new skepticism toward literature's capacity to promote meaningful social change. Between 1934 and 1935 Shen's work would espouse ambivalence over grand narratives, whether of a socialist stripe or in the vein of New Culture idealism. This body of work includes "Unemployed," along with some of his other more melancholic—and intentionally apolitical and utopic—writing, such as *Border Town*, which would cement his identity as a regionalist author.[18]

What is important to note about Shen's brief stint with mass fiction is how it focuses on news, information, and media, particularly the newspaper, to investigate the relationship between reform and a modernizing China. Indeed, "After the War" signals Shen's developing interest in the issue of information and the penetration of mass media into society. But despite its wariness toward mass media's role in manipulating public opinion and maintaining false consciousness among the masses, "After the War" should not be taken as evidence that Shen was categorically "against" the newspaper or mass media. Since his youthful career in the army, Shen had himself worked various positions at newspapers, from printing to editing, and he recognized the important boost the newspaper publishing industry provided to New Culture writing in the form of literary supplements and financial support.[19] Throughout the 1930s, despite (or because of) the perceived encroachment of state manipulation, propagandism, and crass commercialism into newspaper publishing, Shen maintained an idealism toward the continued importance of the newspaper, believing it had the duty of inspiring readers to "love themselves, love those beside them, love justice, love truth, love enterprise, love society, love the nation."[20] All the same, Shen argued that newspapers should not blindly dictate information to the public, but should instead work to connect the public with itself, "published on our behalf, and speaking for us" (*SCQJ*, 14:91). As we shall see, he continued to consider the social impact of the newspaper in his literary work. But whereas in "After the War" Shen centered on the *production* of information and the veracity of newspapers' representations of events, in subsequent works (that is, after 1932) he would shift to the *consumption* of information as circulation and exchange within local society.

This shift is clear in Shen's account of how he became an author. In his memoir, *Congwen's Autobiography* (1934), he attributes his career to his initial introduction to the New Culture movement in the newspaper *Shenbao* 申報.[21] Composed of eighteen chapters primarily describing his youth and military service in western Hunan, this account displays many of the regionalist interests and even literary style that Shen was concurrently developing in his fiction. While scholars have used this text to draw connections between Shen's life and his fiction, the "primal scene" in chapter 11 describing Shen's first exposure to modern knowledge deserves further attention in light of his developing interest in the social life of information. In it, Shen is a teenager during the late 1910s, when he was stationed in the Hunanese city of Huaihua as a military secretary in charge of copying paperwork and keeping accounts. His daily routine is interrupted one day with the arrival of a new coworker, surnamed Wen, whose air of quiet propriety stands out amid the rough-hewn manners and salty talk of the other secretaries. In the course of their interactions, Secretary Wen cannot help but interject in Shen's habitual and uncouth usage of the term *laozi* 老子 to refer to himself. "Don't trifle with such talk. You're bright, you should be learning good things instead. There are many good works in the world worth studying!" (*Congwen zizhuan*, 94). Intrigued, Shen befriends him. Each is drawn to the exoticism of the other's background and experiences. Shen recounts for Wen the howl of a wolf and the roar of a tiger, the difference between the tracks of wild boars and mountain goats, and the heft of a decapitated head. From Wen, Shen learns about the sights and sounds of modern technology: the sounds of train whistles and steamship horns, the appearance of hydrogen balloons, the types of electric bulbs and telephones. Ultimately, Secretary Wen convinces him to go in together on a subscription to *Shenbao*. Shen: "After mailing the subscription off to Shanghai, without having yet received a single issue, I felt as if I were already reading it, and I believed what it said, and that the newspaper was an outstanding thing. And, indeed, I came to learn quite a few things from it. In total, our subscription lasted two months; from the paper I learned to recognize quite a few [new] words" (*Congwen zizhuan*, 97). Thus was Shen drawn into the outside and modernizing world by the paper. The autobiography's reader would have had no trouble inferring the outcome: Shen's fate was to take up these new ideas and new words as a modern author.

Shen places his discovery of *Shenbao* alongside an earlier encounter with another text: the *Ciyuan* (辭源, lit. "origin/source of words," 1915), one of the first modern encyclopedias in China. His edifying exchanges (*jiaohuan* 交換) with Wen take on a new dimension when one day Wen produces from his luggage two volumes. Shen carefully narrates the unfolding scene:

> When I saw that he had two such thick tomes, which despite their minute text were extremely sturdy, I was actually startled. Seeing me so stunned, he said:
>
> "Young man, these are a treasure. Everything in the universe is contained therein—any knowledge which you might wish to know: all is written out clearly and in order so as to impart a thorough understanding of things."
>
> Such words made me even more reverential. Stroking the books with my hand, I only then spotted the two golden characters imprinted on the spine:
>
> "*Ciyuan, Ciyuan,*" I murmured.
>
> "It truly is the 'source of words.' Go ahead and ask me anything, no matter how odd, and I'll immediately find it for you."
>
> While thinking on it, my gaze happened across the relief carving in front of the play hall depicting Zhuge Liang's "Three Frustrations of Zhou Yu,"[22] and I immediately said: "How about Mr. Zhuge Liang?" He right away lowered his head, flipped to the front of the book, then again to the back, and after a moment located the entry. A moment later, he again looked up something else and found it. I was elated. (*Congwen zizhuan*, 95–96)

To a young Shen, the *Ciyuan* really does seem to have everything—even the first-person personal pronoun that he is in the habit of using. Upon looking up the entry for *laozi*, Shen discovers that it refers to the historical figure, Lao Zi, the putative author of the *Daodejing*. Humbled by this discovery, Shen becomes more receptive to the authority of textual knowledge.

As the historian Meng Yue has detailed, the *Ciyuan* was a translingual and monumental text that, when it was published in 1915, was aimed at bridging the gap between new (Western) knowledge and the wealth of information in traditional Chinese sources.[23] But to Shen, its pleasures are not just epistemic but also material: with its handsome gilding and palpable solidity, the *Ciyuan* becomes an object of fascination, to be absorbed as greedily as when he earlier took in the marvels of the telephone and railway as narrated to him by Wen. To Shen, this text does indeed seem to "contain everything." Wen makes Shen wash his hands every time before touching the books, and Shen even dreams of the tomes at night. The account conspicuously repeats the verb *fan* 翻, "to flip through," thus highlighting not only the encyclopedia's materiality but also its nonlinear organization whereby the reader meanders from one entry to another at random or looks up a word using the character index.[24] In turn, the solidity and self-sufficiency of the two *Ciyuan* volumes stand in contrast to the ephemerality of the newspaper *Shenbao*, which arrives from afar first in Shen's own imagination and only afterward as a material thing.

These episodes from the autobiography stage a quintessential New Culture event,[25] in which modern enlightenment spreads via mass media beyond China's urban centers, reaching the relative periphery of western Hunan. In the final chapter, titled "A Turning Point" ("Yi ge zhuanji" 一個轉機; *Congwen zizhuan*, 156–63), Shen details how following his exposure to the world of letters, he eventually gained access to the New Culture journals *The Renaissance* (*Xinchao* 新潮) and *Reconstruction* (*Gaizao* 改造), which ultimately inspired him to head to Beijing in 1922. We must reflect how, in Shen's recounting, the encyclopedia takes privileged place over the newspaper, and how the differences between these two modern textual forms may have inspired or even shaped his literary practice. As Shen tells it, the newspaper instilled in him knowledge of the outside, modern world. While the newspaper essentially refers to the occurrence of historical events (though it also has a self-referential quality, as current news frequently builds on recent news), an encyclopedia like the *Ciyuan* is a totalized collection of knowledge that is self-referential in a more bounded and nonlinear—even labyrinthine—manner. With its transhistorical mix of modern terminology and scientific facts together with Chinese lexicological and literary history, the *Ciyuan* blends the distant past with the present. But there is also an important formal difference between these two textual forms: *Shenbao* produces a kind of serialized grand narrative, the historical present of the nation; the *Ciyuan*, meanwhile, is composed of small narratives in the form of lexical entries that are in turn loosely conjoined in a cross-referential manner. As such, the encyclopedia *formally* resists a singular and linear reading. As Umberto Eco writes, an encyclopedia is without beginning or end—it is rhizomatic and networked in its very essence.[26] As we will see, what fascinated Shen about the *Ciyuan* was not only its wealth of content, but its specific form and structure.

The subjects of literary form and narrative structure were becoming increasingly important to Shen when he began writing this autobiography in 1932. During this period, as we have seen, Shen was undertaking a reassessment of the May Fourth legacy. Coupled with his sporadic teaching duties as a lecturer, this prompted him to articulate his own views of literature for the first time in his career. The literary aesthetic that he consequently developed over a series of works borrows formally from the miniature accounts and nonlinear nature of the *Ciyuan*. For example, between 1934 and 1935, Shen arranged his collection of travelogue essays—later published in 1936 as *Random Sketches on a Trip to Western Hunan*. In his discussion of this text's experimental mode of "transparent" realism, David Wang notes its encyclopedic quality, shaped by the integration of various narrative forms—including gazetteers, biographies, anecdotes, myths, and legends—that ultimately provide the reader with "an accumulation of data—natural and human scenery, detailed biographical information."[27]

While compiling this work, Shen also wrote a number of short essays working through his notion of literature as a form of "craftsmanship" or "craft" (*jiqiao* 技巧, also translatable as "technique," "skill"). The most developed among these is "On Craft" ("Lun jiqiao" 論技巧, 1935),[28] which begins with a reflection on the connotations of "craft" itself:

> In recent years, there has been a noun in literature dictionaries that has suffered particular misfortune: "craft." When most people speak of technique, one gets the feeling of a certain kind of disdain. Then again there are those who, being extremely bashful, are deeply afraid to bring up this word in front of others. The two characters that make up "craft" seem to connote the fine [*xianxi* 纖細, "minute"], the fragmentary and trivial [*suosui* 瑣碎], the empty and vacuous [*kongdong* 空洞], and so on; at times the term even carries the implication of the salacious [*weixie* 猥褻]. When commending or praising a small toy or some small furnishing, inevitably we refer to it as a "craft." . . . Ultimately, "craft" has been limited and restrained by the popular view [*liuxing guannian* 流行觀念], thus becoming an unwanted thing. The establishment of a popular view is worth heeding, and its views of right and wrong are worthy of discussion. (*SCQJ*, 16:470)

In Shen's defensive stance and his association of technique with mundane objects such as handicraft objects (a point to which I will return) can be detected the highly politicized atmosphere of the times. His attempt to salvage the value of craft serves as a way of questioning the contemporary "popular view" that literature must either be simply about ideas (*sixiang* 思想)—in which case artistry is of no concern—or that it should remain "pure" and not engage with current events.[29] In doing so, Shen here takes on two contemporary schools of thought: On the one hand, he is criticizing baldly political works that flatter either the masses or the Nationalists. On the other hand, he is criticizing the "Shanghai school" of writers such as Zhang Ziping who offered entertainment at the expense of engaging with larger historical questions.[30] "Craft" opens a middle ground, then, between the grand narratives of revolution and the meaningless minutiae of the apolitical author.

But what, after all, does Shen mean by craft? In "On Craft," he avoids directly defining the term and instead offers a string of associations, suggesting that "its true implication is something like 'choice' [*xuanze* 選擇], a 'careful disposal' [*jinshen chuzhi* 謹慎處置], 'pursuing a proper arrangement' [*qiu tuotie* 求妥貼], 'pursuing the appropriate' [*qiu qiadang* 求恰當]" (*SCQJ*, 16:471). In a separate essay on the function and social use-value of literature, Shen expands upon his point:

Simply put, literature is just a bunch of words and phrases strung together [*pinpin-coucou chansheng de yi zhong dongxi* 拼拼湊湊產生的一種東西]. . . . One needs patience and relentlessness, a willingness to "to twist and wrench language to learn its malleability, to smash language down hard to test the limits of its brittleness." One has to thoroughly understand the medium's properties. . . . The more a writer understands the properties of written language, the more "proper" [*qiadang* 恰當] is it when he uses it as a tool. I say "proper," not "beautiful" [*meili* 美麗], because "appropriateness" is precisely what it is in great works of literature that so astonishes us about their use of language. The aspiration of every writer is to get across his precise meaning when expressing himself or society, along with the ability to see the kind of impression it will make on certain types of readers, and how they will react. Hence, understanding of the nature [*xingneng* 性能] of written language can itself be called a kind of "knowledge" [*zhishi* 知識], indeed an indispensable knowledge—it is, to put it a little differently, *craft* [*jiqiao* 技巧], *the craft of ordering written words* [*tiaopai wenzi de jiqiao* 調排文字的技巧].[31]

In talking about "twisting" writing and testing "the limits of its brittleness," Shen invokes a materiality of language that is historically characteristic of modernist aesthetics, where "media were no longer serving as a vehicle or instrument of communication or representation of meaning, but as the very *site* of meaning and experience."[32] If writing is an entity with physical properties, then literary form approximates that of the plastic arts: the "knowledge" that Shen advocates here is none other than a knowledge of craft—the skilled manipulation of the material of language. To be a good writer, Shen suggests, is to know how to arrange writing just as handily as one might weave a basket or craft a child's toy. And this emphasis on precise sequencing and lexical exactitude returns us to the logic of the encyclopedia—a text in which all things are defined and positioned within a stable order.

It is the quality of arrangement that distinguishes literary writing from nonliterary writing. Shen illustrates this in "On Craft" by comparing how a newspaper or a piece of fiction would approach a basic love story in which a woman stabs her former lover to death after he abandons her for a different woman. While a newspaper will use a particular formula for narrating the event in a straightforward (but sensational) manner, in the skillful hands of a fiction writer, the plot is reworked into something subtler, thereby transforming the story into something that "resembles a Daoist talismanic character and emits a magic power" over the reader (*SCQJ* 16: 473). The events stay the same; only the form changes. Along these lines, Shen acknowledges that while a literary work cannot dispense with the underlying sequence of events, it must cohere around some organizing truth or idea. Without such motivation, literature risks devolving into pure formalism, becoming "digressive and trifling" (*zhizhi-jiejie* 枝枝節節)— literally "branches and knots [with no trunk]" (*SCQJ* 16: 472)[33]—a horizontal mode of growth that evokes the decentralized figure of the rhizome. What we can deduce is that "craft," and its attention to arrangement, is the knowledge of putting together the branches and knots of writing, of managing the network of basic literary elements like events and characters. Shen further elaborates in a separate essay when he notes that only literature is suitable for representing human experience, for "fiction uses human affairs as its warp and weft [*jingwei* 經緯]; because these affairs can be comprehensively organized into the development of a narrative, even a quick-witted sermon or a dreamful lyric can illustrate abstract principles of human development" (*SCQJ*, 16:494). It is precisely this quality that appears in Shen's story, "Unemployed." Daren manages two networks, the telephone and the web of human affairs, but in his own writing he lacks the wisdom to ground either one, leaving only a record of unemployable digressions and trifles.

For Shen the aesthetic of craft was not merely an expedient metaphor for the importance of editing or emplotment. Instead, his notion of craft directly informed his literary practice. This is beautifully evidenced by Shen's mentee, the author Wang Zengqi 汪曾祺 (1920–1997), in a short commemorative essay he wrote after Shen passed away in 1988. Wang draws on his firsthand experiences with Shen to comment on his approach to composition:

> When Shen Congwen spoke of writing, he rarely used the term "structure" [*jiegou* 结构], preferring instead the word "organization" [*zuzhi* 组织]. I also rather prefer the latter term. "Structure" is overly rational, while "organization" connotes feeling and the subjectivity of most writers. He would take his story, and cut it up line by line [*yi tiao yi tiao de caikai* 一条一条地裁开], and then rearrange it in different manners to see what was most suitable [*heshi* 合适]. He loved to revise [*xiugai* 修改] his own work. He would edit and reedit his manuscripts until the headers, footers, and margins of the pages were covered in handwriting. They resembled a spider's web, with lines leading out of here and there [*zheli qianchu yi tiao, nali qianchu yi tiao* 这里 牵出一条，那里牵出一条] on the page.[34]

At the material level of writing, Shen's idea of literature as craft comes into full view. In its very form—networked, labyrinthine—literary craft stood in opposition to the straightforward and unambiguous style of the propagandistic literature of its day. And, in opposing the grand narratives of the latter, Shen Congwen's literary craft celebrates the small narrative instead. This is not to say that he only produced short anecdotes and avoided larger works; instead, his craft of writing ultimately centers on how small narratives *hang together* and how such interconnectedness infuses a literary text with meaning and beauty.

While the "spider's web" of Shen's original manuscripts may be obscured in the final published form, many critics have nonetheless discerned the presence or logic of network forms in his work. A networked reading of

Shen's work may have been inadvertently undertaken as early as 1932 by the critic He Yubo, in his major work *On Modern Chinese Authors* (*Xiandai Zhongguo zuojia lun* 現代中國作家論). Frustrated with Shen's winding style, He attacks Shen's fiction as being recursive, fragmentary, and lacking in plot. A work like Shen's early avant-garde novella *Letters of a Genius* (*Yi ge tiancai de tongxin* 一個天才的通信, 1930) is a mere "jumble, with unordered paragraphs and an unstructured storyline; it is like a painting with no lines and no coloration—just a bunch of dots."[35] He builds on his visual metaphor to further denigrate the unstructured nature of Shen's narrative. Regarding Shen's short story "Lord Pine Nut" ("Songzi jun" 松子君, 1926): "It has no central characters, it has no central story, the author's pen just writes at random, like a child's meaningless scribble upon a wall." Or, in a summary dismissal of Shen's work as a whole: "It is too mundane and cannot attract our interest. As such, we can only see these pieces as fragmentary impressions, such as when we watch a newsreel. To put it more severely, the author is nothing more than a photographer who shoots passing fragments of the landscape."[36] In retrospect, despite its acerbic edge, He Yubo's visual emphasis is ironically apt because Shen really *did* regularly use sketches and photographs to supplement his writing.[37]

As I investigated in chapter 1, He Yubo was at that time developing his mode of diagrammatic criticism, which he applied to the highly structured plots of Mao Dun's early literature. Here He's contrast between Mao Dun and Shen Congwen is particularly instructive. Mao Dun's stories, in He's eyes, lend themselves to the simplification of the diagram. Shen's more fragmentary and bottom-up approach to storytelling inherently frustrates diagrammatic visualization. As Wang Zengqi notes, Shen was interested not in structure but in arrangement. The encyclopedic and woven quality of Shen's literary craft, from its careful organization and juxtaposition of anecdotes to its web of intertexuality, starkly resists the kind of linearization favored by He Yubo and his contemporaries.[38] And surely He would have found wanting the fragmentary and scattered nature of much of Shen's later work, which, as Jeffrey Kinkley reads it, manifests Shen's "inattention to larger literary structures" and an "unfinished" quality of his major work.[39]

In his study of Shen's mode of fictional realism and what he calls its "iterative lyricism," David Wang invokes a rich array of network metaphors to describe how Shen's storytelling "condenses recurrent events over a period of time into a single narrative and thus renders a synchronic overlay of the diachronicity of events." Wang variously likens aspects of Shen's prose to "an intricate web," "a constellation of sensuous pictures and musical patterns," an "intertextual network," and a tapestry "weaving varied sensory images from natural and human environments into a fabric and giving them correspondences to one another."[40] Reading these formal elements through Bakhtin's notion of the chronotope, Wang argues that they constitute a "topographical system of coordinates . . . which lends itself to anyone wanting to locate the origins of a text. Sites, like texts, are essential loci of remembrance, bounded spaces in which the complexity of human nature and experience are concentrated. More than just his birthplace, Shen Congwen's West Hunan is a textual locus where his discourse about the homeland has germinated, and through which he transports his social/ political ideas."[41] Thus Wang reminds us that, in Shen's major works, we are dealing not with measurable, geographical space but the spaces of memory: writing is in this case a special kind of map. But in addition to *topographically* analyzing the production of space and time in Shen's work as a kind of literary map, Shen's aesthetics and explicit interest in networks call for a *topological* approach to his work, one that accommodates his careful attention to the interrelations and arrangements of the constituent parts of his narratives. Put differently, such a reading would ask how Shen's small narratives are linked together to produce larger network structures, and what these networks signify within the historical, literary, and personal contexts in which they appear. At the same time, the topological stands at the nexus between Shen's aesthetics—his emphasis on "craft" and the arrangement of writing—and his politics: his interest in giving voice to the small becomes a way of speaking back to the grand, a resistance to growing demands that literature be reduced to propaganda.

This nexus is epitomized in a short—but key—passage in *Random Sketches on a Trip to Hunan*, which is emblematic of both the work's anecdotal style and Shen's deep interest in the people of his region. Describing an old friend of his who has now become an innkeeper in Changde in the northwestern part of Hunan, Shen pays homage to the man's rich way of speaking by once again invoking the nonlinear form of an encyclopedia or dictionary:

Everything he said was alive, and even casual remarks and swearwords would have their proper sources and fit the context perfectly [*yanzhichengzhang* 言之成章]. . . . His speech displayed a rich flow of similes which seemed as truly inexhaustible as the waters of a great river. . . .

Listening to him curse the servants, it made me think of all those gentle-men cooped up in Beijing compiling big dictionaries of the national language [*Guoyu* 國語], and of how many books they had cut apart [*jianpo* 剪破] for the usage of a phrase or a word, leafing backward and forward through [*fanlai-fanqu* 翻來翻去] the *Water Margin, Plum in the Golden Vase, Dream of the Red Chamber*, and other novels and dramas of the Yuan, Ming, and Qing. If only they could come to this inn . . . and hear that proprietor give vent to some choice and rare expressions, so that they might feel that a great living dictionary [*huoshengsheng da cidian* 活生生 大辭典] has actually been placed there![42]

Shen's suggestion that the innkeeper offers a living embodiment of a dictionary once again recalls Bakhtin's notion of heteroglossia, which emphasizes the novelistic utterance as a living, social phenomenon. Like the modern dictionary of national language, the novel is composed of "thousands of living dialogic threads, woven by socio-ideological consciousness around the given object of an utterance; [the utterance] cannot fail to become an active participant in social dialogue. After all, the utterance arises out of this dialogue as a continuation of it and as a rejoinder to it—it does not approach the objects from the sidelines."[43] In contrast to dictionaries composed from traditional sources, the innkeeper embodies the social life of language and calls for a new mode of listening—from the margins of both country and canon. On the face of it, by challenging the primacy of the language or style of older novels, this passage appears to echo the New Culture ideology of vernacular writing. But, having identified Shen's aesthetic of literary craft and its structural and material relation to the dictionary or encyclopedia, the network form again comes into view. The passage offers more than a topological rejection of the notion of a cultural or linguistic "center." Underneath the surface layer of Shen's native-soil literature lies the form of the rhizome, at once serving as an aesthetics and a challenge to political or cultural authority.

INFORMATION AND/AS SOCIAL LIFE IN *LONG RIVER*

In late 1937, Shen took the long trip to his home area for the second time in the decade. His earlier return to western Hunan had been marred by skirmishes between Nationalist troops and local forces over control of the region.

This time around, Shen found even the initial stages of his trip thrown into uncertainty as he and several colleagues escaped the impending Japanese occupation of Beijing, fleeing first south toward Nanjing and then up the Yangzi to the interior. In the early spring of 1938 Shen reached western Hunan, where he stayed for several months with his brother in Fenghuang before moving on to Kunming in April. This journey resulted in his second travelogue, *West Hunan* (*Xiangxi* 湘西, 1938), a local ethnography written with the objective of dispelling outsider misconceptions about Shen's home: that the region was, contrary to prevailing stereotypes, not defined by banditry and turmoil, but was instead a place rich in tradition and home to a patriotic people, eager to contribute to the national war effort.[44]

At the outset, *Long River*, which Shen began working on shortly after *West Hunan* in 1938, was to play a similar role. As Shen explains in *Long River*'s preface:

> Just at that time [winter of 1937], the Hunanese provincial government was preparing to send to the countryside several thousand students tasked with educating the common folk [*minxun gongzuo* 民訓工作], an [initiative that was] quite bothersome from a technical standpoint. The situation in Wuhan was taking a turn for the worse, and both public and private institutions, as well as refugees from various provinces, were daily moving into western Hunan. Most of these outsiders lacked any knowledge of the true character of the region, often stereotyping it as a "bandit area." As a result, I produced two small books, one named *West Hunan*, the second, *Long River*. . . . [Through these I] hope to give outsiders—especially students traveling there—an impression relatively closer to the truth. Even more importantly, [I hope] to ignite in them the courage and confidence to overcome such difficulties.[45]

Thus, both *West Hunan* and *Long River* were crafted with a didactic intent, inspired by the mass displacement of the war with Japan. Like Shen's earlier travelogue, *Random Sketches on a Trip to Hunan*, *West Hunan* borrows formal aspects of the encyclopedia, and it similarly manifests Shen's aesthetics of craft as a kind of ordering of words and small narratives. Such an aesthetic, in the observation of David Wang, effects "a sense of accuracy and immediacy by providing us with an excess of information. Names, dates, historical events, anecdotes, personal comments, are poured out without any obvious link with each other. They are not meant to make any specific point but just to exist and state in a mute way that they are there—one of the most powerful ways to achieve the effect of the real."[46] In contrast to the encyclopedic quality of the companion travelogue, *Long River* offers a more novelistic narrative—one that nonetheless embodies Shen's aesthetics of craft to an equally high degree, while also applying that aesthetic directly and reflexively to a critical investigation of modern propaganda.

Despite the novel's target audience, it seems doubtful that the students traveling to Shen's homeland would have had much opportunity to read *Long River*, the first part of which was originally serialized between early August and mid-November in 1938 in the pages of *Constellation (Xingzuo 星座)*, a literary supplement then under the editorship of the modernist poet Dai Wangshu 戴望舒 (1905–1950) at the *Sing Tao Daily* in Hong Kong. But shortly after he began work on it, Shen came to envision leaving a greater mark. *Long River* was to be his career masterpiece: a novel as broad in scope as Leo Tolstoy's *War and Peace*, and one capable of attracting upwards of a million readers.[47] The text was scheduled to be republished as a single volume in Guilin in 1942, but, even after heavy redaction, it failed to garner the approval of the Nationalist censorship apparatus. Only in 1945, following another round of paring down, did a Kunming imprint publish the novel in its final form; this final version was reduced by over twenty percent from the original manuscript. Though Shen intended the novel to span three volumes, perhaps on account of his frustrations with such heavy censorship or a sense of despondency caused by the war, he laid the work aside after completing the first part and never returned to it.[48] It remains his last novel-length creative project of his career.

It is crucial to understand the cultural context of *Long River* in order to appreciate its positioning vis-à-vis the broader institution of modern literature in the late 1930s. While the novel was ostensibly aimed at addressing stereotypes held by students (i.e., would-be propagandists and reformers) headed to western Hunan, the preface poses a more general challenge to the significance of propaganda in the Chinese countryside. During the four-year gestation period of the *Long River* project (1938–1942), the entire institution of literature and criticism in China underwent a dramatic transformation, as the majority of authors effectively became antiwar propagandists by joining the All-China Resistance Association of Writers and Artists (Quanguo wenyi jie kangdi xiehui 全國文藝界抗敵協會; hereafter,

Wenxie) en masse. Indeed, this period marks the culmination of the propaganda era that had begun earlier in the decade (see chapter 3), where literary writing was conscripted as a handmaiden to total mobilization (*zongdongyuan* 總動員). Living in Nationalist-controlled Kunming for most of the war, Shen observed the intensification of propagandizing from the sidelines, and abstained from joining the Wenxie.[49] He reflected that the Chinese literary institution had entered an era in which writers of any political stripe readily embraced the maxim "All writing is propaganda" (*yiqie wenzi dou shi xuanchuan* 一切文字都是宣傳).[50] And he sharply dismissed the literary institution's mobilization efforts as the superficial attempt to stir up *renao* (熱鬧), or "noise and excitement," a term that quickly became for Shen a blanket condemnation of all propaganda-oriented activities.[51]

In seeking space for a subtler form of writing grounded in literary craftsmanship, Shen redoubled his advocacy of a blend of formalism, local description, and small narrative. In "Universal or Restricted?" (*Yiban huo teshu* 一般或特殊, 1939)—an essay that directly addresses the propagandization of literature and arguably serves as the true preface to *Long River* (the standard preface was only written in 1945)—Shen calls on writers to return to the problem of craft, reiterating his earlier gloss of the term as the art of ordering writing.[52] Whereas earlier in the decade Shen had signaled the target of his critique only obliquely, in this essay he adopts a more strident and explicit stance. He peremptorily disavows the notion of "art for art's sake"—a subject position consigned to any writer critical of propaganda—to instead argue that an emphasis on formalism does not equate to a disavowal of the social use-value of literature: good literature produces important knowledge and plays an important role in reshaping social reality.[53] Unlike propaganda, which seeks to dominate modern media of broadcast communication such as newspapers, journals, and radio through a steady stream of amplified and simplified messaging, literature is founded upon an aesthetics of complexity and multi-vocality that delivers a moral message in a subtler and even contingent way.[54] Shen is alluding to his aims with *Long River* when he concludes that, rather than participating in propaganda warfare,

> perhaps some other person should write a little something. His or her work
> might be a mere novel . . . [that] seems to have no connection with the war,

or with politics, and even less connection with propaganda ... it may edu-
cate only a small number of the educated, those who truly love and honor
this nation, who have already been awakened, and thus very modestly seek
such education. Not only might the content of this work enlighten them, the
written language in it can enlighten them too.[55]

Shen envisions for himself a novel that is enlightening but not
propagandistic—the paradox that lies at the heart of his decade-long attempt
to evaluate and redeem the legacy of New Culture literature.

Thus, the political and aesthetic aim of Shen's *Long River* project is a
questioning of the relationship between literary writing, propaganda, and
social change. But Shen's investigation of propaganda also lies at the heart
of the novel's subject matter. By emphasizing the complexity of mass
media through examining its richly multivalent dispensation in Hunan's
countryside, Shen hoped to expose the shortcoming of mass propaganda
itself.[56] That is, instead of depicting social change as an immediate effect
of mass-mediated propagation, Shen frames sociohistorical change as an
architectonic process—one fundamentally beholden to the vagaries of social
communication. As he explains in his preface:

> Just as the beginning of the novel describes, all existence is defined by habit
> and all affairs are shaped by habit, so when currency, goods, and local behav-
> iors circulate, the various modes of life and ideals that they form all seem to
> be developing in a deterministic way. People's oppositional affairs and their
> conflicts all seem to have a fated end. This work is designed to emphasize
> the synthesis of constancy and change, writing out the "past," the "present,"
> and the developing "future." ... [In] taking up this slice of social landscape
> [*shehui fengjing* 社會風景] that so resembles a historical relic, preserving it
> through writing, and contrasting it with the brand-new conditions [of the
> present], [the novel] might help us develop a fresh recognition of society. That
> is, in the midst of the war, how the process of development in a given place
> inevitably includes some conflicts in human sensibilities, and how it entails
> the refashioning of interpersonal relations [*ren he ren guanxi de chongzao*
> 人和人關係的重造]. (Shen, *Changhe*, 102–3)

Shen's philosophy of history is notable not only for its faintly Buddhist
tone—where linear time collapses into an unfolding cycle[57]—but also for

its vision of historical change as an evolving series of nested cycles and ingrained habits (*xiguan* 習慣). Social communication gives shape to individual small cycles and habits—which, on their own, constitute the very substance of small narrative. And acts of exchange or circulation—particularly the movement of *xiaoxi*—in turn reveal the contours of the larger system of social communication and the process of historical change. Crucially, this local system of cycles and communication is not closed off from the outside, but interfaced with external forces, including both national news and state-led initiatives such as the New Life Movement (NLM), which wend their way to Western Hunan through layered and circuitous routes. Through a description of the local percolation of news about the impending arrival of the NLM, the text offers a worm's-eye view of the reception of Nationalist propaganda and how mass media were received—and of their effect (or lack thereof) on changing behaviors. If, as Shen contends, the meaning and impact of propaganda had become unclear even to propagandists themselves, then *Long River* stands as an attempt to reframe propaganda from the perspective of its target on the ground.[58] By approaching the question of societal change through the lens of communication and mediation, the novel offers a unique contribution to the literary articulation of China's information order.

The novel's opening chapter, titled "People and Land" (*Ren yu di* 人與地), displays the kind of ethnographic and naturalistic description for which Shen is famous. Set in the year 1936, the story depicts life in two interconnected places in the mountainous and remote region of western Hunan. The first is Lüjiaping 呂家坪, a small but lively stopping point along the middle section of the Yuan 沅 River, populated by "the usual groups of loafers, supernumerary government clerks, widows who make their living by making small loans, local prostitutes with large breasts and buttocks, and professional fortunetellers and chess players."[59] Besides serving as a port town, Lüjiaping hosts a local market that convenes every five days, making it a commercial, military, and social hub in the area. The second focal point is Turnip Village (Luobo cun 蘿蔔村), a nearby area along a small tributary of the Yuan. Despite its name, Turnip Village is not a village but a collection of farm manors, including the estate of the local well-to-do Teng family. Although the area is only several miles inland from Lüjiaping, it is a far more idealized place, where "the situation is quite different, for the rural traditions are faithfully preserved, not in the least affected by Lüjiaping. For instance, when a traveler passes through the orange groves during the harvest period, he is never charged for the oranges he eats when he is thirsty. But as soon as he gets to Lüjiaping, even the extremely sour tangerines that are completely worthless are sold by the old ladies by the ford" (Chu, "The Long River," 51; Shen, *Changhe*, 138). Directly across the stream from the Teng family's orange groves sits Maple Hill, where the Teng ancestral temple stands.

While these two zones—the timeless and rather idyllic countryside and the market town by the riverside—are reminiscent of the setting of the famous village of Chadong in *Border Town*, there is a significant difference between the two novels. *Border Town* constructs a utopian space that seems hermetically sealed off from modern history. In *Long River*, by contrast, both Lüjiaping and Turnip Village are clearly marked by the arrival of modernity, evident in the influx of new ideas and a variety of material goods. In turn, these imports index what might be thought of as the novel's third significant area: the "rest of China," synecdochally figured by the large, industrialized cities far downriver from Lüjiaping. Through the upstream movement of goods and information, the novel paints a portrait of the integration between national center and relative periphery.

The region's fine oranges and *tong* oil are sent downstream. In return, local boatmen bring back news and newspapers from as far as the eastern seaboard, including major publications like *Shenbao* (Shanghai) and *Dagongbao* (大公報, Tianjin), filled with national and international news. Such news is markedly disconnected from the daily happenings of western Hunan. Making matters worse, since newspapers only travel as fast as the boats themselves, their contents are already stale upon arrival—delivered nearly two weeks after publication. But in this peripheral area, where national newspapers have a relatively weak material presence, the circulation of information depends primarily on personal exchanges rather than mass media. The setting of *Long River* thus marks the outer horizon of mass media's direct reach, where information is remediated and transmitted through a secondary circuit of conversations among farmers, merchants, officials, and the occasional traveler.[60] This circuit occupies the bulk of narrative attention, as all but the first and last chapters of the novel patiently follow characters as they gossip, trade opinions on local politics, share news about market prices, and discuss the broader state of the nation.

The interface between mass media and this secondary circuit can be spatially schematized as two ways of looking at the river that courses through the narrative. Historians of communication in the West have frequently reminded us that until the end of the nineteenth century and the rise of the telegraph and radio, the word "communication" encompassed not just the transmission of information, but also the transportation and circulation of physical goods.[61] The same is true of the Chinese term *jiaotong* 交通, which primarily denotes transportation but also extends to communications networks more broadly. By this token, roads and waterways constitute communications infrastructures. The novel leverages this broader conception of communication by treating the river as a medium in its own right—both as a channel for long-distance communication and as a rich ecosystem of local exchange, especially between communities on either side of its banks. The lengthwise and crosswise orientations of the river-medium correspond to what communication theorist James W. Carey terms the "transmission view of communication" and the "ritual view of communication": the former centers on the speed and effect of messages as an instrumentalized form of control, while the latter foregrounds commonality, community, and the maintenance of social bonds.[62] These competing approaches to the river reveal what might be called the novel's philosophy of communication. A mediological reading of the river recasts Shen Congwen as an ethnographer not only of local society but of forms of the media systems—material and immaterial, long-standing and modern—that collectively structure its modes of communication and rhythms of everyday life.

The novel loosely focuses on the members of the Teng family. Despite intimations that the family's prosperity—and, by extension, the wholesome, idyllic life of the region—will be severely shaken by events of history, there is little plot development. Instead, the narrative details the Tengs' minor interactions with neighbors and friends, thereby highlighting the local social network in which the family is embedded. The character who best indexes this structure is Manman (an affectionate local term for "uncle"), a distant relative of the Tengs who, after an unlucky life that has left him bereft of descendants, has retired from a career as a boatman and now serves as the steward of the Teng family temple. His post is leisurely and solitary, so Manman frequently crosses the stream to chat with the amiable head of the Teng family, Teng Changshun, and the family's young daughters, particularly the beautiful and precocious youngest, Yaoyao. When he is not offering Teng Changshun advice or avuncularly playing with Changshun's girls, Manman chats with passersby or meanders about Lüjiaping, collecting and exchanging gossip and other tidbits of news.

> [He lives] on a mound nearby the highway and overlooking the banks of the river where travelers and boatmen passed back and forth. Many of them would come to the mound to lift the loads from their backs, rest, and smoke. . . . Manman would [also] frequently cross the river at his leisure to pay a visit to Teng Changshun's family. There he would sit awhile and chat about the local gossip. . . . Or, carrying a small bamboo basket, he would go to the market . . . [where] he would listen to the merchants discuss the market conditions, the boatmen talking sales of agricultural goods shipped down the river, and the ups and downs of the boat families of the Yuan River Valley. If he met a Yamen runner [a government messenger], he could learn about the regulations and orders being carried out in the county and hear news [xiaoxi] of the whereabouts of the militia. (Changhe, 146)

Thus, living outside both Lüjiaping and Turnip Village, Manman occupies a topologically central position within the area, serving as a veritable hub of communications connecting the two places and further triangulating them with another space, the docks, where he often visits his former colleagues. Although Teng Changshun often teases Manman by asking him for news—"as the old boatman was the only one in the village who loved asking about xiaoxi, he always had an exceptional quantity of news, but in actuality this news was usually not worth making a big fuss over" (Changhe, 184)—both Changshun and his local ally, the kindly head of commerce, nonetheless find genuine value in Manman's ferrying of oral messages (kouxin 口信) throughout the area. They also depend on the old man's views of local opinion and his updates about the operations of regional security forces. As we shall see, in his capacity as an information broker, Manman both closely resembles and exceeds the kind of information hunter and gatherer portrayed by Mao Dun in his market literature.

As the preceding excerpt notes, passersby frequently pause atop Maple Hill to chat with Manman in front of the Teng family temple. Barely describing these travelers or conveying Manman's impression of them, the narrative turns instead to their minutiae-filled conversations, ranging from this year's orange crop to extraordinary garden yields, such as a bucket-sized winter melon and a legendary thirty-two-pound radish. The extensive use of reported speech, coupled with the way in which the speakers themselves reflect upon the sources of knowledge, question each other's hearsay, and tease one another's ignorance, collectively imparts the narrative with a manifestly heteroglossic quality that is sustained throughout the novel. This multivoiced orality is further augmented by the frequency of words and phrases relating to oral communication, such as "I heard people say" (*wo ting ren shuo* 我聽人說, 120), "as the old saying goes" (*guhua shuo* 古話說, 120), "in one ear and out the other" (*kouli lai, erbian qu* 口裡來, 耳邊去, 128), gossip (*yaoyan* 謠言, 131), and *xiaoxi*. And, in Shen's typical fashion, the narrative also records a mixture of local dialect and folksong lyrics. Throughout such exchanges Manman listens carefully so that he can later relate any valuable information to Teng Changshun or his fellow boatmen. Collectively, Manman's access to this stream of voices gives him—and, by extension, the reader—a privileged window into the opinions and goings-on of local society: as one character describes him in a later chapter, Manman "knows everything under heaven and above earth, and has a mental record [*xin zhong yi ben ce* 心中一本冊] of all of Lüjiaping's affairs" (199).

Though he takes distinct pleasure in maintaining this broad spectrum of social contact, Manman is no simple gossip. He collects information as a preparation strategy against events whose scope and complexity surpass his cognitive horizon. This is not to argue that the novel contains a high level of narrative tension in the text; unlike in Mao Dun's *Midnight*, there is no pivotal moment when a character's fate hinges on a single (mis)communication. What most draws Manman's attention is hearsay about the impending arrival of the New Life Movement. Like the industrialization of local *tong* oil production or the impending war with Japan, the NLM symbolizes a form of modernity that hangs forebodingly over the future of western Hunan—appearing more frequently than these other developments by virtue of its status as an ongoing public propaganda campaign. As discussed in chapter 3, in the mid-1930s the NLM was the Nationalist government's flagship effort to refashion social morals and promote national identity and volunteerism. It was backed by an aggressive expansion of propaganda and mobilization efforts emblematic of the propaganda boom of the Nanjing Decade as a whole. With his unhurried lifestyle and wealth of experience, Manman is particularly attuned to seemingly minor changes and their potentially broader implications. To this end, he is on the constant lookout for signs of the NLM thanks to his superstitious belief in an oral text called the "*Shaobing* Song" (*shaobing ge* 燒餅歌). This millenarian oral text dates back to the mid-Ming period and features a coded language to foretell the coming of a great change (*dabian* 大變). Under its influence, Manman believes that

> regardless of whether things changed for the better or worse, they would never again be "as usual." He got this idea four years previously with the successive arrival of the Communist and GMD troops. He believed that other events would occur in the future and that "tomorrow" would be quite different from "today." Therefore, when he heard that the "New Life" was soon to appear, he was quite excited. He was really the first in the area to cherish some illusion about this New Life, though in fact even though everything else in the world was different, the life of this sailor had long ago become fixed. (Chu, "The Long River," 68; Shen, *Changhe*, 147)

Primed by the "*Shaobing* Song," Manman asks nearly everyone he meets whether they've heard news of the movement, and paranoically scans for signs of its arrival—at one point even suspecting a traveling monkey trainer of being a vanguard of the NLM. He also pumps locals for information about market irregularities in an effort to confirm his suspicions.

But despite his efforts to decipher the timing of the NLM's arrival, Manman remains unsure what the movement actually entails: Is it a Communist takeover? Will it mean conscription or new taxes? Manman's and the other villagers' conspicuous ignorance of a national propaganda campaign as pervasive as the NLM serves as Shen's wry commentary on the national information order and knowledge gap between the countryside and the city—where, the narrative suggests, even urbanites are ignorant, needing written instructions for something as simple as peeling and eating an orange. The locals' struggle to make sense of what the New Life Movement actually *is*—at one point speculating that it might be the name of a cruel general who will order mass beheadings—produces a parodic effect that underscores the dialogic nature of heteroglossia and exposes the epistemic struggle between hinterland and metropole discourses. *Long River* thus shows that when a slogan such as "New Life Movement" reaches the countryside, it can quite literally take on a discursive life of its own.

This dynamic is further illustrated by Manman's relationship to the *Shenbao*. Illiterate, Manman cannot directly access the newspaper. But thanks to his frequent discussions about current events with the educated Teng Changshun and the head of the commerce association, Manman is characterized as a "secondary" reader (*jianjie duzhe* 間接讀者) of the *Shenbao* (198). This category of reader is captured by a contemporaneous woodcut print by Huang Peili 黃培利 titled *Reading the Newspaper* (*dubao* 讀報, 1935). Careful attention to the image (figure 4.1) reveals that beyond the inner ring of readers stands a distinct outer ring of "secondary" recipients, who absorb the news as it lifts off the page and circulates orally. While the image's presumptive focal point is the man who smokes and the newspaper itself, we should not overlook the figure in the upper left

FIGURE 4.1 Huang Peili, *Reading the Newspaper*. Reprinted in *Banhua jicheng: Lu Xun cang Zhongguo xiandai muke quanji* (Shanghai: Lu Xun jinian guan; Nanjing: Jiangsu guji, 1991), 1:253

corner, who appears to be narrating the news to two or three of the other men. We witness here the transformation of "news" (*xinwen*) of the newspaper into socially exchanged *xiaoxi*. Manman is just such a disseminator, as, inspired by his indirect knowledge of *Shenbao* reports about the NLM campaign, he spreads his thoughts and opinions among all he meets. At the same time, despite the apparent information asymmetry between primary and secondary readers of the newspaper, Manman is still able to offer useful knowledge to Teng Changshun and others, as the oral news he gathers often travels at the same pace as the newspapers themselves.[63]

Just as *Reading the Newspaper* constructs a schematic of the social life of information, *Long River* likewise maps a kind of social network along which *xiaoxi* travels. By shuttling between different social strata and trading news, Manman ultimately serves as a kind of information broker within this network. With such a modus operandi, Manman exemplifies a broader pattern of similar characters in Shen Congwen's work—not least of all Daren in "Unemployed."[64] This role is detailed in chapter 6, which features Manman wandering about the docks exchanging words with various boatmen. As the chapter opens:

> When the old boatman arrived in the village, he conveyed [*zhuanda* 轉達] [Teng Changshun's] words to the head of the commerce association, and in turn received some *xiaoxi* at the latter's home regarding the dispatch of armed forces. These items of *xiaoxi* became mixed up with his earlier eccentric conjectures, whereupon, acting in the manner of a "scholar," he felt his abstract musings disrupt his vital energy and his questions bend his back, and thus prepared to return home along the riverside. Along the road he spotted quite a few boatmen carrying canopy rolls, indicating that two groups of shipping boats must have banked, and that he would doubtlessly get some news from them and their boat masters. He hoped that he would hear some news, [which he could] then cross over the river and report to Teng Changshun the following day. (*Changhe*, 193)

The chapter continues with Manman visiting no fewer than four different boats, pausing at each to converse at length with the men aboard in hopes of gathering intelligence about conditions downstream.[65] Crucially, unlike the intelligence gatherers who populate Mao Dun's fiction and who are driven by overt financial self-interest, Manman derives a distinct social pleasure from his peripatetic collection of information. In this way, the transmission of *xiaoxi* serves a particular phatic function, sustaining the social relations and conventions Shen Congwen sought to depict in *Long River*.

Despite its outsized presence in Manman's imagination, the NLM campaign never actually arrives. The final chapter describes preparations for the year-end local drama performance in a manner that echoes the ethnographic quality of the novel's opening chapter. When events foreshadowed by the narrative and anticipated by its characters ultimately fail to materialize, the reader is left with a lingering sense of cyclical recursion: in place of a linearly developing plot, the reader is entangled in a rich web of social communication. In charting the uneven reach of Nationalist propaganda into the countryside, *Long River* reveals how the social life of information eludes central control. Where Ding's fiction imagines revolutionary messages spreading swiftly and seamlessly among the masses, Shen's depiction of the information order underscores its delays, distortions, and at times, its absurdities. Both formally and thematically, *Long River* celebrates a mode of social communication that is diametrically opposed to mass literature, portraying it as more active, purposeful, and reciprocal.

Reciprocity proves to be an important point of tension in the novel as characters demonstrate a growing awareness of the one-directional nature of mass media and propaganda. Indeed, as several poignant episodes show, the hinterland desires to speak back to the Nationalist center. In one scene Manman and Teng Changshun discuss the mechanization of local *tong* oil production and the disruption it will pose to traditional modes of labor. Manman wonders how to send a message to President Chiang Kai-shek in order to warn him of dangers of modernization in Lüjiaping: "That old leader of ours, does he know about our local situation with the oil presses? Why don't we set up a newspaper so that he can read about it? He certainly reads the *Shenbao*. And moreover he had his people set up the *Central Daily* [*Zhongyang ribao* 中央日報]. So he should find out!" Teng Changshun adds: "He sits in Nanjing, and doesn't have ears that catch the wind [*shunfeng'er* 順風耳] or eyes that see a thousand *li* [*qianliyan* 千里眼]— how would he know about our affairs in the countryside!" (189).[66] A similar scene occurs in the following chapter when Manman asks a well-informed boatman why news of recent friction between locals and occupying military forces has not been transmitted (*chuan* 傳) to Nanjing.

The boatman replies: "My old comrade, [the president] is busy the whole day long, his hair has gone completely white, in the course of a day he has so many documents to take care of and so many visitors to see, how could he possibly take heed of this sesame seed-sized affair?" (201). The lesson, plainly, is that the political center only broadcasts information out—Chiang Kai-shek's voice and his NLM campaign may reach the countryside, whether in print or through the ether by radio waves—but such media cannot transmit information from the periphery back to the center.

As the novel's preface suggests, *Long River* itself stands as an attempt to "speak back" to the center. In doing so, the novel offers a powerful alternative vision of literary writing in an age dominated by propaganda: rather than the essentialism and monoglossia of the grand narrative, Shen presents a series of small narratives that foreground the individual voices of seemingly inconsequential folk. Their heteroglossic contributions to the narrative—the "rivulets and droplets" of *xiaoxi* as phatic communication[67]—collectively capture the social consciousness surrounding the signal event of the New Life Movement. These minor moments impart an irony to the novel's grandiose title: instead of a unified and linear narrative of History—a "long river" of national time—the novel presents a complex and vibrant braid of diverse utterances, impressions, and practices. The tension between these two temporal scales is subtly illustrated in a passage describing the view from Maple Hill, where Manman tends to the Teng family shrine. In a novel so steeped in orality, this scene stands out for its distinctly visual emphasis:

> Surrounding the ancestral temple were several mature maple trees whose leaves had already been touched with yellow, red, and purple by several morning frosts. Everywhere beneath the trees lay beautiful leaves spotted with various colors. . . . The orange groves bordering the river offered an outstanding spectacle with their leaves of jade green stretching long and unbroken along both banks of the small river. The trees were adorned [*zhui* 綴] with fruits hanging from their branches, all vermillion and bright yellow, their oranges complexly packed [*fanmi* 繁密] together like stars in the sky. From a distance they look like a plane [*yipian* 一片] of brilliant light, whose magnificence cannot be described. (*Changhe*, 118)

The scene gives the reader a picture of the surrounding countryside and its profound natural beauty. From a distance, the individual leaves and oranges—which recall He Yubo's comment about the "scattered dots" of Shen's writing—dissolve into an undifferentiated plane of light, producing an effect that is purely sublime, evoked only negatively as a sight beyond description. Such an encounter affirms literature's—and language's—capacity to evoke a beauty irreducible to the political imperatives of propaganda. Yet this is not merely another instance of Shen's resistance to the propagandization of literature. By collapsing the leaves and fruits into a unified visual field, the passage presents a fleeting spectacle of abstraction, where the forward momentum of history recedes, yielding to a moment of disembodied perception. In this flash of perceptual stillness, the novel suspends the flow of information, replacing persuasion with presence, transmission with communion—the crossways view of the river medium.

SOCIAL FABRICS

Following Shen's career past the 1949 divide shows that his skepticism of the grand narrative and propagandistic writing forced him to set aside fiction early on in the socialist era. Sensing that his attitude greatly compromised him in the eyes of the Communist Party, on the eve of the Communist takeover of Beijing in the spring of 1949, Shen attempted suicide.[68] Convalescing after the unsuccessful attempt, he recorded in his diary: "It's evident that literature will inevitably become one with propaganda in order to have significance and utility as [a form] of mass education. . . . This will completely destroy opinions of literature like those I previously held, leaving nothing left over. It is inevitable and necessary to put aside my pen."[69] Briefly, however, in late 1951, while traveling in rural Sichuan with a land reform brigade, Shen found a glimmer of literary inspiration back in the countryside—momentarily believing that he might adopt the political imperatives of socialist realism without compromising his authorial eye. He composed several poems and even a short story, with telling titles: "The Land Reform Brigade Arrives in Chongqing" ("Tugai tuan laidao Chongqing" 土改团来到重庆) and "Old Comrade" ("Lao tongzhi" 老同志). He also sent a letter to his youngest son, promising to write a work of land reform fiction (*tugai xiaoshuo* 土改小说) that would outdo even that of the popular Zhao Shuli 趙樹理 (1906–1970) and Zhao's popular peasant hero, Li Youcai 李有才, a character type whom Shen viewed as simplistic and one-dimensional.[70]

More than anything, his return to the countryside renewed Shen's interest in studying the lives of its people. He planned an ethnographically oriented travelogue along the lines of *Random Sketches on a Trip to Hunan* that would also build on his fiction of the 1940s. "If I go on studying here, after three months, I could produce a thick volume of probably fifty episodes, and produce a *Random Jottings of Sichuan* [*Chuan xing sanji* 川行散记]. I already have many outlines among my impressions. Especially the [local] language: I understand its meaning, and I also understand the feeling within its tones [*yuqi zhong de ganqing* 语气中的感情]. This is an extraordinary advantage." And, in moments of loneliness, he rediscovered his passion for reading ancient texts, particularly the *Records of the Grand Historian* (*Shiji* 史記) by Sima Qian 司馬遷 (ca. 145 to 86 BCE), a text that provided Shen solace from the increasing feeling of isolation amid the uproarious transformations of the historical moment.[71] But despite his rekindled hope that literary writing might regain for him some of its previous satisfaction, Shen soon came to realize that it was no longer a viable option. Working through multiple revisions to the manuscript of "Old Comrade," he couldn't get the necessary political tone right: it was impossible to put his literary craft to the purposes of the revolution. The avenue of literature had become permanently closed to him.

No longer able to support himself as an author, Shen absorbed himself in the historical study of Chinese material culture and handicraft art, including objects like jade, porcelain, lacquerware, clothing, fabric, embroidery, paper cutting, woodcut art, bronze mirrors, and fans. In 1949 he began working at the National Museum of History (Lishi bowuguan 历史博物馆). There, while conducting research on the development of craft arts from ancient times through the present, he dreamed of establishing a national crafts school that would help preserve traditional knowledge of silk weaving and embroidery.[72] Craftwork formed a bridge between his life in Beijing and his countryside experiences growing up, and as a writer he closely identified with the wandering mind and attentive eye of the craftsman. As he expressed in an unpublished memoir shortly before his suicide attempt:

After I came to the city, craft art [*gongyi meishu* 工艺美术] expanded my horizon [*yanjie* 眼界, lit. "field of vision"], and my fondness for and familiarity with it were both based in a comprehensive comparison [between object and maker]. What entirely flooded my mind was not simply their zest for the production process, but also the way in which the craftsman's mind fused [*ronghe* 融合] with his work, his industry, desires, passions, even some of his unrealistic calculations. All works of art reflect their creators' struggles with life, as well as their measured intelligence—this I understood in depth and in detail.[73]

Handicrafts constituted a kind of "small narrative" in their own right—one that came under siege in the new socialist era, as Mao Zedong's push for industrialization led to the widespread "deskilling" of rural artisans.[74] In an effort to counter this decline, Shen quietly pursued a series of detailed studies on China's premodern material culture over the next two decades—they now constitute five whole volumes of his *Collected Works*. What can Shen's prolonged interest in handicrafts in his later life tell us about his earlier career and identity as a writer? And, conversely, what does Shen's approach toward the craft of writing suggest about his interest in handicrafts? Given how often he was called upon—and refused—to return to writing in service of the socialist cause (including a personal suggestion from Mao Zedong), Shen's work at the museum can be read as a sublimation of his earlier artistic self-expression through literature.[75] As such, his antiquarian scholarship should not be taken as escapism into a remote past; instead, it stands as a creative foray into what was, for Shen, a living history.

The juxtaposition between craft and writing is expediently illustrated in the front-cover design Shen consigned from his cousin, the artist Huang Yongyu 黄永玉 (1924–2023), for a 1960 collection of his essays on material history, *Longfeng Art* (*Longfeng yishu* 龙凤艺术). The cover image (figure 4.2) pictures a girl sitting alongside a handwoven basket, upon which she props an open book. Not directly related to the specific objects presented in *Longfeng Art*, the picture instead speaks to handicraft as a living tradition. Or perhaps the book in the girl's hands is the text itself, suggesting the masses' interest and participation in scholarship on their own material history. Overall, the proximity between book and basket draws them together into a metaphorical relationship and even similitude—a likeness further suggested by the lineation of basket and text on the book's open page—in which each stands in for the other, a visual literalization of Shen's longstanding aesthetic of writing as handicraft or weaving and vice versa.

FIGURE 4.2 Cover image of Shen Congwen's first collection of writing on material culture, *Longfeng Art* (Beijing: Zuojia chubanshe, 1960)

Indeed, one of the craft arts that most interested Shen was fabrics and weaving. Throughout his second career as a historian of material culture, he indulged this fascination by extensively documenting both textual and material histories of decorative fabric. He repeatedly bemoaned the fact that fabric art, despite its centrality in popular rural and traditional culture, had been relatively ignored by specialists and collectors; perhaps he also identified with the neglect into which the handicraft of weaving (a distinctly feminine mode of labor)[76] had fallen the new era. Though fabric was hard to preserve, in many places—particularly in the southwest region he called homeland—weaving and embroidery were still active practices. As such, they offered a vital link to the living histories of their communities, where older modes of production and sociality might still coexist. Decorative fabrics also helped preserve local legends. In an article discussing the tradition of decorative cross-stitching (*tiaohua* 挑花), Shen observes: "It is primarily produced by women in their spare time. They don't use a set plan for the image, but generally recreate situations close at hand. . . . But as the subject of the images reflects social customs and habits, the images are invariably of auspicious and hopeful things, like bearing children, good marital relations, and copious harvests. They also sometimes integrate scenes from popular plays and stories" (*SCQJ*, 30:124).[77] Looking upon one of the images that Shen included with this article—a close-up of a cross-stitched scene of a boat race (figure 4.3)—one is tempted to see decorative fabric as a practice of visual-material storytelling that parallels Shen's literary aesthetic. Displayed serially in Shen's study, these individual pieces/scenes collectively exude the kind of heteroglossia he strove for in his fictional narratives.

In the final analysis, there is a mutually constitutive relationship between Shen's aesthetics of craft—with its emphasis on assemblage and

FIGURE 4.3 Close-up of a cross-stitch featuring a scene of a boat race. Reprinted in *Shen Congwen quanji* (Taiyuan: Beiyue wenyi chubanshe, 2002), 30:125

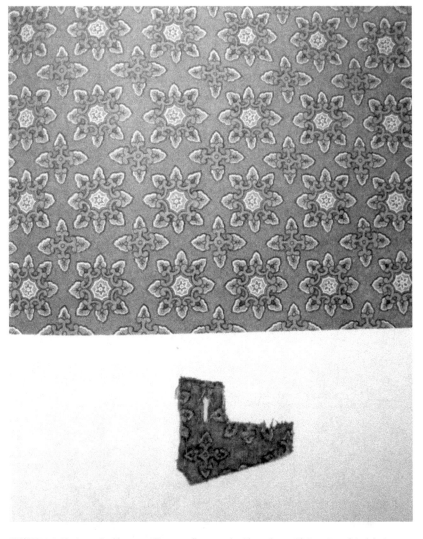

FIGURE 4.4 Photograph of fragment Tang-era flower embroidery along with its extrapolated design. Reprinted in *Shen Congwen quanji*, 30:17

network—and his social vision, marked by a deep suspicion of mass politics and propagandization. Tracing this relationship demands that we look beyond conventional readings of Shen's work and attend to his persistent concern with information and its social circulation. By way of conclusion, one final image from Shen's late scholarship on fabrics (figure 4.4) appears as a plate in his first full-length study on Chinese handicrafts, *Chinese Silk Design* (*Zhongguo sichou tu'an* 中国丝绸图案, 1957).[78] Across twenty-seven images, *Chinese Silk Design* surveys various patterns and designs in the history of silk production in China. The research also poses a study in *technique* and *arrangement*: how an image emerges from warp and weft, how pattern arises through visual repetition. This plate is unique insofar as it reveals Shen's technique for reconstructing designs from the material fragments of old samples. The top register displays the reconstructed pattern; the bottom, a photographic image of the fabric fragment. Serving as an archival anchor, the lower image "authorizes" the reconstructed design above, demonstrating how a full pattern can be extracted from a fragment through inference. In turn, the top register contextualizes the lower one, evoking the broader design and visual field to which the original fragment once belonged. Exemplifying what Xiaojue Wang identifies as Shen Congwen's aesthetics of fragments—the cultural details that constitute a mode of representation and focalization that stands apart from the grand narratives of socialist revolutionary ideology[79]—the image, in its totality, is nevertheless more than a document of a partial thing, indexing a broader, living structure of meaning. Indeed, the plate testifies to the connection between materiality and representation. Through their mutually supplementary relationship, the two registers offer a key for critically reflecting on one another. By turning back on itself in this way, the plate functions as a metapicture capable of reflecting upon its own ontology.[80] I see the dual registers as an analog of Shen's two careers—first as author and then as historian of craft—and of the dialectical resonance between them. Quietly published amid the roar of high socialism, this metapicture offers a fleeting revival of Shen's earlier literary project and critique of mass politics via the figure of the network: as the eye shuttles between the two registers, it moves from fragment to emergent pattern and back again—from individual node to constellated aggregate, only to return once more to the fragment, now newly seen.

CONCLUSION

Seeing Through Abstraction

Thus did abstraction and "information" became part of the cultural imaginary of modern China.

In the preceding chapter, Shen Congwen's withdrawal from writing fiction during the onset of the modern propaganda era, coupled with his character Daren's failure as an author, powerfully symbolizes the death of the storyteller. With this we return to the introduction, where Walter Benjamin's critique of *Mitteilung* in "The Storyteller" serves as a touchpoint for examining the encounter between literature and information. It is difficult to resist drawing further parallels between these two figures. Similar to Shen, Benjamin likens the storyteller to a craftsperson, noting how both "rework the raw material of experience in a solid, useful, and unique way."[1] Though armed with different understandings of information, both writers sound the alarm about its threat to literature and its essential features of polysemy and depth. And yet by directly adopting—rather than sidestepping—the modern discourse of information that had emerged in China by the 1930s, Shen's *Long River* complicates any clear-cut opposition between literary writing and information. Indeed, the novel's ethnographic description of the percolation of tidbits of news and gossip in the countryside demonstrates storytelling's ability to animate the information order. Alongside Shen Congwen's long-standing interest in other informational genres, such as encyclopedias and newspapers, *Long River*'s engagement with the discourse of information positions him as a key contributor to the broader zone of experimentation outlined in this book. The contemporaneity of Shen's and Benjamin's projects attests to the global nature of this discourse—and of the encounter between modern literature and modern information—while reminding us that, like any global event, it unfolded differently in various contexts.

In China, following Mao Zedong and the CCP's ascendance to power and the foundation of the People's Republic in 1949, the experimental zone that had opened during the preceding era largely vanished. Undoubtedly, the general decline of literary experimentation stemmed from the severe strictures placed on cultural production. In effect, literature and even language itself was subjugated into an overarching genre of information that was as politicized as it was unified. The critic Li Tuo has written extensively about this transformation, calling it "Mao-style prose" (*Mao wenti* 毛文体), under which literature was reduced into a channel for reproducing and disseminating Mao's language and thought.[2] Consider, for example, the following lines from Guo Moruo's 1953 poetry collection *Odes to New China* (*Xin Hua song* 新华颂):

Steel can be made into needles,
Gems can be carved into flowers—
Who says our minds aren't enlightened.
In past days we were beasts of burden—
Don't even mention reading or being literate.
Even the biggest mouths didn't dare utter a word.
But now we've become the masters:
The culture is now our culture.[3]

The patently self-explanatory transparency of the language—representing "the worst lines that Guo produced in his entire life, and perhaps some of the worst poems written since the advent of poetry," declares Li—leaves no space for interpretation. Nor do works rendered in Mao-style prose show much interest in the kind of modernistic meta-reflection that was characteristic of the literary experiments with information in earlier decades. By exclusively treating it as a medium for Mao's thinking and authority, socialist-era writers recast literature as a set of ideological coordinates, locatable upon the grid of Mao-style prose. (In this light, Zhang Yaoxiang's earlier drainage of the text Guo Moruo's "Morning Peace" into an abstract data table was something of a blossom that bloomed prematurely—its emptied lines are as meaningful as those of Guo's Mao-era poetry.) Shen's deepest fears as an author had come to pass.

Woodcut art met a similarly rapid demise as a site for seeing *through* abstraction. With the Nationalists squarely deposed from the mainland, the form's original raison d'être as an instrument of political protest faded.[4] Nevertheless, the broadcast aesthetic that woodcut helped to establish during the 1930s inspired the ubiquitous iconography of Mao Zedong's face as a red sun beaming over the masses, echoing earlier depictions of the horizon as an ethereal space saturated with signals. Such evocation of a communications-filled ethereal space was not limited to graphic art; in terms of the actual soundscape of the earliest period, Mao Zedong similarly dominated the airwaves. In his study of Maoist "quotation songs" (*yulu ge* 语录歌) popularized by the *Quotations of Chairman Mao* (*Mao zhuxi yulu* 毛主席语录, a.k.a. "the little red book"), Andrew Jones notes how the state's "emphasis on the ability of these songs to record, broadcast, and enable Mao Zedong thought to saturate social, somatic, and psychological space reads almost uncannily like an account of the ethereal yet ubiquitous powers of mass media itself."[5]

Even so, the self-conscious depiction of information did not disappear entirely from literature and images. One need look no further than the many pulp novellas of "adventure fiction" (*maoxian xiaoshuo* 冒险小说) and "counterespionage fiction" (*fante xiaoshuo* 反特小说) from the 1950s.[6] These works characteristically feature tales of the detection and elimination of Nationalist or pro-American spies—and titles like *The Signal Gun* (*Xinhaoqiang* 信号枪, 1954) and *The Secret of the Table* (*Biao de mimi* 表的秘密, 1957) reinforced in particular the importance of the masses in contributing to the socialist information order. Film, too, depicted the abstract entity of information. For example, the story of *The Red Lantern* (*Hong deng ji* 红灯记, 1963) centers on the heroic actions of a railroad switchman delivering a telegraph code from an underground Communist operative to a group of guerrilla fighters hiding out in the nearby mountains. In his analysis of the film, Yomi Braester observes that the fact the code is revealed neither to the switchman nor the film's audience suggests the Communist Party's total control over information flow and the interpretation of signs.[7] This authority was further manifest in the state's deployment of literature in the propagandistic fight for hearts and minds abroad, an integral front in what Richard Jean So describes as an "information war" between the PRC and the United States, where writers like Ding Ling and Eileen Chang were consigned to produce competing narratives about the revolution in China.[8]

In the cultural renaissance that followed Mao's death and the end of the Cultural Revolution (1966–1976), the dominant position of Mao-style prose was breached by writers seeking fresh modes of expression. Not coincidentally, the post-Mao period also saw the revival of the zone of literary experimentation with information that had opened half a century before. In her detailed study of the 1980s, Xiao Liu shows how the concepts of "information" (*xinxi* 信息) and "information society" (*xinxi shehui* 信息社会) became popular buzzwords following the introduction of digital computing and Chinese translations of systems theory and books such as Alvin Toffler's *The Third Wave* (1980). This renewed information discourse in turn inspired a growing number of intellectuals, authors, and filmmakers to grapple with information from a variety of angles.[9]

We might now view literature's encounter with information during the post-Mao era as a sequel chapter in China's twentieth-century cultural history. But drawing too bold a line of continuity with the Republican era risks being more misleading than illuminating. Where directly articulated, the terms of engagement—*xiaoxi* and *xinxi*—are different: in the context of the early twentieth century, the former was more wide-ranging and functioned quite loosely as the translational counterpart for "information." The meaning of the *xinxi* in the 1980s, meanwhile, came to be completely determined by the post–World War II redefinition of information initiated by Claude Shannon. In this more recent and etic instantiation, *xinxi*/information presents itself as a transparent and universal concept. It is perhaps on account of such newfound resistance to historicization that the earlier and more subtle discourse of information of the Republican period has escaped our notice until now.

It is time to take stock of this discourse's history as I have attempted to reconstruct it in this book. This project's underlying aim—to understand how "information" as a concept and word shaped modern Chinese literature—was originally prompted by my encounter with Mao Dun's "sketch" describing his fateful visit to the floor of one of Shanghai's main stock exchanges.

When I came across this short piece, the Great Financial Crisis of 2008 was still reverberating strongly in the United States. Writing in the early 1930s, Mao Dun was familiar with the social upheaval wrought by financial crises. But in the wake of an American housing bubble fueled by increasingly intricate financial instruments like collateralized debt obligations (CDOs) that left the value of underlying assets obscured, Mao Dun's insight into the centrality of abstraction to the operation of fictitious capital struck me as particularly poignant.[10] In response to the spectacle of information and noise at the exchange, Mao Dun attempted to use literary realism to see through or unmask capitalism's production of abstraction itself. By doing so, he had directly opposed realism and information. What other scenes of abstraction had entered into modern Chinese literature? And had they similarly both produced and been produced by articulations of information?

Let the mutual imbrication between modern literature and informatic abstraction serve as a key takeaway of this book. Whether articulated directly as a word-concept or more obliquely, the appearance of information simultaneously points to abstract domains such as "markets," "publics," or "history," as well as to systems of abstraction like the apparatus of the stock exchange, statistical models, or propaganda science. In other words, information's emergence as an object of literary consciousness was no mere side effect of the many new technologies of communication and information management. Instead, its piecemeal appearances index the information order of modern society as a whole—and one in which literature itself was a participating agent.

Throughout this study, if I have made liberal use of the historian C. A. Bayly's formulation of an "information order," it is because it so aptly captures the stakes of seeing through abstraction. For Bayly, the information order serves as a heuristic device for retroactively mapping out the fissures and overlaps between the knowledge of English administrators and various indigenous groups in nineteenth-century colonial India. But in the present case, it is necessary to recognize how historical actors *themselves* identified and analyzed the asymmetries between epistemes that constitute their information order. In other words, when Chinese writers consciously took up the subject of information, they were opening a field of investigation to probe the present as well as the past. For example, how did propagandistic efforts to mobilize a population run up against counterpropaganda or even simply social inertia? Or how could data visualization reveal something about society or literature that an individual reader could not? Information was always part of some larger order. As such, it was inextricable from relations of power and competing modalities of knowing—including literary and pictorial modes of knowledge. As a result, the investigation of information as a "thing" in modern literature and woodcut art formed the grounds for the self-reflexive examination of these media within the information order at large, as we have seen in all four chapters. In sum, the information order (itself a significant abstraction) offered critical leverage for pursuing the urgent mission of social, cultural, and literary modernization, bestowing the writers and artists examined here with excitement and anxiety in turns.

A second key takeaway is that the information order was made imaginable and even thinkable in modern China through the emergence of a new mode of perception primarily organized around vision. In addition to instances of exposing modern mechanisms of abstraction, "seeing through abstraction" also refers to a distinctly modernist mode of abstractive seeing. Like the film camera, this mode (which is not limited to a single medium) expanded the limitations of individual human perception. While the invention of the camera newly revealed what Benjamin calls the "optical unconscious" of physical reality, the informatic mode of perception offered a bird's-eye view of reality at scale—encompassing populations, systems, infrastructures, and patterns of social change. Along these lines, John Durham Peters briefly describes such informatic visuality in reference to an eighteenth-century Western subject who, thanks to the advent of statistics, came to

"see" something intellectually they could not see sensually . . . [and to] know something they can never experience themselves. They have a kind of knowledge no mortal can have . . . a kind of gnosis, a mystic transcendence of individuality, a tasting of the forbidden fruit of knowledge. But what a strange and ironically modern kind of gnosis. . . . This new kind of knowledge—knowledge that absolves individuals from the claims of deixis, of existing at one place and at one moment—is of course none other than information.[11]

James C. Scott offers a similar conception of an abstract and simplifying mode of seeing or "synoptic view" in his classic study *Seeing Like a State*.[12] The title phrase bears a significant conceit—after all, an individual sees, but states do not. For Peters, too, statistical information offers a figural rather than literal act of seeing, as indicated by his usage of quotation marks. In all cases, seeing specifies a particular mode of knowing at a distance, one that accounts for an entire field while reducing the complexity of the individual components—quite literally, in Scott's discussion of scientific forestry, a matter of seeing the forest rather than the trees.[13]

Throughout this book, a similarly transcendental vision recurs in the many instances of seeing, whether in narrative or image. As a form of informatic seeing, the visuality on display here extends beyond the statistical (and statist) register described by Peters and Scott to include the communicative aspect of information. This more expansive mode of abstractual seeing thus encompasses both Liang Qichao's and Zhang Yaoxiang's efforts to detect patterns in texts using statistics, together with Shen Congwen's investigation of the social life of information in the countryside, as well as woodcut artists' depiction of the ether as a contested field of information flows. In accordance with the dual character of information, seeing through abstraction entails not just seeing like a state, but also seeing like a telecommunications system, a stock market, or a radio broadcast tower. As apparatuses that "see" from afar, their perspectives make visible what otherwise remains inaccessible to the individual human subject.

Crucially, this abstract perceptual mode was both predicated upon and dramatized through the recurring appearance of a new figure in modern Chinese literature: the individual as a subject of insufficient knowledge, one whose agency is superseded by systems that remain largely unseen by them.[14] The method of historical statistics, for example, justifies itself by the imaginative construction of a reader of limited capacity—one who is unable to tap into the data latent within a corpus of texts. In chapter 2, the fate of speculators, farmers, and factory laborers is collectively at the mercy of the stock exchange, posed as a contest of information that is too intricate and fast-moving for any single player to comprehend. Emblematically, Mr. Zhao, the hypersensitive broker, keenly tracks the rises and dips in stock prices but cannot step back to understand how or why prices move in the first place. Likewise, the propaganda apparatus, as imagined by Chen Yuxin and other writers during the 1930s, not only reshapes the individual's knowledge of the world but employs them as a vector for the further dissemination of messages. In chapter 4, the frustration of Shen Congwen's telephone operator, Daren, arises directly from his inability to make sense of the tangled network of corruption and abuse that he accesses through his switchboard. On the whole, early twentieth-century Chinese literature is littered with characters of limited understanding who remain unable to grasp some elemental truth—one that remains hidden in plain view—and must go on serving as cogs in the machine. The literary project of seeing through abstraction thus emerged through the epistemological interplay between proximity and distance, fragmentary information and holistic knowledge, the worm's-eye view of complexity and the bird's-eye view of totality.

In the final analysis, the literary encounter with information reflects an attempt to wrestle with this epistemological interplay as a defining structure of modern subjectivity. As literature confronted the abstractions of the market, the state, and technological systems, it became a space where the infrastructures of power and perception were made legible in new ways—if only sporadically, and in forms that require attentive reading today. In engaging with information as both a narrative device and a conceptual field, modern Chinese writers and artists did more than document the onset of a new age; they illuminated the new conditions under which knowledge—especially literary forms of knowing—became contested in the ongoing negotiation of reality and its representation. If modern Chinese literature evolved alongside—and apart from—modern information, this book argues that this difference made a difference.

TRANSLATIONS

MAO DUN, "SKETCH OF THE STOCK EXCHANGE"
(*JIAOYISUO SUXIE* 交易所速寫)

1936

The street in front of the gate is not broad—only with some effort would it be possible for two cars to pass through side by side. Nor is the gate anything grand. Compared to the large doors of the Textile Exchange on Edward Avenue with its twenty steps out front, this stock exchange is lacking in majesty. And in this vicinity, it's the only large building. What I'm describing, of course, is the new building of the Shanghai Stock Exchange.[1]

Looking in directly through the front doors, one sees a corridor of considerable length, with two rows of four great stone columns blocking one's line of sight. Advance another more step, and you have reached the "market" itself. The scene is similar to the main hall of a large theater. Above, in the rear section, there is a "clapper-board stage" [*paiban tai* 拍板台] that makes many laugh, and many cry.

At exactly 11:00 in the morning, a critical moment has arrived, and the trading is pitched. The hall very much resembles a beehive. Please don't imagine that the hall is filled with row upon row of seats, like the hall of a large playhouse. One could not even squeeze in a small bench. Everyone is standing: the outer ring of people has come to watch the market conditions [*shimian* 市面], all prepared to buy or sell—one could say that the majority of them are individual traders with small amounts of capital, though naturally there's also no shortage of "inside traders" [*qiangmaozi* 搶帽子].[2] These are not the principal instigators who loudly, ear-piercingly scream out numbers. But among them some raise their heads and look toward the stage—though please don't be mistaken, the men on the clapper-board stage who roll up their sleeves all the way to their shoulders are not at all handsome, and one can't spot at the front anything of guiding value. [Instead, these traders] are looking at the "background" on the stage that is exhibiting 'XXXX Treasury Bonds,' 'X period of time' . . . a sort of "theater program" (if I may make such a comparison), especially with its illuminated number board above this "stage." The face of the board is inlaid high above the small stage in the back, with rapidly shifting red Arabic numerals, which are lined up four side by side, where two digits are for the (sub)unit of yuan and lower, like the format we frequently see on a bill; under these two small numbers there is a horizontal line of digits, also red. The board's font size is not small, so that from anywhere in the hall one can see it clearly. These compact, crimson, electrically lit numbers are created by people, and it is people that make them change every moment, but they control people's "fate."

No—we should instead say that it is a minority of people that creates this red, electrically lit record, causing it to change every moment, thus making any estimation of the majority's "fate" impossible. Who is the majority, then? Naturally, the people on the outer ring within the hall, who, haunted with fear, gaze at these numbers. But, at the same time, these traders are enablers—blind though they are—of the magical, red, electrically lit record. Outside of the hall there are an even greater number of people who have not personally seen their "fate" rising and sinking, who live in different areas of Shanghai, in different areas of China. But here upon the stage, when the red lights leap, the numbers determine these masses' bankruptcy or fortune.

At the center of the ring mills a group of traders, an ear-piercingly loud motor that yells out a tide of numbers. A circular, dirty railing, like the edge of an enormously round table, forms the boundary between this group and the outside ring. This interior group represents a number of big timers: these are the brokers. Their hands and mouths are driving the movement of the red electrically lit numbers displayed on the wall. But they are just like the red lights, themselves nothing more than a sort of machine, used by others. Some also stand to the side, arms folded, yelling over the noise into one another's ears. Suddenly an assistant excitedly comes running into the fray, or a broker anxiously runs off to a small side room to speak over the telephone, only to hang up the receiver and again race back to the hall. Perhaps the red electrically lit numbers will take another jump. All the people in the hall on the outside circle experience a new wave of anxiety. They can't help but grimly smile, grinding their teeth and swallowing their tears. Who knows which direction the numbers will move? Even the broker himself didn't know before he took the phone call. It is thus no stretch to say that he himself is nothing more than a machine.

On either side of the hall there are rooms that look like the spectator boxes at a theater. There one sees small chairs that look as if they are rarely occupied by the same backside for more than fifteen or twenty minutes. These are the back seats. Here sit two people secretively conversing into one another's ears; over there, another two argue over something in suppressed tones. In a chair against one of the side columns, a person bows his back, holding his head in his hands as if ruminating: Should he escape the city? Or commit suicide by swallowing a dose of opium? Over there is another, sitting in view of the magical, red, electrically lit placard. He holds a small notebook and pencil, mindfully recording the changes. It looks like he's drawing a treasure map—he probably believes that the fluctuation of government bonds follows a certain "path."

There are also women about. Hanging on the shoulders of their men, these ladies are youthful and fashionable. They look like they're just tagging along to take a look about. Over there is a middle-aged one in first-rate clothing, but in a style that is not the most fashionable, standing together with a middle-aged man, their faces upturned. When the electrically lit red digits jump up slightly, she pushes the man's shoulder; when the red numbers jump again, she agitatedly pulls the man closer and twitters at length in a low tone.

A man, completely clean-shaven and wearing only an embroidered short robe and pants, paces back and forth as throngs of people come and go around him. While pacing, he also repeatedly smacks his forehead with his palm. At this moment, the cries of trading and exchange within the hall resemble a cyclone or a tidal wave.

If you go up to one of the upper floors and stand at the iron railing and look downward, you might suddenly think of the supernatural spirits described in old tales: "Hearing the roar of killing rushing up from below, they parted the clouds to peer downward." From here one can clearly make out the actions of the interior group—how they extend and withdraw their palms, and how the people of the outer group make their way in and out, moving like ants do just before a great rainfall. Also frequently seen are small, balled-up things flying through the air. These are wads of paper, about the size of a button, thrown from all sides toward the central throng. How can we but not think of supernatural beings casting their magic spells!

Even now such a ball of paper is tossed down from the "theater box." Your attention alights on the half-circular platform, which looks like the border of a cloud. Within this semicircle sit several people recording something. Their desolation is soundless. On the wall behind them there hang several numerical placards of broker agents. Who can predict whether the wads of paper that they throw will cause the empty-headed masses to sob or to laugh?

A wild rumor blown through the stock exchange can excite large waves of fluctuation in the prices of bonds and stocks. These people fantasize within the rumors, get excited by them, or are rendered spiritless by them. No one is more sensitive than these people. But, if they didn't have such sensitivity toward rumor, the bond market wouldn't become a market. The human heart is just this sort of weird thing.

QIU SHENG 秋生 (MAO DUN), "OLD ACCOUNTS" (*JIU ZHANGBU* 舊賬簿)

1935

Last year a member of the older generation in my village expressed a wish to compile a local gazetteer [*zhi* 誌].[3] Originally, our area did have an old gazetteer, one compiled by a fellow who served as a local official during the Qianlong period [1735–1799]. He was an outsider and only compiled materials during his time off; thus, he did not concentrate his abilities on the project. As a result, some oversights were inevitable. But this stands as our locality's first "gazetteer."

This time around, the old fellow vowed to improve upon the earlier version. As for the budget, it went without saying that he himself would cover it. But the old fellow was busy with numerous affairs, and in truth he was only nominally involved in the compilation. Aside from passing judgment on the final version of the manuscript, he entrusted all the work of surveying and collection to several friends.

It was when the style sheet for publication [*tili* 體例] was being put together that the old man got really involved. He pored over a number of recently compiled county- and village gazetteers and inspected their formats. In addition, he invited over as many compilers of gazetteers as he could locate. To that end, he played host more than ten times.

One of his guests, a real big timer, was a dignified and sanctimonious man: the long-bearded Old Mister Jin. He was of the older generation from the neighboring town who was involved in compiling a "gazetteer" of his native place. Among recently compiled gazetteers, his was considered the most comprehensive. He had quite a few good opinions. I recall one was that a "town gazetteer" could contain a section on "taxation" as a way of recording the rise or drop in the burdensomeness of taxes in past years. He said one could also add an index of the past prices of goods, which, though it could not constitute its own section, should be paid special attention to in the relevant sections. For example, in the "agricultural production" section, it would be ideal if the compiler could check the historical rise and fall in agricultural prices and organize them onto a detailed table. The same went for the "industry" section.

There was no one who did not approve of the old man's opinion. But how could we come up with these materials? The old man twisted his beard and said, smiling, "In this matter the old account books of previous decades have a use."

After that dinner, I often thought of the wooden chest full of old annual ledger books that was stored in the attic in the back of my family home during my childhood. I don't know for what reason, but these old account books were kept around, and as a ten-year-old I often went and flipped through them, ripping out the blank pages at the back for scrap paper for my math exercises. By now, I am sure, that chest full of old annual account books no longer exists. Whether it was incinerated or traded for sweets, I don't remember clearly. At any rate, twenty years ago, it had reached its fate. And I had already long forgotten about my family's previous collection of these worthless "antiques."

Now, upon hearing the words of this Old Mister Jin, I recalled just how each heavy volume had not only provided me with scrap paper for calculations but also how I had moved them back and forth to serve as a stepping stone for when I wanted to locate some old woodblock-printed work of literature on top of the cabinet; in those times, it never occurred to me that these old "stepping stones" were a part of the historical record of my family—no, I should say a component for the "town gazetteer."

In truth, if we want to know how our grandfathers' grandfathers lived, among the resources that can tell us the most authentic information [*xiaoxi*],[4] I'm afraid nothing surpasses these old account books!

We know that our history is also but a type of "old annual account." It is lamentable, however, that there are so many "fake" [*xuzhang* 虛賬] and "embellished" [*huazhang* 花帳] accounts! We also know that we need "discernment" [*yanguang* 眼光] when reading the so-called "history" of these old annual account books. Besides "discernment," we also need a correct "method of interpretation" [*dufa* 讀法]. It's just like how that Old Mr. Jin has his own proper "viewpoint" [*kanfa* 看法] regarding these "old annual accounts."

Here I thought of a fellow villager that I knew, and his attitude toward the "old annual accounts" that were piled up in his own house.

These days this man is very badly off. But in the past his family really got by—the several decades' worth of "old annual accounts," stacked as high as a person, are proof of this. When his father placed the last account book, filled out in his own hand, on top of the stack, the volume joined a collection that had accumulated over generations. This happened over thirty years ago. As for the son, after his old man's "treasure" fell into his own hands, year after year he also added to the stack a new, thick volume. In those times, life was comfortable. But the recent couple of years have been different. The evidence is that, of late, his account books are getting thinner and thinner. Last year, heaving a sigh, he proclaimed: "This one is only fifty pages!" Who knows, perhaps this year his account will only fill twenty pages.

However, regarding the value of these "old annual accounts," his attitude has all along remained unchanged. No—I should say, as his circumstances become meaner, the attitude toward the "old annual accounts" passed down from his forefathers becomes in him ever more resolute and intransigent. For instance: three or five years prior, before he had fallen into complete ruin, hearing people discussing how much the Zhang family were demanding for a daughter-in-law or how much the Li family had to spend to marry off their daughter, he would simply chuckle and remark: "Previously when an elder handled the wedding of fifth paternal aunt, he spent the same amount as the Li family; during the big ceremony for my father's wedding, our family also asked for a bit more than the Zhang family. You can check the old accounts about all of this! But don't forget: in those times, a cruller sold for three *wen*!" But since year before last, he hasn't been able to laugh lightly at any affairs. The day before yesterday, on New Year's Eve, when the clerk from the grain shop sat in his home demanding that he clear his debt of thirteen yuan and eight jiao, the old man leaped back and forth as if crazed, blue veins popping out over his entire face, and made an uproar. "I tell you, I must delay through the New Year's celebration, but I'll certainly pay you back by the Lantern Festival! You don't believe it? You don't trust my household? Go have a look at the stack of our family's old accounts, passed down since my forefathers: every year is full of expenses and incomes in the thousands and tens of thousands! *Me*, disclaim your thirteen yuan, eight jiao?! What a joke, what a joke!" He really did proffer forth a large pile of "old annual accounts," urging the grain shop clerk to have a "look for himself." It is said that this New Year's Eve he reverentially reviewed his "old annual accounts" the entire night, then began to shed grateful tears, mumbling to himself: "Our ancestors in every year really did have expenses and incomes in the thousands and tens of thousands . . . in our village, among the wealthy families, who has as tall a stack of old accounts as this! Hm! There are only three households able to bring out as big a stack, one totaling several decades' worth of old accounts: Old Mister Zhao on the East Street, Second Brother Qian on South Street, and, on this street, there is only me!" Amid those "old account books" passed down through generations, he was only able to maintain conviction in his own self-arrogance. Thus returning to the "golden era" of the past, his "pain of frustration" was lightly kneaded away.

SHEN ZHAO 沈著 (SHEN CONGWEN),
"UNEMPLOYED" (*SHIYE* 失業)

1935

The busy period having not yet arrived, the office was strangely peaceful and the employees rather idle.[5] In a corner sat the long-distance telephone operator, Daren, who had only recently taken up the post. He was inspecting

that odd machine used for transmitting civilization [*chuandi wenming* 傳遞
文明]: its porcelain body, its copper ribbons, its staples and dots, its wires
and threads, its string of small lights. He felt bewildered. He was a bit short
on sleep, his digestion wasn't too good, and right then he looked like he was
working up a temper. Right, he was a little angry. A new life was pressing
hard down upon him, constricting him, making him mad. He had been
writing in his diary, recording an incident he overheard yesterday afternoon, where a call came from a soldier to a tobacco merchant, pressing the
latter for payment for a load of tobacco, resulting in a quarrel between the
two. The soldier and the merchant worked together distributing that poi-
sonous substance to the county, and the merchant as a rule received a
16 percent commission. But when it came time for the merchant to deliver
the money, he didn't have it. The soldier was anxious to get back his capital,
but there wasn't much he could do about it. Anyway, the matter couldn't be
cleared up over the phone, leaving no alternative but a round of severe verbal
abuse. That's just how things were! Every day there'd be one or two incidents
resembling this one.

After jotting down in the diary more fragments of confused language,
he stopped to read it over to himself and became really angry. Abandoning
the unfinished entry, he unconsciously flipped back to previous days' entries
and began reading them.

What inexplicable fate made it possible for me to come to this small
county to serve as a telephone operator? For such a job, one needs a gigantic
belly in order to swallow up all its depression and boredom. Is this a job for
humans? [Engineers] crisscrossed the area within several hundreds of li with
lines containing copper wiring from abroad and in various strategic places
installed these complex connectors [*jiexianji* 接線機] and transmitter
machines [*chuanhuaji* 傳話機]: "Hello." "Hello." "OK." "OK." Once they
have installed this "implement of civilization," connected the line and trou-
bleshot it, they return to the provincial capital to collect their commission
with the "Wawa" foreign company. Thereupon that location an auspicious
day is chosen for a grand opening of the telephone bureau, attracting the
county's head commissioner, the government messengers [*chuanda* 傳達],
the shopkeepers, as well as all the common families, on down to the crip-
ples and old ladies, aunties, temple nuns, and whomever else could scrounge
up two coins. "Sir, recite for me the regulations, I demand to answer the

call . . ." "I have here only eighty-four coppers, I'm short four cents, but at any rate please take them so that I can make the call. I'll just speak a little less!" If you try to make the person read the regulations for themself, well, no go! Education has not been universalized, so a Mrs. Wang doesn't recognize the characters. They need to scrape together the correct amount, but the pitiful thing is that the eighty-four coppers were already scraped together from various places. Yamen affairs are even harder to deal with: if one is slow in connecting the line, the county government's office messenger assumes the airs of a functionary and accuses you of "holding up public affairs." Hah! Even usury counts as public affairs! Then there are the conversations between military showoffs. Their first words are always something like: "Connector, damn you, are your ears stuffed with cock?" Replying that your ears are only filled with their words—now that would be a good one. It would be good to tell him that, for these are exactly the people who are always seeking "to get to the bottom of things." These guys, who receive endless scolding and countless beatings, constantly drill and stand guard, suppress bandits and abuse young women. For this, they get a monthly payment of three kuai and four mao, though they are completely unengaged in anything productive, these odd ducks who are known as "deputy gentlemen!" Between the northern and southern provinces of China, there are over a million of these types. Who knows where they come from, or of what use they are to our country.

This is the true university for training people to understand what it means to be Chinese. I should keep studying. I should continue enduring this hardship and tolerating this suffering. This career will tell me what China is and what it has. For one who wants to live on in China, they must understand how the majority there live.

Only twenty-one years old and having recently graduated from a high school established by the province, Daren was still a youth. After graduating, he didn't move to the next level of schooling. At that time, his mind was full of idealism about a career, about work, and about scholarship. By lucky coincidence, the province was investing in new construction projects and had just completed building a long-distance telephone network. An advertisement was published in the paper announcing that, out of six hundred people, only thirty outstanding and excellent fellows would be selected for the job of operator. After being chosen, Daren was dispatched to work in this county town. How many people covet such a stable and profitable job! How many hope for such a position but can't attain it!

In all truth, this job really was worthy of others' envy and admiration. For the kind of person who was willing to learn a bit from society, who had the courage to prepare to face "life," and who hoped to in the future use their brains and hand alike in pursuit of a career as an author, for such a person, there really was no better opportunity. When you think about it, who has more experience than the long-distance telephone operator and his ear? This was a central exchange hub for the corrupt souls of the region. What vulgar language would fool one such as the operator? What novel and strange affairs did he not know?

Especially those of the *yamen*. All the games of government office, from fraud to bribery, repaying small deeds with great favors, flouting the law, filing lawsuits over asking prices or remuneration . . . all the disreputable affairs that are nowadays widely recognized as entirely natural in China: these must all be set up, discussed, and negotiated over the phone. Anyone knows that regarding such affairs, one can fool heaven and earth, but there's no fooling the telephone operator.

And precisely for this reason, all the institutions in the county are completely willing to be on good terms with the telephone operator, taking anyone who works at the telephone department as a reliable confidant or intimate other [*xinfu zhiji* 心腹知己], they are at once unreservedly burdensome and totally polite toward him.

As for the common folk, because these people are completely ignorant and are unsuited for using this tool of civilization, they are always up for troubling the operator. And yet they harbor a certain fear of him, just like how they see the employees at the post and telegraph offices: don't worry about the officials, worry about the gatekeepers. Although the telephone office will connect for as little as two mao, it also controls their talk by making use of "There is no free line," and "Time's up" to resist these burdensome people. Regardless of whether you're a country bumpkin or a city dweller, there's no way to negotiate with the operator. The ones who really bind the hands of the operator are soldiers, but then again, the affairs of soldiers are also completely in the hands of the telephone operator.

This operator recalled yesterday's report on the military's bandit suppression initiative, which made him very uneasy. Looking at the time, it was still at least three hours before business would pick up, so he walked out of the office and onto the street to have a look about. Across from the telephone office was a noodle shop, where a fat shopkeeper was standing atop a wooden stool. His small assistant supported the legs of the stool, as the master worked to post a banner announcing the shop's anniversary celebration and a sale on noodles. Several unemployed idlers stood along the street with their hands in their sleeves, watching the action. To the east of the street was a pool of water, toward which a woman across the street was just then leading her ducks, as if to take them to the water. A gray-uniformed "deputy gentleman" suddenly ran out of the alley, putting on an air of astonishment, while eyeing up the three ducks. After settling on one, he looked at the woman while hatching his strategy. With great big steps, he immediately set upon the duck, saying, "Hey! As if I wouldn't find you, you feathered, flying beast, you went so far as to fly all the way over here!"

The woman, sensing danger, pursued the soldier, saying, "What? What? Sir, you've snatched my duck! That won't do, it's mine!"

The soldier had sharp eyes and quick hands, and by now he had already gotten hold of the duck's white-feathered neck. "This is mine! You're stealing my duck! Did you buy it or steal it? . . . " The woman blurted out in a sharp voice: "This won't do, this won't do. Sir, you can't take it away. It's mine, I raised it!"

The soldier replied in an equally loud voice, "You raised it? You hussy, you stole my duck and now you're even lying! Off we go to the East Yue Palace!"

With its ten halls, the East Yue Palace had been a yamen fit for the King of Hell, but nowadays was the camp for the Forty-fifth Army Brigade from Sichuan. The woman momentarily made a blank expression. Taking advantage of her lapse, the soldier grasped the duck and walked off. In response, she sat down at the side of the pool and quietly began crying. The loafers watching the action approached her. They understood what had happened, and some even laughed. The woman wiped her tears and began narrating the event to one individual she recognized among the group. This acquaintance was afraid of getting involved, and, looking in all four directions, said, "Sister, forget it. The duck can't speak, so even if you go to the yamen and find Judge Bao, it won't matter! Atop his lofty stage, Judge Bao doesn't care about our village's small affairs!"

The telephone office operator also approached the woman, but she had already stopped crying. Someone else asked her, "Was that duck yours?"

The woman replied, "How could it belong to anyone else?"

"If it's yours, then go ask for it back!"

"I'm afraid they'll beat me. Forget it, it's like seeing an evil spirit in broad daylight." The woman seemed to be resorting to fate to comfort herself, while at the same time lightly cursing, "On top of our grain they snatch away everything else, robbing us—begging for a beheading or shooting." So saying, she raised her pole and, clucking at the two remaining ducks, led them down to the water.

Originally the telephone operator was preparing to ask some questions of the woman, but, seeing her circumstance, he kept his mouth shut and promptly returned to the office.

Just when he returned to his switchboard, he thought, "This woman is definitely a local prostitute. Last night the soldier brought his duck when he came to sleep with her, then she took advantage of the situation, and in the middle of the day he came back for his duck. Otherwise, how could he just steal a duck in broad daylight?"

Glancing at the clock, he saw it was still early. On account of what he had just witnessed, he was very unhappy and finally decided to go back and ask the woman whether ultimately it was the soldier who stole the duck, or whether she had first stolen the duck from him, and he was just retrieving it by force. Just as he came out from the office, he ran into the village head from Xinyiji Village, sitting astride a healthy-looking black and white mule. The two men recognized each other, but before Daren had opened his mouth, the village head half rose out of the saddle and bowed with clasped hands, saying "Sir, good morning, good morning, good morning!"

"Village head, good morning!"

The village head dismounted and said, "It's a trouble, but please connect me to our village."

After the line was connected, the village head asked to speak with the other village elders, whereupon the operator learned that the man had yesterday gone to the city to report a young brigand named Li and request that troops be dispatched to capture him. At the break of dawn, the troops had issued forth, including a captain, two assistant captains, and a further 120 "gentlemen." This village head managed affairs earnestly and even exhorted the village elders that the expenses of hosting the brigade leader and the troops were to be paid by him personally. This wasn't a trifling expense—it takes real dough to feed 120 people!

After concluding the phone call, the village head chatted about the weather and some local gossip, then busily mounted the mule and headed back toward Xinyiji. Daren, the telephone operator, spotted two villagers trailing after the village head's mule. They were proffering two large loads of noodles along with meat and vegetables while seeming to think out loud, "Let's accumulate some virtue and let this fellow Li escape, wouldn't that be far less work?" The operator knew that once the troops came out, it wasn't simply a matter of the village head hosting them, and that the costs would also fall upon the villagers. Daren also knew that afterward there would come an official report, the kind circulated by telephone to one's superiors all the way up to the highest ranks. As a rule, such reports extolled the troops' incredible battle accomplishments, and they always concluded with the same old stuff: a triumphant return and the presentation of prisoners of war. All of this was like a formula, unavoidable, because it, too, was a "custom," and so very few people harbored any doubts about it.

In the afternoon, as expected, a telephone call came from Xinyiji. It was the voice of the major captain, asking to be connected to the public office. Even though the line was transferred to the county government office, Daren could still overhear the conversation clear as day. The captain's report was also to be copied by the telephone office for the sake of record-keeping.

"This guy Li was the head of a bandit mob, he was tenaciously resistant, but through the courage and determination of our soldiers, we advanced upon him and captured him. Seeing how things were unfolding, five other bandits scattered off . . . in all directions. Through the course of our campaign, approximately six hundred bullets were expended, and one rifle was damaged. But luckily no one in our unit was injured . . ." A while later, the county government office called the assistant commissioner office, and the county head made a similar report to the commissioner: ". . . the minute I heard from the village head, I personally led the troops into the countryside . . . in total about a thousand bullets were expended."

What a business! After copying down three similar reports, the unvisited became visited, the undone done, and, as for the "battle," it became ever more impressive, with an ever greater bullet count. No wonder the newspapers always reported the thoroughness with which the anti-bandit campaigns were undertaken, and the gusto with which the troops entered the countryside!

On the following day, the major captain, his ears tufted with hair, was the first to visit the phone office.

"Thanks for your trouble, thanks for your trouble! Thanks, captain, for going into the countryside!"

"Say nothing of it, it's our duty. If there's something about here that needs doing, we can't just ignore it, now, can we? In fact, you're the ones doing the hard work! This office does good business, but the troubles of the country folk are many! And you also take care of army affairs . . ." After finishing up this official-speak, he continued on in a more private vein.

The phone operator Daren asked: "Captain, what was up with that bandit? I heard it said the guy could leap onto roofs and vault over walls!"

"Erm, I wouldn't put it that way! He was a regular nobody, with no superpowers. A deserter, a shriveled-up youngster. A wasted youth like that, I don't know where he was stationed originally, but he saw an opportunity and was brave enough to make off with a few rifles, and he then returned to his home area to hide out. He had never committed a crime in the area, so he never reckoned someone would sell him out. When the troops surrounded his farmstead, the kid was just sunning himself atop some millet stalks. If the locals didn't make it into a case, there'd be no reason for a guilty conscience, heh! Once the fellow realized someone ratted on him and that the army had come out, he scurried into his stockade, hid away in a trough, and popped off a couple of shots. The situation wasn't hard to handle: 120 versus one—catching a guy alive is as easy as plucking a mollusk from a water can. 'Good brother, don't fire, the stockade is surrounded. Throw over the weapons, and we can talk things over.' The youth looked about. He really was surrounded. Realizing the situation, he threw us the rifles. Afterward, we tied him up, fastened him to the trough, and gave him a thrashing. . . . The village chief Zhou said to me: 'Captain, captain, thanks for your trouble, leave the rifles with us, on another day I'll send a separate report to the county. Here's 120 foreign dollars for you brothers to drink a little tea. You're my good elder brother,' that kind of thing. And that's how things ended."

"How old?"

"Twenty-two, a stripling!"

"Did you transport him to the city?"

"*Hai*, what's the use of transporting him to the city? I ask you: if we tie him up and bring him in, what good is that 120 dollars?"

"Then did you submit for reimbursement for the bullets?"

"In total we used five and a half clips."

"*Hai*, and that was it for him?"

"Didn't we just give him a single pop! What use would it be for us to leave him alive? Come on," said the captain, getting annoyed.

Telephone operator Daren wrote a letter to his brother, saying: "Brother, help me switch jobs. I can't do this! I can't do this! I can't do this!" His brother wrote back, "You can't? OK, if you can't do this job, then let someone else do it. We'll figure out a way for you to continue studying in Beijing." But in response to Daren's second letter of supplication, his brother instead wrote: "Wherever you go, isn't it still the same? If you don't continue on as is, you'll be unemployed!" Finding himself unable to advance in his studies, this young man really did join the ranks of the unemployed.

NOTES

ACKNOWLEDGMENTS

1. Liang Qichao 梁啟超, *Intellectual Trends in the Ch'ing Period*, trans. by Immanuel C. Y. Hsü (Cambridge, MA: Harvard University Press, 1959), 11. Translation modified for precision.

INTRODUCTION: LITERARY ENCOUNTERS WITH INFORMATION IN MODERN CHINA

1. Originally titled simply "Zhengquan jiaoyisuo" 證券交易所, the piece first appeared in a centerfold in the February 15 issue (no. 114) of the magazine *Liangyou Huabao* 良友畫報, 24–25. In October of that year, the essay was recategorized as a "sketch" (*suxie* 速寫) and included shortly thereafter in a collection of Mao's works titled *Yinxiang, ganxiang, huiyi* 印象、感想、回憶, published by Wenhua shenghuo chubanshe. Because the original only appears across two pages of the *Liangyou Huabao*, I omit page numbers for the quotes I use from it.
2. Though he does not specifically focus on stock and bond exchanges (instruments which, as Friedrich Engels notes in his supplement, become more important after volume 3 of *Das Kapital* was written in 1865), Marx remarks the concurrent rise of speculation, quoting a contemporary source to make his point: "It is the object of banking to give facilities to trade, and whatever gives facilities to trade gives facilities to speculation. Trade and speculation are in some cases so nearly allied, that it is impossible to say at what precise point trade ends and speculation begins. . . . Wherever there are banks, capital is more readily obtained, and at a cheaper rate. The cheapness of capital gives facilities to speculation, just in the same way as the

cheapness of beef and of beer gives facilities to gluttony and drunkenness" (532). He goes on to note that innovations in bank lending and borrowing resulted in a state where, by the 1850s, as many as *nine-tenths of all the deposits in the United Kingdom may have no existence beyond their record in the books of the bankers."* Karl Marx, *Capital: A Critique of Political Economy*, trans. David Fernbach (New York: Penguin Books, 1991), 3:533 (emphasis in original).

3. Rey Chow, *Primitive Passions: Visuality, Sexuality, Ethnography, and Contemporary Chinese Cinema* (New York: Columbia University Press, 1995), 8.

4. Here I find useful Bernard Geoghegan's exploration of an apparatus both as a set of material instruments and techniques, on the one hand, and, on the other hand, as an attendant ideology by which such media and practices "transform into epistemological figures that coordinate, suspend, or rationalize difference [and knowledge]." See "From Information Theory to French Theory: Jakobson, Lévi-Strauss, and the Cybernetic Apparatus," *Critical Inquiry* 38, no. 1 (Autumn 2011): 99.

5. Quoted in Richard Menke, *Telegraphic Realism: Victorian Fiction and Other Information Systems* (Stanford, CA: Stanford University Press, 2008), 16 (emphasis in original).

6. BBVA, "The Five Vs of Big Data," updated May 26, 2020, https://www.bbva.com/en/five-vs-big-data/.

7. See Zhou Yongming, *Historicizing Online Politics: Telegraphy, the Internet, and Political Participation in China* (Stanford, CA: Stanford University Press, 2006), 33. For an account of the substantial Danish efforts in promoting telegraph infrastructure in China, see Erik Baark, *Lightning Wires: The Telegraph and China's Technological Modernization, 1860–1890* (Westport, CT: Greenwood Press, 1997).

8. Xie Liuyi 謝六逸, "Qingnian yu xinwen" 青年與新聞, in *Qingnian jie* 青年界 6, no. 2 (1934): 49–51. Reprinted in *Xie Liuyi wenji* 谢六逸文集, ed. Chen Jiang and Chen Gengchu (Beijing: Shangwu Yinshuguan, 1995), 295–96.

9. See China Telecom Shanghai Company, ed., *Dianxin de jiyi: Shanghai dianxin 138 nian* 电信的记忆：上海电信138年 (Shanghai: Wenhui chubanshe, 2009). As of now, a comprehensive account of the history of telephony in China awaits further research.

10. "Every year the service continues to expand; more and more places are brought within the postal net; speedier and more frequent deliveries are effected, and with each step forward the Post Office takes, China is knit more closely together." Chu Chia-Hua 朱家驊, *China's Postal and Other Communications Systems* (Shanghai: China United Press, 1937), 27. See also Lane Jeremy Harris, "The Post Office and State Formation in Modern China, 1896–1949" (PhD diss., University of Illinois at Urbana-Champaign, 2012).

11. Radio: John Alekna, *Seeking News: Making China: Information, Technology, and the Emergence of Mass Society* (Stanford, CA: Stanford University Press, 2024), along with Michael A. Krysko, "Forbidden Frequencies: Sino-American Relations and Chinese Broadcasting during the Interwar Era," in *Technology and Culture* 45, no. 4 (2004): 712–39. Phonograph: Andrew F. Jones, *Yellow Music: Media Culture and Colonial Modernity in the Chinese Jazz Age* (Durham, NC: Duke University Press, 2001). Film: Mary Farquhar and Chris Berry, "Shadow Opera: Toward a New Archaeology of Chinese Cinema," in *Chinese-Language Film: Historiography, Poetics, Politics*, ed. Sheldon Lu and Yueh-Yu Yeh (Honolulu: University of Hawai'i Press, 2005), 27–52; Laikwan Pang, "Walking into and out of the Spectacle: China's

Earliest Film Scene," *Screen* 47, no. 1 (2006): 66–80; Zhang Zhen, "Teahouse, Shadowplay, Bricolage: Laborer's Love and the Question of Early Chinese Cinema," in *Cinema and Urban Culture in Shanghai, 1922–1943*, ed. Yingjin Zhang (Stanford, CA: Stanford University Press, 1999), 27–50.

The body of literature on modern press and print is too expansive to list more than a sample of its representative works. For estimated print runs and circulation reach, see in particular Leo Ou-fan Lee and Andrew Nathan, "The Beginnings of Mass Culture: Journalism and Fiction in the Late-Qing and Beyond," in *Popular Culture in Late Imperial China*, ed. David Johnson, Andrew J. Nathan, and Evelyn S. Rawski (Berkeley: University of California Press, 1983), 360–95. See also Bryna Goodman, "Networks of News: Power, Language, and Transnational Dimensions of the Chinese Press, 1850–1949," *China Review* 4, no. 1 (2004): 1–10; Henrietta Harrison, "Newspapers and Nationalism in Rural China, 1890–1929," in *Twentieth-Century China: New Approaches*, ed. Jeffrey Wasserstrom (London: Routledge, 2003), 83–102; Joan Judge, "The Power of Print: Print Capitalism and the News Media in Late Qing China and Republican China," *Harvard Journal of Asian Studies* 66, no. 1 (2006): 233–54; Barbara Mittler, *A Newspaper for China? Power, Identity, and Change in Shanghai's News Media, 1872–1912* (Cambridge, MA: Harvard University Press, 2003); Rudolf Wagner, ed., *Joining the Global Public: Word, Image, and City in Early Chinese Newspapers, 1870–1910* (Albany: State University of New York Press, 2007); Alexander Des Forges, *Mediasphere Shanghai: The Aesthetics of Cultural Production* (Honolulu: University of Hawai'i Press, 2007). On publishing and print capitalism, see Christopher Reed's detailed description in *Gutenberg in Shanghai: Chinese Print Capitalism, 1876–1937* (Honolulu: University of Hawai'i Press, 2004).

12. On print culture, see Reed, *Gutenberg in Shanghai*, 4–12; and for studies of political information see Silas Wu, *Communication and Imperial Control in China: Evolution of the Palace Memorial System, 1693–1735* (Cambridge, MA: Harvard University Press, 1970), along with Chelsea Zi Wang, "More Haste, Less Speed: Sources of Friction in the Ming Postal System," *Late Imperial China* 40, no. 2 (2019): 89–140.

13. I adopt the framework of "information order" from the social historian C. A. Bayly's landmark social history of the Indian uprising of 1857 and the surprise it posed to British colonial administration. Bayly teases out the overlaps and gaps in what he calls the "information order" of British and Indian sources about local, regional, and transnational realities. Demonstrating that access to and production of local and regional knowledge were negotiated between indigenous and colonial groups, his point is less about how the British administration knew at least *something* true of the Indians it governed (contra claims that orientalist knowledge was completely insular and totalizing), but rather an insistence upon positioning knowledge or information as a relatively autonomous sphere of social life, integral to the "world of power and economic exploitation" but not be reducible to it. See *Empire and Information: Intelligence Gathering and Social Communication in India, 1780–1870* (Cambridge: Cambridge University Press, 1996), 4.

14. It is Marshall McLuhan who famously brings the "antennae" metaphor to literature and art; see *Cybernation and Culture* (Notre Dame, IN: University of Notre Dame Press, 1966), 100–101.

15. Menke, *Telegraphic Realism*, 4.

16. Simon DeDeo, "Information Theory for Intelligent People," September 9, 2018, https://wiki.santafe.edu/images/a/a8/IT-for-Intelligent-People-DeDeo.pdf.

The context of the "difference which makes a difference" quote was the Nineteenth Annual Korzybski Memorial Lecture (1970), where Gregory Bateson took up the topic of the difference between map and territory (i.e., the relationship between objects and their representations, or substance and mind). See his *Steps to an Ecology of Mind: Collected Essays in Anthropology, Psychiatry, Evolution, and Epistemology* (Northvale, NJ: Jason Aronson, 1987 [1972]), 321. On the originary nature of difference in psychology and communication, Bateson writes: "In the world of mind, nothing—that which is *not*—can be a cause. In the hard sciences, we ask for causes and we expect them to exist and be 'real.' But remember that zero is different from one, and because zero is different from one, zero can be a cause in the psychological world, the world of communication" (320, emphasis in original). Notably, the binarism of the *Yijing* was also a major inspiration in the binary philosophy of Leibniz. See Lydia H. Liu, *The Freudian Robot: Digital Media and the Future of the Unconscious* (Chicago: University of Chicago Press, 2010), 68–70.

17. Ann Blair, "Foreword," in *Literary Information in China: A History*, ed. Jack W. Chen, Anatoly Detwyler, Christopher M. B. Nugent, Xiao Liu, and Bruce Rusk (New York: Columbia University Press, 2021), xvi.

18. Many more examples could be marshaled, but these two studies by Ann Blair and Mary E. Berry stand out as particularly strong demonstrations of what an etic approach to information can do for historians. For each scholar's justification of anachronism and metaphor to study information, see *Too Much to Know: Managing Scholarly Information Before the Modern Age* (New Haven, CT: Yale University Press, 2010), 1–2, and *Japan in Print: Information and Nation in the Early Modern Period* (Berkeley: University of California Press, 2006), 15, respectively.

19. Michael E. Hobert and Zachary S. Schiffman offer one of the earliest examples of this view in *Information Ages: Literacy, Numeracy, and the Computer Revolution* (Baltimore: Johns Hopkins University Press, 1998), though their argument that information originates with the invention of writing, which "created new entities, mental objects that exist apart from the flow of speech, along with the earliest systematic attempts to organize this abstract mental world" (2), is too logocentric. Language also has the capacity to separate information out of experience. Science writer James Gleick provides an updated universalist account of information in *The Information: A History, A Theory, A Flood* (New York: Pantheon, 2011).

20. Claude Shannon, "A Mathematical Theory of Communication," *Bell System Technical Journal* 27, nos. 3–4 (1948): 379–423, 623–56.

21. This example comes from Bruce Clarke's entry on "Information" in *Critical Terms for Media Studies*, ed. W. J. T. Mitchell and Mark B. N. Hansen (Chicago: University of Chicago Press, 2010), 160.

22. John Durham Peters, *Speaking Into the Air: A History of the Idea of Communication* (Chicago: University of Chicago Press, 1999), 23.

23. To give but a sampling of critical scholarship on the history of the new fields inspired by Shannon's insights: Liu, *The Freudian Robot*; Lily E. Kay, *Who Wrote the Book of Life? A History of the Genetic Code* (Stanford, CA: Stanford University Press, 2000); N. Katherine Hayles, *How We Became Posthuman: Virtual Bodies in Cybernetics, Literature, and Informatics* (Chicago: University of Chicago Press, 1999).

24. William R. Paulson, *The Noise of Culture: Literary Texts in a World of Information* (Ithaca, NY: Cornell University Press, 1988).

25. Put differently, etic categories are abstractions, and information is the ultimate form of abstraction. "Behind the late-twentieth-century idiom, then, are the historically grounded notions of information as something informed, shaped by a pattern, and something preserved, set aside from the immediacy of experience. Each notion requires the other. The pattern, the indwelling form, is an abstraction (from the Latin verb *abstrahere*, 'to pull,' 'to drag,' or 'draw away from'), the product of a reflective mental operation that fixes the flux of experience, both ordering and preserving it. This act involves two closely intertwining movements, (1) 'drawing away from' experience, such that we are no longer immersed in it and can see it from a critical perspective, and (2) 'pulling' or 'dragging' something out of it. The twofold movement of abstraction is the sine qua non of information, without which it cannot exist." Hobert and Schiffman, *Information Ages*, 4.

26. John Durham Peters, "*Information*: Notes Toward a Critical History," in *Journal of Communication Inquiry* 12, no. 2 (1988): 10. My discussion here is also inspired by Eric Hayot's discussion of the term's universalism and how to move beyond or around it. See *Information: A Reader*, ed. Eric Hayot, Anatoly Detwyler, and Lea Pao (New York: Columbia University Press, 2021), 1–14.

27. Mary Poovey, *A History of the Modern Fact: Problems of Knowledge in the Sciences of Wealth and Society* (Chicago: University of Chicago Press, 1998). See also Theodore M. Porter, *Trust in Numbers: The Pursuit of Objectivity in Science and Public Life* (Princeton, NJ: Princeton University Press, 1995). My condensation of Peters's illuminating genealogy necessarily leaves out a great deal of his original nuance. Suffice it to say that his essay, "*Information*," is a must-read for anyone remotely interested in this historical field.

28. Bayly, *Empire and Information*, 3–4.

29. Bayly, *Empire and Information*, 5.

30. Lydia H. Liu, *Translingual Practice: Literature, National Culture, and translated Modernity—China, 1900–1938* (Stanford, CA: Stanford University Press, 1995), 1–42.

31. Hilde De Weerdt, *Information, Territory: and Networks: The Crisis and Maintenance of Empire in Song China* (Cambridge, MA: Harvard University Asia Center, 2015); Devin Fitzgerald and Carla Nappi, "Information in Early Modern East Asia," in *Information: A Historical Companion*, ed. Ann Blair, Paul Duguid, Anja-Silvia Goeing, and Anthony Grafton (Princeton, NJ: Princeton University Press, 2021), 38–60; Wu, *Communication and Imperial Control in China*.

32. Lee Cronk, *That Complex Whole: Culture and the Evolution of Human Behavior* (Boulder, CO: Westview Press, 1999), 12; Charles Sanft, *Communication and Cooperation in Early Imperial Culture: Publicizing the Qin Dynasty* (Albany: State University of New York Press, 2014), 12, 19; Chen et al., *Literary Information in China*, xxii.

33. Liu, *Information Fantasies: Precarious Mediation in Postsocialist China* (Minneapolis: University of Minnesota Press, 2019).

34. Michael C. Lazich, "The Diffusion of Useful Knowledge in China: The Canton Era Information Strategy," in *Mapping Meanings: The Field of New Learning in Late Qing China*, ed. Michael Lackner and Natascha Vittinghoff (Leiden: Brill, 2004), 305. See also Alexander Welsh's discussion of the Society as representative of new

consciousness of the importance of knowledge and information in Victorian England, *George Eliot and Blackmail* (Cambridge, MA: Harvard University Press, 1985), 39–41.

35. Tong Lam, *A Passion for Facts: Social Surveys and the Construction of the Chinese State, 1900–1949* (Berkeley: University of California Press, 2011).

36. Genealogized by Tie Xiao, *Revolutionary Waves: The Crowd in Modern China* (Cambridge, MA: Harvard University Press, 2017).

37. Paize Keulemans made this point during a presentation at our panel at the Association for Asian Studies annual conference in 2017.

38. Specifically, the 23rd and 55th hexagrams. Here I use the popular Wilhelm/Baynes translation. See *The I Ching or Book of Changes: The Richard Wilhelm Translation rendered into English by Cary F. Baynes* (Princeton, NJ: Princeton University Press, 1950), 501.

39. The *Hanyu da cidian* 汉语大词典 cites such a usage in a poem by the Eastern Han poetess, Cai Yan 蔡琰 (dates unknown), daughter of Cai Yong 蔡邕 (133–192).

40. *Ciyuan* 辭源 (Shanghai: Shangwu yinshuguan bianshenbu, 1915), vol. 1, p. 99 of the *si* [巳] section.

41. See the *Hanyu da cidian* entry under *xinxi* 信息, which gives it as a compound of "message and news" (*yinxin xiaoxi* 音信消息). The term *xinxi* also commonly appeared in nineteenth-century newspaper column titles, particularly in missionary publications. Curiously, however, by the Republican period, it was less commonly used than *xiaoxi* but came back into vogue in the 1980s with the advance of digital technologies and cybernetic science in China. Another term used to translate "information" is *qingbao* 情報 (it can also mean "a piece of intelligence"). This term is derived from the Japanese *jōhō* 情報, a much stabler translational counterpart to "information," as in the origination of "information society" *jōhō shakai* 情報社会 or "informatized society" *jōhōka shakai* 情報化社会 in the work of Yoneji Masuda and others during the 1960s. See Masuda, *The Information Society as Post-Industrial Society* (Tokyo: Institute for the Information Society, 1980).

42. Xie Liuyi, "Baozhang wenxue suotan" 報章文學瑣談, in *Xin daxia* 新大夏 1, no. 3 (1938). Reprinted in *Xie Liuyi ji* 谢六逸集 (Liaoning: Liaoning renmin chubanshe, 2009), 112–14.

43. "Xiandai tongxun shiye zhi qushi" 現代通訊事業之趨勢, originally published in Xie's wartime journal, *Wenxun yuekan* 文訊月刊 2, no. 1 (1942). The journal was the primary publication outlet for the Guiyang branch of the Wenxie (of which Xie was the director). Reprinted in *Xie Liuyi wenji*, 327.

44. *Xie Liuyi wenji*, 328.

45. Xie Liuyi, "*Wenxun* chuangkan ci" 《文訊》創刊辭, in *Wenxun yuekan* 1, no. 1 (1941): 1. Reprinted in *Xie Liuyi wenji*, 306–7. On the reformation of the Chinese literary institution as a network after the fall of Shanghai in 1938, see Charles Laughlin, "The All-China Resistance Association of Writers and Artists," in *Literary Societies of Republican China*, ed. Kirk A. Denton and Michel Hockx (Lanham, MD: Lexington Books, 2008), 379–412.

46. Found in Mittler, *A Newspaper for China?*, 23.

47. In *Seeking News, Making China: Information, Technology, and the Emergence of Mass society*, John Alekna does an admirable job reconstructing listeners' experiences of

radio in modern China, but even his account necessarily relies primarily on print sources.

48. A point that I and my collaborators expand on in our introduction to *Literary Information in China*, xxv.

49. Guido Isekenmeier, "Literary Visuality: Visibility—Visualization—Description," in *Handbook of Intermediality: Literature—Image—Sound—Music*, ed. Gabriele Rippl (Berlin: De Gruyter, 2015), 327.

50. On microscopy, see Ari Larissa Heinrich, *The Afterlife of Images: Translating the Pathological Body between China and the West* (Durham, NC: Duke University Press, 2008), 149–156, as well as Liu Lu, "Away/With the Pest: Science, Visuality, and Socialist Subjectivities in Modern China's Biosocial Abjection" (PhD diss., University of Wisconsin–Madison, 2019), 25–62; on photography, William Schaeffer's *Shadow Modernism: Photography, Writing, and Space in Shanghai, 1925–1937* (Durham, NC: Duke University Press, 2017); regarding film, see Chow, *Primitive Passions*, along with Zhang Zhen, *An Amorous History of the Silver Screen: Shanghai Cinema, 1896–1937* (Chicago: University of Chicago Press, 2006).

51. Andrew Plaks explains: "the evocation of meaning in [traditional] narrative must . . . lie only in the overall configurations, rather than in the specific patterns, of structure and characterization [in the text]. Or, more precisely, it is only as the specific figures of Chinese narrative tend to fall into larger patterns of alternation and flux that they take on a dimension of what we may call 'meaning.'" The fact that mimetic details are "pumped into the pages of works in effect guarantees that certain existential patterns of alternation or recurrence will manifest themselves sooner or later," thus revealing the abstract cosmic principles behind the work. "Towards a Critical Theory of a Chinese Narrative," in *Chinese Narrative: Critical and Theoretical Essays*, ed. Andrew Plaks (Princeton, NJ: Princeton University Press, 1977), 350.

52. "Wenyi yu geming" 文藝與革命, *Yusi* 語絲 4, no. 16 (1928): 38–46.

53. *Literary Information in China* makes the case comprehensively for such an approach.

54. *Liang Qichao quanji* 梁启超全集, ed. Yang Gang and Wang Xiangyi (Beijing: Beijing chubanshe, 1999), 5610.

55. Preface to the novel, reprinted in *Liang Qichao quanji*, 5609. On the novel's mixture of traditional lyricism with futuristic utopia, see Satoru Hashimoto, "Liang Qichao's Suspended Translation and the Future of Chinese New Fiction," in *A New Literary History of Modern China*, ed. David Der-wei Wang (Cambridge, MA: Belknap Press of Harvard University Press, 2017), 161–65.

56. Liang Qichao, "Lun xiaoshuo yu qunzhi zhi guanxi" 論小說與群治之關係, in *Xin xiaoshuo* 新小说 no. 1 (1902). The English translation, by Gek Nai Cheng, appears in Kirk A. Denton, ed., *Modern Chinese Literary Thought: Writings on Literature, 1893–1945* (Stanford, CA: Stanford University Press, 1996), 74–81. Both in China and North America, Liang's essay remains the starting point for many a modern Chinese literature survey course. See also Theodore Huters's comprehensive account of the rise of "new fiction" and Liang's role in it in *Bringing the World Home: Appropriating the West in Late and Early Republican China* (Honolulu: University of Hawai'i Press, 2005), 100–120.

57. Liu, *Translingual Practice*, 235–36.

58. Marston Anderson, *The Limits of Realism: Chinese Fiction in the Revolutionary Period* (Berkeley: University of California Press, 1990), 3.

59. Marshall McLuhan, *Understanding Media: The Extensions of Man* (New York: McGraw-Hill, 1965), 302.

60. Walter Benjamin, "The Storyteller: Reflections on the Work of Nikolai Leskov," in *The Storyteller Essays*, trans. Tess Lewis, ed. Samuel Titan (New York: New York Review of Books, 2019), 51–52, 54–55. See also Benjamin's earlier essay from 1933, "The Art of Storytelling," in the same volume: "Information is valuable only for the moment in which it is new. It lives only in that moment. It must be completely subject to it and declare itself immediately without losing any time. A story is different: it does not use itself up. It preserves its inherent power, which it can then deploy even after a long period of time has passed" (35–36).

61. See, respectively, Richards, *The Imperial Archive*, 11–44; Kataoka Teppei, "The Linesmen," trans. Gregory Golley, in *For Dignity, Justice, and Revolution: An Anthology of Japanese Proletarian Literature*, ed. Norma Field and Heather Bowen-Struyk (Chicago: University of Chicago Press, 2016), 159–71; and Jahani Ramazani, *Poetry and Its Others: News, Prayer, Song, and the Dialogue of Genres* (Chicago: University of Chicago Press, 2013), 75–81. Overall, the scholarship on information in/as literature has expanded too rapidly in the last decade to attempt a comprehensive enumeration of it here. But, in addition to Richards's, two early studies that remain among the finest examples of this subfield are Richard Menke's *Telegraphic Realism* and Alexander Welsh's *George Eliot and Blackmail*, all three of which focus on Victorian-era English literature.

1. "DISTANT READING" AND THE PULL OF LITERARY ABSTRACTION IN NEW CULTURE CHINA

1. Two notable, albeit brief, treatments of information graphics are Tong Lam's discussion of Cai Yuanpei's celebration of a small volume of data visualization and Kate Merkel-Hess's account of the richly complex organizational chart used in Nationalist rural reform during the 1930s. Tong Lam, *A Passion for Facts: Social Surveys and the Construction of the Chinese State, 1900–1949* (Berkeley: University of California Press, 2011), 44–49; Kate Merkel-Hess, *The Rural Modern: Reconstructing the Self and State in Republican China* (Chicago: University of Chicago Press, 2016), 84.

2. Chen Heqin 陳鶴琴, "Tubiaoshi de tongji baogao fa" 圖表式的統計報告法, *Xin jiaoyu* 新教育 8, no. 1 (1924): 46–59.

3. This is the summary definition of Francesca Bray, who follows the opposition of *tu* and writing proposed by the Song dynasty polyhistor Zheng Qiao 鄭樵 (1104–1162). Francesca Bray, "Introduction: The Powers of *Tu*," in *Graphics and Text in the Production of Technical Knowledge in China: The Warp and the Weft*, ed. Francesca Bray, Vera Dorofeeva-Lichtmann, and Georges Métailié (Leiden: Brill, 2007), 1–78.

4. The lecture was transcribed and published in several venues. See *Liang Qichao quanji*, 4045–50. The original appeared in the widely circulating *Chenbao fukan* 晨報副刊, November 28–30, 1922, 1–2. The lecture was then again reprinted in the *Shidi xuebao* 史地學報 2, no. 2 (1923): 1–8.

5. Lam, *Passion for Facts*, 32–34.
6. Wei Juxian, "Yingyong tongjixue de fangfa zhengli guoxue" 應用統計學的方法整理國學, *Dongfang zazhi* 東方雜誌 26, no. 14 (1929): 73–84. Wei Juxian was but one of a larger group of scholars interested in developing historical statistics as a method. In a 1935 review of the field, Yang Chengbo lists half a dozen projects that adopt Liang's method. See "Lishi tongjixue di genben wenti" 歷史統計學地根本問題, *Yanjiu yu pipan* 研究與批判 1, no. 1 (1935): 75–78. The studies surveyed here mainly involve attempts to map the spatial distribution of China's "historical personages" (*lishi renwu* 歷史人物), that is, either successful civil service examinees or simply those figures prominent enough to be included in the mainstream historical record.
7. *Liang Qichao quanji*, 4045.
8. Fernand Braudel, *On History*, trans. Sarah Matthews (Chicago: University of Chicago Press, 1980), 39.
9. Wei Juxian, *Lishi tongjixue* 歷史統計學 (Shanghai: Shangwu yinshuguan, 1934), 15.
10. If we follow along this line, we see the absurdity in Liang's agenda of a set of "comprehensive tables" to be equal in number to the number of dynastic histories themselves: it is like an imperial map that is exactly the size of the empire itself, as caricatured by Jorge Luis Borges in his well-known story "On Exactitude in Science," in *Collected Fictions*, trans. Andrew Hurley (New York: Penguin Books, 1998), 325.
11. Franco Moretti, "Conjectures on World Literature," *New Left Review* 1 (January–February 2000): 57.
12. Franco Moretti, *Graphs, Maps, Trees: Abstract Models for Literary History* (London: Verso, 2005), 4.
13. As with any field, the newness of quantitative cultural study is being challenged. One notable aspect of the recent conversation about digital humanities' prehistory is the diversity of case studies, which range from Russian formalism and Natsume Sōseki's critical work to the nineteenth-century tables of the American educator Elizabeth Peabody. See *Journal of Literary Theory* 13, no. 1 (March 2019), special issue, "Moscow Formalism and Literary History"; Hoyt Long, *The Value of Numbers: Reading Japanese Literature in a Global Information Age* (New York: Columbia University Press, 2021), 19–68; and Lauren Klein et al., "The Shape of History: Reimagining Elizabeth Palmer Peabody's Historical Visualization Work," at http://shapeofhistory.net. Ted Underwood provides a helpful survey of further work in "A Genealogy of Distant Reading," *Digital Humanities Quarterly* 11, no. 2 (2017).
14. Liang himself credits Qing evidentiary scholars such as Gu Donggao 顧棟高 (1679–1759) and his monumental *Chunqiu dashi biao* 春秋大事表 (1748) as already effecting the "spirit of statistical study" (*Liang Qichao quanji*, 4045). For a recent attempt to read China's literary tradition in terms of information, see Chen et al., *Literary Information in China: A History*.
15. Lydia H. Liu, *Translingual Practice*, 235–36.
16. D. W. Y. Kwok, *Scientism in Chinese Thought, 1900–1950* (New Haven, CT: Yale University Press, 1965), 135–60; Lydia H. Liu, "Life as Form: How Biomimesis Encountered Buddhism in Lu Xun," *Journal of Asian Studies* 68, no. 1 (2009): 21–56.
17. Joseph North, *Literary Criticism: A Concise Political History* (Cambridge, MA: Harvard University Press, 2017), 109–16.

18. Especially with the case of the *biao*, these older forms are closely connected to the production of literary knowledge. For an in-depth review of *biao* both in Sima Qian and in archaeological fragments that antedate the *Shiji*, including the *biao*'s materiality, function, and rhetorical appeal, see Griet Vankeerberghen, "The Tables (*Biao*) in Sima Qian's *Shiji*: Rhetoric and Remembrance," in Bray et al., *Graphics and Text*, 293–311; and Michael Nylan, "Mapping Time in the *Shiji* and *Hanshu* Tables 表," *East Asian Science, Technology, and Medicine* 43 (2016): 61–122.

19. See Whitney Battle-Baptiste and Britt Rusert, eds., *W. E. B. Du Bois's Data Portraits Visualizing Black America: The Color Line at the Turn of the Twentieth Century* (New York: Princeton Architectural Press, 2018); Dennis Tenen, "Stalin's Powerpoint," *Modernism/Modernity* 21, no. 1 (2014): 253–67.

20. See Wei-Chih Liou, "An Analysis of Doctoral Dissertations from Chinese Students at Teachers College, Columbia University (1914–1929)," *Bulletin of Educational Research* 59, no. 2 (2013): 1–48.

21. Geraldine Joncich, *The Sane Positivist: A Biography of Edward L. Thorndike* (Middletown, CT: Wesleyan University Press, 1968).

22. Norbert Wiener, *Cybernetics and Society: The Human Use of Human Beings* (Boston: Houghton Mifflin, 1954), 7–12.

23. Joncich, *Sane Positivist*, 282–83, 289, 293; Benoit Godin, "From Eugenics to Scientometrics: Galton, Cattell, and Men of Science," *Social Studies of Science* 37, no. 5 (2007): 691–728.

24. Joncich, *Sane Positivist*, 308.

25. Yurou Zhong, *Chinese Grammatology: Script Revolution and Literary Modernity, 1916–1958* (New York: Columbia University Press, 2019).

26. After further counting and the assimilation of other counts, Thorndike's list was expanded and republished twice, first in 1931 (doubling the original number of words to twenty thousand) and again in 1944 (now with a whopping thirty thousand words). A fuller explication of the project is provided by Thorndike in the *Teachers College Record* 22 (1921): 334–70. Dating back to the nineteenth century, word counting represents one of the oldest methods of quantitative textual analysis. David Masson, in his *British Novelists and Their Styles* (Boston: D. Lothrop & Co., 1875), enumerated novels and novelists to show the expansion of the literary field, in the process explicitly making the case for a statistical approach and datafication of criticism. See Jonathan Farina, "'The New Science of Literary Mensuration': Accounting for Reading, Then and Now," *Victorians Institute Journal Digital Annex*, no. 38 (2010), https://nines.org/exhibits/Literary_Mensuration.

27. Charles Kay Ogden, *The Basic Vocabulary: A Statistical Analysis* (London: Kegan Paul, 1930), 18, 24, 38–41; Charles Kay Ogden, ed., *The System of Basic English* (New York: Harcourt, Brace, 1934), 21–30.

28. Edward Thorndike, *The Teacher's Word Book* (New York: Teachers College, Columbia University, 1921), iii.

29. Thorndike, *Teacher's Word Book*, iv.

30. Chen Heqin, "Yutiwen yingyong zihui: Zihui yanjiu zhi lishi" 語體文應用字彙：字彙研究之歷史, *Xin jiaoyu* 5, no. 5 (1922): 74.

31. Yao-Chiang Chang [Zhang Yaoxiang], "Factors Affecting the Speed and Clearness of Reading Chinese" (MA thesis, Columbia University, 1919), 1.

32. Thomas Mullaney, "Quote Unquote Language Reform: New-Style Punctuation and the Horizontalization of Chinese," *Modern Chinese Literature and Culture* 29, no. 2 (2017): 206–50.

33. Zhang Yaoxiang 張耀翔, ed., *Xinli zazhi xuancun* 心理雜誌選存 (Shanghai: Zhonghua shuju, 1932), 2:679.

34. Zhonghua xinli xuehui 中華心理學會, "Ben zazhi zongzhi" 本雜誌宗旨, *Xinli* 心理 1, no. 1 (1922): 1.

35. See Zhang Yaoxiang, "Zhihui celiang" 智慧測量, *Beijing nügao shi youzhi jiaoyu de yanjiu* 北京女高師幼稚教育的研究 1, no. 1 (1920): 92–97; Zhang Yaoxiang, "Zhihui celiang: Shi gaizao . . ." 智慧測量：是改造, *Jiaoyu congkan* 1, no. 4 (1920): 1–8; Zhang Yaoxiang, "Zhili ceyan: Zhili ceyan yuanqi" 智力測驗：智力測驗緣起, *Xinli* 1, no. 1 (1922): 87–89; Zhang Yaoxiang, "Shizi shiyan" 識字試驗, *Xinli* 1, no. 1 (1922): 113–133; and Liao Shicheng 廖室誠, "Dufa ceyan" 讀法測驗, *Xinli* 1, no. 2 (1922): 1–20.

36. Jingyuan Zhang, *Psychoanalysis in China: Literary Transformations 1919–1949* (Ithaca, NY: Cornell University Press, 1992); Wendy Larson, *From Ah Q to Lei Feng: Freud and Revolutionary Spirit in 20th Century China* (Stanford, CA: Stanford University Press, 2008).

37. Siegen K. Chou, "The Present State of Psychology in China," *American Journal of Psychology* 38, no. 4 (October 1927): 665.

38. See, for example, Tao Deyi 陶德怡, "Shan'e zihui" 善惡字彙, *Xinli* 3, no. 2 (1924): 1–33, and 3, no. 3 (1924): 1–44; and especially the enumerative work by the linguist and society member Chen Heqin, "Yutiwen yingyong zihui: zihui yanjiu zhi lishi" and *Yutiwen yingyong zihui* 語體文應用字彙 (Shanghai: Shangwu yinshuguan, 1928).

39. Zhang Yaoxiang, "Beijing shangdian zhi zhaopai" 北京商店之招牌, *Chenbao liu zhounian zengkan* 晨報六週年增刊, December 1924, 137–44.

40. Zhang Yaoxiang, "Beijing shangdian zhi zhaopai," 138.

41. Zhang Yaoxiang, "Beijing shangdian zhi zhaopai," 144. I thank Gregory Patterson for furnishing the English translation. As a game of making sense out of nonsense, I asked Greg to translate the poem before sharing anything about its origins.

42. Zhang Yaoxiang, *Xinli zazhi xuancun*, 2:771–72.

43. Zhang Yaoxiang, "Zayin" 雜音, *Xinli* 1, no. 2 (1922): 15.

44. Qian Zhongshu, *Limited Views: Essays on Ideas and Letters*, ed. and trans. Ronald Egan (Cambridge, MA: Harvard University Press, 1998), 294.

45. Zhang Yaoxiang, "Zayin," 15.

46. A classmate of Zhang's wife, one Sun Xiangji 孫祥偈, added another twenty-eight noise entries in the following issue of *Xinli*. See her article "Zayin" 雜音, *Xinli* 1, no. 3 (1922): 1–3. On the other projects, see Ouyang Xiang 歐陽湘, "Zase" 雜色, *Xinli* 2, no. 3 (1923): 1–15. Ouyang identified a total of 203 colors. The next issue of *Xinli* (vol. 2, no. 4, 1923: 1–12) carried a supplementary second article by Cheng Junying, who, with her greater knowledge of literature, more than doubled the number of colors by adding 206 further entries. Zhang Yaoxiang, "Wenxuejia zhi xiangxiang" 文學家之想像, *Xinli* 1, no. 3 (1922): 1–20; and Cheng Junying, "Shiren zhi zhuyi ji xingqu" 詩人之注意及興趣, *Xinli* 2, nos. 1 and 2 (1923): 1–30 and 1–32, respectively.

47. Zhang Yaoxiang, "Xinshiren zhi qingxu" 新詩人之情緒, *Xinli* 2, no. 3 (1924): 1–14.

48. Liu, *Translingual Practice*, 94.

49. Lin Chuanding 林傳鼎, *Tang Song yilai sanshisi ge lishi renwu xinli tezhi de guji* 唐宋以來三十四個歷史人物心理特質的估計 (Beijing: Furen daxue xinlixi, 1939).

50. Michelle Yeh, *Modern Chinese Poetry: Theory and Practice Since 1917* (New Haven, CT: Yale University Press, 1991), 23.

51. Yu Pingbo 俞平伯, "Shehui shang duiyu xinshi de gezhong xinliguan" 社會上對於新詩的各種心理觀, *Xinchao* 2, no. 1 (1919): 169.

52. Haiyan Lee, *Revolution of the Heart: A Genealogy of Love in China, 1900–1950* (Stanford, CA: Stanford University Press, 2007), 7.

53. Zhang Yaoxiang, "Xinshiren zhi qingxu," 1.

54. Zhang Yaoxiang, "Qingxu shiyan" 情緒試驗, *Xinli* 1, no. 4 (1922): 1–12.

55. Zhang Yaoxiang, "Xinshiren zhi qingxu," 2.

56. Henry Y. H. Zhao, *The Uneasy Narrator: Chinese Fiction from the Traditional to the Modern* (Oxford: Oxford University Press, 1995), 46–47, 101–15, 230.

57. Zhang Yaoxiang, "Xinshiren zhi qingxu," 2–3.

58. On this point, see John A. Crespi's analysis of Zhang's article within the context of recitational practices and aesthetics in Republican China, in his *Voices in Revolution: Poetry and the Auditory Imagination in Modern China* (Honolulu: University of Hawai'i Press, 2009), 50–51.

59. The list in total: Hu Shi's 胡適 *Changshi ji* 嘗試集 (1920); Kang Baiqing's 康白情 *Cao'er* 草兒 (1921); Yu Pingbo's *Dongye* 冬夜 (1922); Bing Xin's 冰心 *Chunshui* 春水 (1923) and *Fanxing* 繁星 (1923); Zhang Jinfen's 張近芬 *Langhua* 浪花 (1923); Guo Moruo's 郭沫若 *Nüshen* 女神 (1921); and two general collections—*Xinshi nianxuan* 新詩年選 (1922) and *Baihuashi yanjiu ji* 白話詩研究集 (1921).

60. Zhang Yaoxiang, "Xinshiren zhi qingxu," 10–11, 12–13.

61. Crespi, *Voices in Revolution*, 51. His argument that Zhang's article is not also driven by scientific principles does not square with the biography of Zhang that is sketched out here. Although Zhang's methodology is crude and problematic, it is quite clear that he and his cohort saw their work as an important conduit for promoting modern psychological knowledge and the experimental method.

62. This translation is from Stephen Owen, *Readings in Chinese Literary Thought* (Cambridge, MA: Harvard University Press, 1992), 43.

63. Zhang Yaoxiang, "Da moujun chao baihuashi" 答某君嘲白話詩, *Liumei xuesheng jikan* 留美學生季刊 6, no. 1 (1919): 237–38.

64. Lu Xun, "Zailun Leifengta de daodiao" 再論雷峰塔的倒掉, *Yusi* 1, no. 15 (1925): 1.

65. Heinrich, *The Afterlife of Images*, 113–56; Liu, "Life as Form."

66. Zhang Yiping 章衣萍, "Gantan fuhao yu xinshi" 感嘆符號與新詩, *Chenbao fukan*, September 15, 1924, 3–4.

67. Zhang Yaoxiang, "Baihuashi zhong gantanfu" 白話詩中感嘆符, *Chenbao fukan*, September 22, 1924, 2–3.

68. This anecdote comes from a manuscript of interviews undertaken in 1960 by a team of workers at the Shanghai film studio, Tianma, in preparation of a biopic about Lu Xun. Production on the film was canceled in 1963. In 2004, the author Chen Cun 陈村 obtained a portion of the original mimeograph copy of the interviews and put much of the text online. See http://bbs.tianya.cn/post-books-54175-1.shtml.

69. Bray, "Introduction: The Powers of *Tu*," 5; Heinrich, *Afterlife of Images*, 113–47.

70. Wang Xipeng 汪錫鵬, "Xiaoshuo de tujie" 小說的圖解, *Wenyi yuekan* 文藝月刊 6, no. 3 (1934): 16–23.

71. Fu Donghua, "Wenxue zhi jindai yanjiu" 文學之近代研究, *Xiaoshuo yuebao* 小說月報 17, no. 1 (1926): 14–43; Richard Green Moulton, *The Modern Study of Literature* (Chicago: University of Chicago Press, 1915).

72. Yu Dafu 郁達夫, "Jieshao yi ge wenxue de gongshi" 介紹一個文學的公式, *Chenbao fukan: Yilin xunkan* 晨報副刊：藝林旬刊, no. 15 (1925): 3–4. On the original, see Natsume Sōseki 夏目漱石, *Theory of Literature and Other Critical Writings*, ed. and trans. Michael K. Bourdaghs, Atsuko Ueda, and Joseph A. Murphy (New York: Columbia University Press, 2010); and Long's discussion of Sōseki's interest in formulas in his book, *The Values in Numbers*, 19–68.

73. He Yubo 賀玉波, "Xiaoshuo de tujie" 小說的圖解, *Dushu yuekan* 讀書月刊 2 (1931), nos. 4–5: 125.

74. He Yubo, "Xiaoshuo de tujie," 126.

75. He Yubo, "Mao Dun chuangzuo de kaocha" 茅盾創作的考察, *Dushu yuekan* 2, no. 1 (1931): 268.

76. Wang Xipeng, "Xiaoshuo de tujie," 16, 18.

77. Delightfully, one of my book's reviewers observes that an undercurrent to He Yubo's choice of Zhang Ziping's work is that Zhang was known (and in some circles criticized) for a kind of formulaic geometry of his fiction, one expressed as love triangles or other patterns and in telling titles such as "Love's Focal Point" (*Ai zhi jiaodian* 愛之焦點) and "Lopsided Forces" (*Bu pingheng de ouli* 不平衡的偶力).

78. Michael Friendly, "The Golden Age of Statistical Graphics," *Statistical Science* 23, no. 4 (2008): 502–35.

79. Eric Hayot, *On Literary Worlds* (New York: Columbia University Press, 2012), 42–47.

80. Mao Dun 茅盾, *Wo zouguo de daolu* 我走过的道路 (Beijing: Renmin wenxue, 1997), 1:481–82, 490–99.

81. See He Yubo, *Xiandai Zhongguo zuojia lun* 現代中國作家論 (Shanghai: Guanghua shuju, 1932), 2:139.

82. Mao Dun, ed., *Zhongguo de yi ri* 中國的一日 (Shanghai: Shenghuo shudian, 1936); Sherman Cochran and Andrew C. K. Hsieh, ed. and trans., with Janis Cochran, *One Day in China: May 21, 1936* (New Haven, CT: Yale University Press, 1983).

83. Mao Dun, "Bei kaowen le 'Zhongguo de yi ri'" 被考問了《中國的一日》, *Shenghuo xingqikan* 生活星期刊 1, no. 18 (1936), 207, 213.

84. Rosalind Krauss, *Grids: Format and Image in 20th Century Art* (New York: Pace Gallery, 1980), n.p.

85. Krauss, *Grids*, n.p.

86. Boris I. Yarkho, "Speech Distribution in Five-Act Tragedies (A Question of Classicism and Romanticism)," *Journal of Literary Theory* 13, no. 1 ([1935–38] 2019): 13–76.

2. PIERCING THE ROAR OF NUMBERS: MISINFORMATION AND FICTITIOUS CAPITAL IN MAO DUN'S MARKET-THEMED LITERATURE

1. Bi Shutang 畢樹棠, "Shuping: Duojiao guanxi: Mao Dun zuo" 書評：多角關係：茅盾作, *Yuzhou feng* 宇宙風 36 (1936): 73–74.

2. A representative list of Mao Dun's market literature would include famous works such as "Spring Silkworms" ("Chuncan" 春蚕, 1933), "Mr. Zhao Can't Fathom It" ("Zhao Xiansheng xiangbutong" 赵先生想不通, 1934), and "The Lin Family Store" ("Linjia puzi" 林家铺子, 1932), along with some of his less read works, such as the novella *Polygonal Relations, The Story of the First Stage* (*Di yi jieduan de gushi* 第一阶段的故事; 1938, 1945), *Department Store* (an adaptation of Émile Zola's *Au bonheur des dames* [1883]; *Baihuo shangdian* 百貨商店, 1934), "Shanghai" (1935), and the array of shorter essayistic and critical works that supplement *Midnight*.

3. See Jack Burnham, "Systems Aesthetics," in *Networks*, ed. Lars Bang Larsen (Cambridge, MA: MIT Press, [1968] 2014), 42–46.

4. Mao Dun, *Midnight*, trans. Hsu Meng-hsiung (Beijing: Foreign Languages Press, 1979), 33. For the original citation, see *Ziye* 子夜 (Shanghai: Kaiming shuju, 1933), 39. Hereafter citations are in text, with the original Chinese edition followed by the English version. In places I make minor adjustments to the latter for the sake of precision and consistency with pinyin romanization.

5. Founded in November 1920, the exchange was merged with the Chartered Stock and Produce Exchange (Shanghai zhengquan wupin jiaoyisuo 上海證券物品交易所) in 1933 following the Nationalist government's Exchange Law (promulgated in 1929), which mandated the consolidation of redundant exchanges. By 1935 there remained five stock exchanges in Shanghai. In order of descending size following the Merchants Exchange, they were the Chinese Cotton Goods Exchange, the Shanghai Gold Stock Exchange, the Shanghai Flour Stock Exchange, and the Shanghai Provision Exchange. For an overview of the exchanges, see "Shanghai jiaoyisuo zhi faduan yu xianzhuang" 上海交易所之发端与现状 from the 1935 *Shanghai Yearbook* (Shanghai: Municipal Archive, 1992), 341–53. It ought to be noted that Mao Dun's literature concentrates on government bonds rather than corporate stocks. As Liu Zhiying 刘志英 explains in her history of the Merchants Exchange, bond trading dwarfed stock trading during this period; see *Jindai Shanghai Huashang zhengquan shichang yanjiu* 近代上海华商证券市场研究 (Shanghai: Xuelin chubanshe, 2004). Bonds were an integral index of the performance of—and public confidence in—the Nationalist government, as recent economic historians have emphasized. See Felix Boecking and Monika Scholz, "Did the Nationalist Government Manipulate the Chinese Bond Market? A Quantitative Perspective on Short-Term Price Fluctuations of Domestic Government Bonds, 1932–1934," *Frontiers of History in China* 10, no. 1 (2015): 126–44; and Chun-yu Ho and Dan Li, "A Mirror of History: China's Bond Market, 1921–1942," *Economic History Review* 67, no. 2 (2014): 409–34.

6. See *Scenes of City Life* (*Dushi fengguang* 都市風光, dir. Yuan Muzhi 袁牧之, 1935), which features highly stylized (i.e., not on location) scenes of stock trading at 34:20 and 1:24:49. For Liu Xian, see *Ziye zhi tu* 子夜之圖 (Shanghai: Weiming muke she, 1937), 1. Today one widely accessible image of an exchange is the diorama of the floor of the Flour Stock Exchange, on display as part of a permanent exhibit at the Oriental Pearl Tower in Shanghai's Pudong District.

There *were* literary treatments of the speculation during the 1920s. Authors of the popular Saturday Group (*Libailiu pai* 禮拜六派) targeted first the mushrooming of small exchanges across China and then the bursting of a large speculation bubble in 1922 that bankrupted many overeager amateur speculators. See Bryna Goodman, "Things Unheard of East or West: Colonialism, Nationalism, and Cultural

Contamination in Early Chinese Exchanges," in *Twentieth-Century Colonialism and China: Localities, the Everyday, and the World*, ed. Bryna Goodman and David S. G. Goodman (New York: Routledge, 2012), 57–77. Among advocates of the new vernacular style, only members of the Neoperceptionist School (*Xinganjue pai* 新感覺派) took any interest in exchange, celebrating it as a symbol of urban decadence. Mu Shiying discusses Shanghai's financial management schemes in a number of his works; see *Mu Shiying quanji* 穆时英全集 (Beijing: Beijing shiyue wenyi chubanshe, 2008), 1:266–87 and 2:358–434, for instance. A notable episode also appears in Japanese author Yokomitsu Riichi's famous novel *Shanghai*, trans. Dennis Washburn (Ann Arbor: University of Michigan Press, [1935] 2001), 34–35. Another exception to the larger absence during the Republican period is *Jiehun* 結婚, by Shi Tuo 師陀 (Beijing: Huaxia chubanshe, [1947] 2010), 3–120.

7. C. T. Hsia, *A History of Modern Chinese Fiction*, 2nd ed. (New Haven, CT: Yale University Press, 1971), 533–34.

8. Joseph Lau, "Naturalism in Modern Chinese Fiction," *Literature East & West* 12 (1968): 155.

9. David Der-Wei Wang, *Fictional Realism in Twentieth-Century China: Mao Dun, Lao She, Shen Congwen* (New York: Columbia University Press, 1992), 59–66.

10. On the importance of seemingly superfluous details, see Roland Barthes, "The Reality Effect," in *The Rustle of Language*, trans. Richard Howard (Berkeley: University of California Press, 1989), 141–48. Jiwei Xiao provides a fascinating account of this technique in early modern and modern Chinese "detail novels" in *Telling Details: Chinese Fiction, World Literature* (New York: Routledge, 2022).

11. This was the stockbroker Zhang Yu'an 章郁庵 (1901–1940). He and his brother, Zhang Naiqi 章乃器 (1897–1977), a prominent theorist of finance and credit and the founder a credit service bulletin, were influential figures in the finance world of 1930s Shanghai.

12. Mao Dun, *Wo zouguo de daolu* 我走过的道路 (Beijing: Renmin wenxue, 1997), 1:507 (my emphasis).

13. David Wang asks: "If the speculator, by generating money, is a kind of producer, isn't the producer a kind of speculator by modulating his production against the fluctuation of [the] market?" *Fictional Realism*, 64.

14. Mao Dun, *Wo zouguo de daolu*, 1:507.

15. In "Spring Silkworms," the producer, Old Tongbao, has a bumper crop of silkworm cocoons but cannot sell them because, as he finds out too late, that year silk buyers are purchasing only Japanese-style cocoons.

16. I borrow the term from ethnographic work on floor trading. See Daniel Beunza and David Stark, "How to Recognize Opportunities: Heterarchical Search in a Trading Room," in *The Sociology of Financial Markets*, ed. Karin Knorr Cetina and Alex Preda (Oxford: Oxford University Press, 2005), 84–101.

17. My emphasis. See the appendix for the full piece in translation.

18. Marston Anderson, *Limits of Realism: Chinese Fiction in the Revolutionary Period* (Berkeley: University of California Press, 1990), 150.

19. James Beniger, *The Control Revolution: Technological and Economic Origins of the Information Society* (Cambridge, MA: Harvard University Press, 1986), 8.

20. David Novak, "Noise," in *Keywords in Sound*, ed. David Novak and Matt Sakakeeny (Durham, NC: Duke University Press, 2015), 125–38.

21. Noise is now also identified as a general feature of all stock exchanges. See Nicholas A. Knouf, *How Noise Matters to Finance* (Minneapolis: University of Minnesota Press, 2016).

22. This was the classicist literary scholar at Tsinghua University, Wu Mi 吳宓 (1894–1978). Although Wu gave *Midnight* high praise (to Mao Dun's surprise), he called the narrative's weather "contrived," as Mao Dun reminisces in his autobiography, *Wo zouguo de daolu*, 1:523.

23. Although, as we have seen in the previous example, Wu Sunfu himself does not operate on complete information. Here the level of privilege of Liu Yuying's knowledge converges with that of the novel's reader.

24. Anderson, *Limits of Realism*, 148–50.

25. Consider the depiction of the roaring tidal bore at Haining, a sonic metaphor for the coming revolutionary fight by Ye Shengtao 葉聖陶 in *Ni Huanzhi* 霓煥之 (Shanghai: Kaiming shuju, 1978), 281, as well as the allusion to this scene in experimental representations of mass voice and urban noise in Ding Ling's novella *Eventful Autumn* (*Duo shi zhi qiu* 多事之秋), which I address in chapter 3. See Yeh Shengtao, *Schoolmaster Ni Huan-chih*, trans. A. C. Barnes (Beijing: Foreign Languages Press, 1978); as well as Charles Laughlin, "Narrative Subjectivity and the Production of Social Space in Chinese Reportage," *boundary 2* 25, no. 3 (1998): 25–46. Mass noise also featured prominently in early sound film, for example *Children of Troubled Times* (*Fengyun ernü* 風雲兒女, dir. Xu Xingzhi 許幸之, 1935), as well as in leftist woodcut art, per Xiaobing Tang, *The Origins of the Chinese Avant-Garde: The Modern Woodcut Movement* (Berkeley: University of California Press, 2008).

26. Mao Dun, *Spring Silkworms and Other Stories*, trans. Sidney Shapiro (Beijing: Foreign Languages Press, 1979), 183.

27. This point is demonstrated by Mary Poovey's magisterial study of early modern English novel in *Genres of the Credit Economy: Mediating Value in Eighteenth- and Nineteenth-Century Britain* (Chicago: University of Chicago Press, 2008).

28. Lydia H. Liu, *Translingual Practice: Literature, National Culture, and Translated Modernity—China, 1900–1938* (Stanford, CA: Stanford University Press, 1995), 116 (emphasis in original). In *Limits of Realism*, Marston Anderson makes a related observation about realist literature of the period in general: "Reading the oeuvre of any of the major Chinese realists of the 1920s or 1930s, one is struck by their high degree of formal self-consciousness. Again and again authors introduce frankly reflexive elements into their work, often in the form of authorial alter egos or ironical foregrounding of the very techniques that identify their works as realist" (7).

29. Mao Dun, *Mao Dun quanji* 茅盾全集 (Beijing: Renmin wenxue chubanshe, 1984–2006), 16:372–74.

30. *Mao Dun quanji*, 16:373.

31. The term "figuration" or "visualization" was introduced as a critical word in Geng Jizhi's 耿濟之 translation of an essay by the Russian scholar L. Timofeyev. See "Zenyang chuangzao wenxue de xingxiang" 怎樣創造文學的形象, *Wenxue* 7, no. 2 (1936): 406–16.

32. *Mao Dun quanji*, 11:327–31.

33. Joseph Dennis, *Writing, Publishing, and Reading Local Gazetteers in Imperial China, 1100–1700* (Cambridge, MA: Harvard University Press, 2015), 3.

34. Notable as an atypical usage of *xiaoxi* to mean information in the sense of historical data, rather than as a bit of current news.
35. *Mao Dun quanji*, 11:328.
36. *Mao Dun quanji*, 11:484–489. See Robert Gardella, "Squaring Accounts: Commercial Bookkeeping Methods and Capitalist Rationalism in Late Qing and Republican China," *Journal of Asian Studies* 51, no. 2 (1992): 317–39.
37. *Mao Dun quanji*, 18:220–40.
38. A traditional style of accounting, the four-column method was widely employed by both family operations and the state since at least the late Tang (ca. 900–950) and still widely in use in the 1920s and 1930s, where it coexisted alongside Western methods of double-entry bookkeeping that had been introduced in the 1900s and 1910s. As Robert Gardella notes in his review of late imperial history of accounting, the four-column method was the basis of state accounting through the Qing dynasty and so called because of its four categories of noting receipts and disbursements: balance forwarded, new receipts, outlays, and present balance ("Squaring Accounts," 323–24). Even relatively simple accounting systems (including the four-column account) would track both short-term profits and losses and long-term movement of a business's value based on the difference between its stock/capital and its claims.
39. *Mao Dun quanji*, 18:226. Here Mao Dun takes aim at the long-standing literary and historiographical practice of meting out praise and blame such that a perceptive reader can calculate in advance the ending of every character in the narrative. Cf. Chu Renhuo's preface to his *Romance of the Sui and Tang* (1695), as discussed by Robert Hegel, "*Sui T'ang Yen-I* and the Aesthetics of the Seventeenth-Century Suchou Elite," in *Chinese Narrative: Critical and Theoretical Essays*, ed. Andrew Plaks (Princeton, NJ: Princeton University Press, 1977), 137–38.
40. *Mao Dun quanji*, 18:227–28.
41. Erich Auerbach, *Mimesis: The Representation of Reality in Western Literature*, trans. Willard R. Trask (Princeton, NJ: Princeton University Press, 1953), 3–23.
42. *Mao Dun quanji*, 4:1–117. *Midnight* closes with Wu Sunfu preparing to leave Shanghai for Guling and escape the fallout of his unsuccessful speculation gambit. In *Polygonal Relations*, the wealthy magnate Tang Zijia has just returned to his hometown to temporarily flee his debtors in Shanghai. Like Wu, Tang Zijia is a patriotic capitalist who at once draws on hometown assets (rental income, a pawnshop, etc.) and his silk factory to speculate as a bear in Shanghai's stock markets. The similarities between Wu and Tang, as well as the dovetailing between plots, did not escape the attention of contemporary critics. See Yu Lie 余列, "Shuping: Duojiao guanxi: Mao Dun zuo" 書評：多角關係：茅盾作, *Qinghua zhoukan* 清華週刊 45, nos. 10–11 (1936): 102–5.
43. See Hong Xuecun 洪雪邨, "Guanyu 'Duojiao guanxi'" 關於"多角關係," *Chuangjin yuekan* 創近月刊 3, no. 8 (1936): 67–70. Hong observes that since the publication of *Midnight*, all of Mao Dun's works had dealt with the financial crisis and economic depression. Picking up on the narrative's synchronic, networked structure, Hong likens Mao Dun's deftness in describing the characters' social connections to a "weaver who takes a bale of hemp floss and weaves out of it a bolt of cloth."
44. The title also gestures to the sexual relations between individuals from two families. But this dimension is only developed by the narrative insofar as it augments

the asymmetrical power relations between creditor and debtor structuring the story's social relations.

45. Tomoko Shiroyama, *China During the Great Depression: Market, State, and the World Economy, 1929–1937* (Cambridge, MA: Harvard University Press, 2008), 140–67.

46. *Mao Dun quanji*, 4:48.

47. *Mao Dun quanji*, 4:9–10, 4:16. The quotation is at 4:9.

48. *Mao Dun quanji*, 4:13, 4:28.

49. *Mao Dun quanji*, 4:13, 4:58–59, 4:78.

50. *Mao Dun quanji*, 4:104.

51. *Mao Dun quanji*, 4:104.

52. "Because the ledger does not initiate the incomes and outgoes (paying a debt, receiving income) it records, it is a *de facto* trace of a 'real world' event that has already occurred. The ledger . . . is a social order in which traces of real action simultaneously come to be represented and stand in for economic actions." Rekha Rosha, "Accounting Capital, Race and Benjamin Franklin's 'Pecuniary Habits' of Mind in *The Autobiography*," in *Culture, Capital and Representation*, ed. Robert J. Balfour (London: Palgrave, 2010), 41.

53. *Mao Dun quanji*, 4:29, 4:61, 4:114–16.

54. One need look no further than the major land reform novels such as Ding Ling's *The Sun Shines Over the Sanggan River* (*Taiyang zhao zai Sangganhe shang* 太陽照在桑干河上, 1948) and Zhao Shuli's 赵树理 *Sanliwan Village* (*Sanliwan* 三里湾, 1955), both of which prominently feature discourses of social-moral calculation.

55. Anderson, *Limits of Realism*, 17.

3. RIPPLE EFFECTS: ETHER AND THE INFORMATION ORDER DURING THE PROPAGANDA ERA

1. On speech-giving as a modern form of political participation, see David Strand, *An Unfinished Republic: Leading by Word and Deed in Modern China* (Berkeley: University of California Press, 2011).

2. Tie Xiao, *Revolutionary Waves: The Crowd in Modern China* (Cambridge, MA: Harvard University Press, 2017).

3. The problem of mass address is dealt with in a notably different way in a slightly later novel, *Electric World* (*Dian shiji* 電世界), a science fantasy story by an anonymous author in which a godlike inventor, the Electricity King, addresses a gathering of several tens of thousands of his subjects by using an electric amplification tube (*chuanyintong* 傳音筒; 55). In a separate episode, for the sake of implementing mass education, the King invents a two-way, radial telephone network that allows an instructor to remotely interact with hundreds of students in a kind of virtual classroom (24). See *Xiaoshuo shibao* 小說時報 1, no. 1 (1909): 1–58.

4. Xiaobing Tang with Michel Hockx, "The Creation Society (1921–1930)," in *Literary Societies of Republican China*, ed. Kirk A. Denton and Michel Hockx (Lanham, MD: Lexington Books, 2008), 122. I have adjusted the translation for precision. The original passage appears in Guo Moruo zhuzuo bianji chuban weiyuanhui 郭沫若著

作编辑出版委员会, ed., *Guo Moruo quanji* 郭沫若全集 (Beijing: Xinhua shudian, 1992), 13:167.

5. *Guo Moruo quanji*, 13:167.

6. For the etymology of the two characters that make up the compound word *xuan-chuan*, see Shao Peiren 邵培仁, ed., *Xuanchuanxue he yulunxue* 宣传学和舆论学 (Shanghai: Fudan daxue chubanshe, 2002), 30–31, as well as Sun Xupei 孙旭培, *Huaxia chuanbolun* 华夏传播论 (Beijing: Renmin chubanshe, 1997), 23. *Xuan* 宣 originally referred to a room (*xuanshi* 宣室) at the imperial palace and appears already in Shang-era texts. Because this room was a place where air could circulate, it came to metaphorically denote the transformation of something small into something large (*you xiao bian da* 由小變大). By the Han period, *xuan* became a metonym for the emperor's proclamations, which naturally were to be disseminated. The etymology of *chuan* 傳 is equally old and, given its importance to the discursive history of communication in China, deserves some attention here. The second-century dictionary, *Shuowen jiezi* 說文解字, glosses the character as *ren* 人 and *zhuan* 專, with the latter specifically denoting the spool of a spinner and by extension meaning to turn or spin (as in the related verb, *zhuan* 轉). The *Shishuqi* 釋書契 section of the *Shiming* 釋名, a dictionary from circa 200 CE, provides the following gloss for *chuan*: "That with which something is transmitted, and held as proof/evidence [of such transmission]" 轉移所在執以為信也. However, Shao Peiren argues, in early texts *chuan* appears most often in the compound *chuanche* 傳車, a chariot or vehicle used to travel between relay stations (*yizhan* 驛站). *Chuan*'s secondary meaning, pronounced as *zhuan*, is also notable: it means to transmit or, by extension, an individual's "biography" or "records." The etymologies of *xuan* and *chuan* thus offer one expedient entry into the long history of political communication in China.

7. Kirk A. Denton, ed., *Modern Chinese Literary Thought: Writings on Literature, 1893–1945* (Stanford, CA: Stanford University Press, 1996), 74.

8. John Fitzgerald, *Awakening China: Politics, Culture, and Class in the Nationalist Revolution* (Stanford, CA: Stanford University Press, 1996), 197–213.

9. The document is reprinted in Zhongguo Shehui kexue yuan xinwen yanjiusuo 中国社会科学院新闻研究所, ed., *Zhongguo Gongchandang xinwen gongzuo wenjian huibian* 中国共产党新闻工作文件汇编 (Beijing: Xinhua chubanshe, 1980), 1:6–7. Another useful resource is Xu Dongping 徐东平, ed., *Shiyong xuanchuanxue cidian* 实用宣传学辞典 (Anhui: Anhui renmin chubanshe, 1989).

10. For a good review of debates among critics and writers of the time, see Kirk Denton's introduction to *Modern Chinese Literary Thought*, 44–49. Although my focus is on literature and woodcut images, these were certainly not the only media of leftist experimentation with propaganda. For a discussion of the Communist Party's cooptation of traditional popular culture, see David Holm, *Art and Ideology in Revolutionary China* (Oxford: Clarendon Press, 1991), and Chang-tai Hung, *War and Popular Culture: Resistance in Modern China, 1937–1945* (Berkeley: University of California Press, 1994). The latter offers a compelling survey of how both Nationalists and Communists during the Second Sino-Japanese War used folk songs, drum singing, and storytelling to "create new channels for the dissemination of information . . . [and] activate an unprecedented, ambitious propaganda campaign aimed at mobilizing every citizen and utilizing every resource in the country" (3).

11. In Mao Dun, *Wo zouguo de daolu* (Beijing: Renmin wenxue, 1997), 1:359–81.

12. The distinction between integration and agitation propaganda is drawn from the classic work of Jacques Ellul. See *Propaganda: The Formation of Men's Attitude*, trans. Konrad Kellen and Lean Lerner (New York: Vintage Books, 1973), 70–79.

13. Sa Mengwu 薩孟武 and Lin Yimin 林懿民, "Xuanchuan zhi lilun ji qi shiji" 宣傳之理論及其實際, *Duli qingnian* 獨立青年 1, no. 3 (March 1926): 13–17. Sa was a rightist who was opposed to the increasing influence of the Communist faction within the GMD, and in 1927 he joined the GMD's Ministry of Politics' propaganda department.

14. Mao Zedong, *Selected Works of Mao Tse-tung*, vol. 1 (Beijing: Foreign Languages Press, 1967).

15. See Shao's recapitulation of the document, *Xuanchuanxue he yulunxue*, 7. John Fitzgerald also offers an in-depth discussion of the GMD Central Propaganda Bureau's internecine struggles in 1925–1926, which, under the leadership of Mao Zedong, increasingly engaged in attacks with "counterrevolutionary" factions (*Awakening China*, 252–53).

16. Fitzgerald, *Awakening China*, 3.

17. On GMD censorship, particularly relating to literary production, see Michel Hockx, *Questions of Style: Literary Societies and Literary Journals in Modern China, 1911–1937* (Leiden: Brill, 2002), ch. 7; Lee-hsia Hsu Ting, *Government Control of the Press in Modern China, 1900–1949* (Cambridge, MA: Harvard University Press, 1974); and San Mu 散木, *Yu wusheng chu ting jinglei: Lu Xun yu wenwang* 于无声处听惊雷:鲁迅与文网 (Nanchang: Baihuazhou wenyi chubanshe, 2002).

18. On the conceptualization of propagation as a communications problem, see also Fitzgerald, *Awakening China*, 21. Carol Gluck offers a parallel case in her study of nationalist ideology in Meiji Japan. See *Japan's Modern Myths: Ideology in the Late Meiji Period* (Princeton, NJ: Princeton University Press, 1985), 10–12. Both Fitzgerald and Gluck mention "noise" as a reminder that the state propaganda apparatus was never totally unified but instead comprised competing voices. It goes without saying that the issue of noise extended beyond factional and intra-institutional propagation to the communication strategies of rival parties.

19. Xu Yi 徐怡, *Xuanchuanshu yu qunzhong yundong* 宣傳術與群眾運動 (Shanghai: Zhonghua shuju, 1931), 4–11.

20. One influential example is the work of an early communications expert, Harold D. Lasswell, *Propaganda Technique in the World War* (New York: Peter Smith, 1927). In the 1930s, Lasswell directed the Social Science Research Council's module on "Pressure Groups and Propaganda," which resulted in a voluminous and translingual bibliography of contemporary propaganda studies. See Lasswell, ed., *Propaganda and Promotional Activities: An Annotated Bibliography* (Minneapolis: University of Minnesota Press, 1935).

21. A representative list of relevant works includes Ji Da 季達, *Xuanchuanxue yu xinwen jizhe* 宣傳學與新聞記者 (Jinan: Jinan daxue wenhuabu, 1932); Zhang Zhizhong 張致中, "Xinwen zhanzheng yu *Propaganda*" 新聞戰爭與 *Propaganda*, *Liudong xuebao* 留東學報 2, no. 2 (1936): 95–100; Mu Chao 穆超, *Feichang shiqi de xuanchuan zhengce* 非常時期的宣傳政策 (n.p.: Zhengzhong shuju, 1938); Ren Baitao 任白濤, *Riben dui Hua de xuanchuan zhengce* 日本對華的宣傳政策 (Changsha: Shangwu yinshuguan 1940); Huabei Zhengwu Weiyuanhui 華北政務委員會, *Xuanchuan jishu* 宣傳技術 (n.p.: Huabei zhengwu weiyuanhui zongwu ting qingbao ju, 1944); Wang Yizhi

王一之, *Zonghe xuanchuanxue* 綜合宣傳學 (Chongqing: Guomin tushu chubanshe, 1944); and Sa Kongliao 薩空了, *Xuanchuan xinli yanjiu* 宣傳心理研究 (Shanghai: Gengyun chubanshe, 1948). The last is a translation of Amber Blanco White's *The New Propaganda* (1939), an influential text in China during the war period.

22. *Xuanchuan zhan* 宣傳戰 (Beijing: Guomindang lujun daxuexiao, 1931), hereafter cited in text. Recently the book has been reprinted, see *Xuanchuan zhan* 宣传战 (Beijing: Beijing guotu shudian, 2010). In his survey of propaganda scholarship from the 1930s and 1940s, Liu Zixiong 刘自雄 ranks this work as the most systematic and substantive. "Lun woguo xiandai xuanchuan yanjiu de di yi bo gaochao" 论我国现代宣传研究的第一波高潮, *Sichuan ligong xueyuan xuebao* 四川理工学院学报 23, no. 4 (August 2008): 7–10.

23. On the indigenization of modern propaganda as a long-standing Chinese practice, see Dai Jingsu 戴景素, ed., *Zhongguo xuanchuan wenxuan* 中國宣傳文選 (Chongqing: Shangwu yinshuguan, 1939). In selecting classic and seminal propaganda documents from China's tradition, Dai begins with the famous Tang Proclamation (*Tang shi* 湯誓), Shang Tang's exhortation to overthrow the Xia ruler, Xia Jie 夏桀, ca. 1600 BCE, and chronologically moves forward from antiquity to early imperial China and into the Republican period, spanning a total of twenty-nine texts.

24. Michael North, *Reading 1922: A Return to the Scene of the Modern* (New York: Oxford University Press, 1999), 126.

25. Chen sets this definition in opposition to contemporary Soviet practices of agitprop, which he sees as limited to extraordinary circumstances (such as incitation) rather than appealing to the totality of the senses/faculties (*quanbu guanneng* 全部官能).

26. The arrow metaphor parallels the formulation of Mao Zedong—which itself draws from Mencius—that propaganda should "drawing the bow without shooting, [and instead] just indicate the motions" (that is, lead the masses to a revolutionary consciousness without mandating their actions directly). From Mao Zedong, *Selected Works*, 1:46.

27. Notably, Chen excludes film, a curious omission given how important cinema was as a propagation tool in Britain, America, and, increasingly, in China. See Matthew David Johnson, "International and Wartime Origins of the Propaganda State: The Motion Picture in China, 1897–1955" (PhD diss., University of California San Diego, 2008). See also Weihong Bao's discussion of propaganda film theory in the late 1930s in her article, "'A Vibrating Art in the Air': Cinema, Ether, and Propaganda Film Theory in Wartime Chongqing," *New German Critique* 41, no. 2 (Summer 2014): 171–88.

28. For an exploration of the translingual dimensions of "ether" in Tan's masterwork, *Renxue*, see David Wright, "Tan Sitong and the Ether Reconsidered," *Bulletin of the School of Oriental and African Studies* 57, no. 3 (1994): 551–75. See also David Derwei Wang, *Fin-de-Siècle Splendor: Repressed Modernities of Late Qing Fiction, 1849–1911* (Stanford, CA: Stanford University Press, 1997), 279.

29. Peng Leshan 彭樂善, *Guangbo zhan* 廣播站 (Chongqing: Zhongguo bianyi chubanshe, 1943), 1. Besides building on Chen's work, Peng relies on a wide range of American and British source materials that he had read in English.

30. Bao, "A Vibrating Art in the Air," 186 (emphasis in original). See also Weihong Bao, *Fiery Cinema: The Emergence of an Affective Medium in China, 1915–1945* (Minneapolis: University of Minnesota Press, 2015), 7–9.

31. See Bao, "A Vibrating Art in the Air," 186.

32. See Yun Zhen 惲震 and Wang Chongzhi 王崇植's comprehensive study of China's place in world wireless communications sovereignty (*tongxun zhuquan* 通訊主權), *Wuxiandian yu Zhongguo* 無線電與中國 (Shanghai: Wenrui yinshuguan, 1931). Yun and Wang argue that the era of wired communications dominated by the British Empire and its "imperial chain" (*diguo wang* 帝國網; original in English) is coming to an end as the telegraph's power is outpaced by wireless communications such as radiotelegraphy. Their interest in radiotelegraphy leads to a discussion of the "world wireless telegraphy network" (*shijie wuxiandian tongxin wang* 世界無線電通信網) (42), though they ultimately see radio as primarily a broadcast medium that harnesses the global sphere of "ether" (52). Yun and Wang's list of the uses of radio includes broadcasting information, international communication, land-to-sea and land-to-air communications, domestic industry, and colonial administration (79). On the issues of modern communications sovereignty and empire in Japan at the time, see Daqing Yang, *Technology of Empire: Telecommunications and Japanese Expansion in Asia, 1883–1945* (Cambridge, MA: Harvard University Press, 2011). And, from a Korean perspective, see Michael Robinson, "Broadcasting, Cultural Hegemony, and Colonial Modernity in Korea, 1924–1945," in *Colonial Modernity in Korea*, ed. Gi-Wook Shin and Michael Robinson (Cambridge, MA: Harvard University Press, 1999).

33. Film trumped radio in one important way: the latter relied on spoken language and thus ran up against linguistic barriers, particularly among the listenership in the Chinese hinterlands. This problem emerged in cinema too with the rise of talkies in the mid-1930s. On the universal visual language of film and the search to redeem the language of talkies, see Weihong Bao, "In Search of a 'Cinematic Esperanto': Exhibiting Wartime Chongqing Cinema in a Global Context," *Journal of Chinese Cinemas* 3, no. 2 (2009): 135–47.

34. John Alekna, *Seeking News, Making China: Information, Technology, and the Emergence of Mass Society* (Stanford, CA: Stanford University Press, 2024).

35. Laura DiGiorgi, "Communication Technology and Mass Propaganda in Republican China: The Nationalist Party's Radio Broadcast Policy and Organisation during the Nanjing Decade (1927–1937)," *European Journal of East Asian Studies* 13, no. 2 (2014): 305–29.

36. Federica Ferlanti, "The New Life Movement in Jiangxi, 1934–1938," *Modern Asia Studies* 44, no. 5 (2010): 961–1,000.

37. Chiang Kai-shek, "The Object of a New Life Movement," in *Sources of Chinese Tradition*, ed. Wm. Theodore de Bary (New York: Columbia University Press, 1960), 801.

38. Alekna, *Seeking News, Making China*, 99–100.

39. On the viability of wireless communication to surpass older infrastructures, see Yun and Wang, *Zhongguo yu wuxiandian*, 81.

40. Achieving a standardized and centralized way to discipline bodies remained a fantasy of mass media advocates. In reality the construction of new modes of "cultural citizenship" varied widely between regions and institutions, representing a plurality of political views among citizen groups (e.g., schoolteachers) even in places under heavy influence of the Nationalists (such as in Zhejiang, near Nanjing). See Robert Culp, "Rethinking Governmentality: Training, Cultivation, and

Cultural Citizenship in Nationalist China," *Journal of Asian Studies* 65, no. 3 (2006): 529–54. The illusoriness of remote social control via propaganda and broadcast media is precisely Shen Congwen's point in *Long River*, as we will see in the next chapter.

41. *Broadcast Weekly* was by no means the only radio-related publication produced by the GMD. It was preceded by *Radio Monthly* (*Wuxiandian yuebao* 無線電月報, 1928) and *Radio Bi-Monthly* (*Wuxiandian xinbao* 無線電新報, 1929) and later joined by a host of other official publications, including *Wireless* (*Wuxiandian* 無線電, 1934–1937), *Receiver Periodical* (*Shouyin qikan* 收音期刊; 1935), *Radiowave* (*Wuxiandianbo* 無線電波, 1935–1936), *Radio Broadcast Weekly* (*Dianyin boyin zhoukan* 電音播音週刊, 1935–1936), as well as by a host of commercial journals. In contrast to its relatively short-lived counterparts, *Broadcast Weekly*'s long print run underscores its status as the preeminent official journal.

42. As Peng Leshan mentions, by the early 1940s the signal of the GMD central radio station signal was strong enough to clearly reach the occupied areas of northeastern China, as well as Taiwan, Korea, Japan, the Dutch East Indies, New Zealand, Hawai'i, and, on certain days, even North America. Peng, *Guangbo zhan*, 25.

43. See Mark Wollaeger's *Modernism, Media, and Propaganda: British Narrative from 1900 to 1945* (Princeton, NJ: Princeton University Press, 2006).

44. Fitzgerald, *Awakening China*, 95–97.

45. See Qian's contemporary polemic, "Guanyu 'Ping *Duankudang*'" 關於"評短褲黨," *Taiyang yuekan* 太陽月刊, no. 2 (1928).

46. Mao Dun, "On Reading *Ni Huanzhi*," trans. Yu-shih Chen, in Denton, ed., *Modern Chinese Literary Thought*, 300.

47. "It will not do to write fiction in the enthusiastic style of mass meeting agitation. One who prepares to devote himself to the new art and literature must first have a head for organization, judgment, observation, and analysis; it is not enough to be equipped with a trumpet that will serve to transmit one's voice. One must first be able to analyze by oneself the mixed noises of the masses and quietly listen to the dripping of the underground spring, and then structure these into the consciousness of fictional characters." Mao Dun, "On Reading *Ni Huanzhi*," 301.

48. As with propaganda discourse more generally, a Manichean logic is at work here: only three months after the League formed and announced its agenda of promoting social change and leading the way for the development of proletarian literature (*puluo wenxue* 普羅文學), the GMD formed a literary countermovement promoting "nationalist literature" (*minzuzhuyi wenxue* 民族主義文學). The feedback loop between these ideologically opposed camps helped precipitate a very active (and acerbic) publication atmosphere, characterized in particular by dueling *zawen* (雜文, "miscellaneous essays").

49. Marston Anderson, *The Limits of Realism*, 182 (my emphasis). Besides Anderson, see also Tie Xiao, *Revolutionary Waves*.

50. On this episode, see Wang-chi Wong, *Politics and Literature in Shanghai* (Manchester: Manchester University Press, 1991), 100–112. See Leo Ou-fan Lee, *The Romantic Generation of Modern Chinese Writers* (Cambridge, MA: Harvard University Press, 1973), 263. See also Tani Barlow, "Introduction," in *I Myself Am a Woman: Selected Writings of Ding Ling*, ed. Tani Barlow with Gary Bjorge (Boston: Beacon Press, 1989), 1–46.

51. On this transition, see Barlow, "Introduction," 29–34, as well as Xiaobing Tang, *Chinese Modern: The Heroic and the Quotidian* (Durham, NC: Duke University Press, 2000), ch. 3. Tang ascribes Ding Ling's turn toward propaganda to the general politicization of writing in Shanghai during the period. While I agree with Tang's perceptive analysis of the reworking of the corporeal body in Ding's fiction, I would argue that the sort of mobilization that Tang discusses is just as much about ethereality and immateriality (and the informatic) as it is about the body. In short, mobilization is an act of communication. On Ding's transformation, see also Meng Yue 孟悦 and Dai Jinhua 戴锦华, *Fuchu lishi dibiao: Xiandai funü wenxue yanjiu* 浮出历史地表：现代妇女文学研究 (Zhengzhou: Henan renmin chubanshe, 1993), 126; Tsi-an Hsia, *Gate of Darkness: Studies on the Leftist Literary Movement in China* (Seattle: University of Washington Press, 1968); Yi-tsi Mei Feuerwerker, *Ding Ling's Fiction: Ideology and Narrative in Modern Chinese Literature* (Cambridge, MA: Harvard University Press, 1982).

52. Here I have significantly altered the extant translations. Both the original English translation and Tang's adjustment fail to capture the original construction, where the subject of the final clause is information itself: 這裡有許多消息都攢集到他腦中了 (267). Interestingly, the narrative embeds a commentary on news sources in contemporary Shanghai: Wangwei was "most interested in *Western Newsworld* [*Zilin xibao* 字林西報], because its information [*xiaoxi*] was more accurate than the major Chinese newspapers," and faster and more detailed (*lingtong xunsu* 靈通迅速) than that of smaller papers, with quite a bit of touching news (*xiaoxi*, again).

53. See Tang, *Chinese Modern*, 113–62.

54. For a biographical treatment of Ding Ling during this period, see Charles J. Alber, *Enduring the Revolution: Ding Ling and the Politics of Literature in Guomindang China* (Westport, CT: Praeger, 2002).

55. Feng's "New Fiction" (*xin de xiaoshuo* 新的小說) should not be confused with the prior category of "new fiction" (*xin xiaoshuo* 新小說). For Feng and other leftist writers, the older category (along with the New Culture movement more generally) had proven inadequate to the task of promoting a revolution and was thus in need of replacing. I henceforth capitalize New Fiction when referring to the Feng's concept.

56. *Beidou* 北斗 2, no. 1 (1932): 240–44. Of course, Feng's comments also fit within the larger contemporary debate on the formation of "mass literature" (*dazhong wenxue* 大眾文學) or proletarian literature that took as its focus the proletariat rather than the petit-bourgeois class. It should also be noted that New Fiction's attempt to portray the masses as a literary protagonist by no means stands as the first attempt in Chinese literature to disperse narrative focalization across a wide variety of characters. As Yiheng Zhao points out, such scattered focalization was common in traditional vernacular novels and even definitive of more modern stories such as Lu Xun's "A Public Example" (*Shizhong* 示眾). See Henry Y. H. Zhao, *The Uneasy Narrator: Chinese Fiction from the Traditional to the Modern* (Oxford: Oxford University Press, 1995), 98–99.

57. The story was partly translated into English by Agnes Smedley in 1932 as part of a broader campaign to mobilize Western readers to put pressure on the GMD for jailing Ding Ling. On Smedley and company, see Richard Jean So, *Transpacific Community: America, China, and the Rise and Fall of a Cultural Network* (New York: Columbia University Press, 2016), 1–40.

58. See Agnes Smedley's adapted and abbreviated translation, "The Flood," *Asia Magazine* (October 1935): 634.
59. My translation. From *Beidou* 1, no. 3 (1932): 71.
60. *Ding Ling lun chuangzuo* 丁玲论创作 (Shanghai: Shanghai wenyi chubanshe, 1985), 99–102. Ding characterizes the fragment as the "failure of a great dream."
61. *Beidou* 2, no. 1 (January 20, 1932): 25–37, and nos. 3–4 (July 20, 1932): 153–166, 516–529. The journal was discontinued after issue 3–4 due to tightening GMD censorship. Ding Ling published the story under the pseudonym Binzhi 彬芷. Subsequent citations are given in text, with issue number followed by page number.
62. See Linda Dalrymple Henderson, "Vibratory Modernism: Boccioni, Kupka, and the Ether of Space," in *From Energy to Information: Representation in Science and Technology, Art, and Literature*, ed. Bruce Clarke and Linda Dalrymple Henderson (Stanford, CA: Stanford University Press, 2002), 126–48. See also the collection of essays in Anthony Enns and Shelley Trower, eds., *Vibratory Modernism* (London: Palgrave Macmillan, 2013). The aural nature of Ding's story also places it in the lineage of late imperial Chinese oral storytelling explored by Paize Keulemans in his *Sound Rising from the Paper: Nineteenth-Century Martial Arts Fiction and the Chinese Acoustic Imagination* (Cambridge, MA: Harvard University Press, 2014); but Ding's modernism imparts the movement of sound and the general soundscape with the distinctive shape of radial expansion or broadcast.
63. See Charles A. Laughlin, "Narrative Subjectivity and the Production of Social Space in Chinese Reportage," *boundary 2* 25, no. 3 (1998): 25–46.
64. This is a clear allusion to a famous scene in chapter 24 of Ye Shengtao's *Ni Huanzhi*, which likens mass politics to the roar of the tide: "the thunderous roar that jarred the eardrums and made the heart quiver . . . is just what the state of mind of people in Shanghai is like at this present moment. No matter who he may be, provided only that he is in Shanghai at the present moment, he must already have heard that thunderous roar and in consequence harbouring a mysterious feeling of extreme tension." From *Schoolmaster Ni Huan-chih*, 281.
65. Or, as Ellul puts it, "information not only provides the basis for propaganda but gives propaganda the means to operate; for information actually generates the problems that propaganda exploits and for which it pretends to offer solutions." Ellul, *Propaganda*, 63.
66. *Wenxue yuebao* 文學月報 1, no. 2 (1932): 33–38. Because the story is so short, I do not give page citations.
67. For example, the publication of a Kathe Kollwitz print in the first issue of *Big Dipper* in 1931. See Xiaobing Tang, *The Origins of the Chinese Avant-Garde*, 110.
68. Julia F. Andrews and Kuiyi Shen, "The Modern Woodcut Movement," in their co-edited volume, *A Century in Crisis: Modernity and Tradition in the Art of Twentieth Century China* (New York: Guggenheim Museum, 1998), 213–25, 230. See also Andrews's description of the emergence of the modern woodcut through the lens of one artist, Jiang Feng, in Andrews, *Painters and Politics in the People's Republic of China, 1949–1979* (Berkeley: University of California Press, 1994), 12–27.
69. On Lu Xun's early promotion of woodcut in his four-volume series, *Banhua jicheng* 版畫集成, see Tang, *Origins of the Chinese Avant-Garde*, ch. 3.
70. Andrews and Shen, "The Modern Woodcut Movement," 213. See also Xiao, "In the Name of the Masses," ch. 4.

71. See Ellen Johnston Laing, "Reform, Revolutionary, Political, and Resistance Themes in Chinese Popular Prints, 1900–1940," in *Modern Chinese Literature and Culture* 12, no. 2 (Fall 2000), 123–75. Laing synthesizes recent Chinese research to examine how traditional (and popular) imagery, via media of woodblock prints and modern lithography, was put into the service of spreading political messages first in the late Qing and again in the early years of the Republic. For an abbreviated survey of visual forms of propaganda in premodern China, see the introductory chapter to Stefan Landsberger, *Chinese Propaganda Posters: From Revolution to Modernization* (Armonk, NY: M. E. Sharpe, 1995), 18–24.

72. See Tang, *Origins of the Chinese Avant-Garde*, 102–3, for the formation of the Mei-lian and its connection to the League of Left-wing Writers and Shanghai artist collectives.

73. Quoted from Wang Xinqi, *Lu Xun meishu nianpu* 鲁迅美术年谱 (Guangzhou: Lingnan Art Press, 1986), 189.

74. Tang, *Origins of the Chinese Avant-Garde*, 120–21.

75. Tang, *Origins of the Chinese Avant-Garde*, 194, 218. Tang suggests this "aural turn" was "compelled by contemporary events," but does not elucidate why the voice and the depiction of sound were foregrounded during the period. At the "Multimedia Lu Xun" workshop held at Columbia University in February 2009, Tang suggested that the rise of woodcuts was in part fueled by leftist artists' frustrations with the dry objectivism of documentary photography in its depiction of the Japanese bombing of Shanghai in 1932. In this sense, like the contemporary rise of reportage literature, woodcuts would offer a subjective account of events containing a social truth inaccessible to the lens of the camera.

76. On the subject of orality and May Fourth spoken drama, see Colin MacKerras, *The Chinese Theatre in Modern Times: From 1840 to the Present Day* (Amherst: University of Massachusetts Press, 1975). The most prominent attempt to bring writing closer to speech during the vernacularization movement were the many proposals to replace Chinese characters with a phonetic script. See Yurou Zhong, *Chinese Grammatology*.

77. See W. J. T. Mitchell, *Picture Theory* (Chicago: University of Chicago Press, 1994), 35, as well as ch. 2.

78. On this point, see Tang, *Origins of the Chinese Avant-Garde*, 168, 197.

79. Shanghai Lu Xun Jinianguan 上海鲁迅纪念馆 and Jiangsu Guji Chubanshe 江苏古籍出版社, ed., *Banhua jicheng: Lu Xun cang Zhongguo xiandai muke quanji* 版画集成：鲁迅藏中国现代木刻全集 (Nanjing: Jiangsu guji chubanshe, 1991): 4:1372. Lu Xun had multiple versions of this image. See *Banhua jicheng* 5:1717; this second version (which appears in an undated collection of Luo's works, most likely from 1936), carries the alternate title. Further examples of woodcut representation of propagandization are Luo Qingzhen's *Labor Day* (*Laodongjie* 劳動節; 1933) and *Propaganda Lecture* (*Jiangyan xuanchuan* 講演宣傳; undated, but pre-1936), by Zhang Hui. They are reprinted in *Banhua jicheng*, 3:883 and 5:1589.

80. On such lines, see Henderson, "Vibratory Modernism," 135.

81. From *Zhang Hui mukehua di er ji* 張慧木刻畫第二集 (Shanghai: Kaiming shudian; Beiping: Lijian shuju, 1935), 7. Similar horizons appear in the pastoral scenes in Luo Qingzhen's *Returning Herd* (*Fangmu guilai* 放牧歸來; 1935) and Zhang's *Sunset's Glow Over the Forested Hills* (*Shanlin wanzhao* 山林晚照; 1935). See *Luo Qingzhen*

muke zuopin xuanji 罗清桢木刻作品选集 (Shanghai: Renmin meishu chubanshe, 1958), 14; and *Zhang Hui mukehua di er ji*, 13.

82. *Luo Qingzhen muke zuopin xuanji*, 25.

83. *Xinbo banhua ji* 新波版画集 (Beijing: Renmin meishu chubanshe, 1978), 10.

84. On the advent of sound films and the rise of leftist ideology around 1934 and 1935, see Yingjin Zhang, *Chinese National Cinema* (New York: Routledge, 2004), 68–69.

85. *Banhua jicheng*, 4:1241.

86. *Banhua jicheng*, 3:986.

87. These images also show the influence of Frans Masereel. On Masereel in China, see also Tang, *Origins of the Chinese Avant-Garde*, 168–69.

88. *Banhua jicheng*, 3:992.

89. On the issue of multivalence of postures as a formalization of a social network, see my analysis of Liu Xian's *Midnight* illustration in chapter 2. Such multivalence stands in direct opposition to the figuration of the masses, which constitute an organic and univocal body.

4. NARRATING NETWORKS: SHEN CONGWEN'S LITERARY CRAFT AND THE SOCIAL LIFE OF INFORMATION

1. The story first appeared in the journal *Shuixing* 水星 2, no. 3 (1935). It is reprinted in Shen Congwen and Zhang Zhaohe 张兆和, eds., *Shen Congwen Quanji* 沈从文全集 (Taiyuan: Beiyue wenyi chubanshe, 2002), 8:311–18. Hereafter, I abbreviate citations of the *Collected Works* as *SCQJ*, followed by volume and page number.

2. Perhaps this is due to the story's provenance: when it was later republished, Shen playfully appended an endnote disavowing authorship, explaining that he had merely "revised" the work of a "friend [he] didn't know personally," and stating that he "didn't dare take undue credit" for it (*SCQJ*, 8:318). Shen is without doubt the story's author, which explains its inclusion in his collected works.

3. M. M. Bakhtin, *The Dialogic Imagination: Four Essays*, ed. Michael Holmquist; trans. Caryl Emerson and Michael Holmquist (Austin: University of Texas Press, 1981), 263, 271.

4. On Shen's usage of dialect, see Jeffrey C. Kinkley, *The Odyssey of Shen Congwen* (Stanford, CA: Stanford University Press, 1987). Kinkley notes that by the 1930s, perhaps because Shen was writing with a national audience in mind, he had largely shifted away from emphasizing dialect in his work. Certainly his mature works from this period contain their share of dialect words: Shen even wrote a short vocabulary list that was to accompany the work I focus on in this chapter, *Long River* (though the list is hardly necessary, since the terms' meanings are mostly understandable by their context).

5. Bakhtin, *The Dialogic Imagination*, 276–77.

6. This is particularly the case with C. T. Hsia's treatment of Shen in *A History of Modern Chinese Fiction*, 2nd ed. (New Haven, CT: Yale University Press, 1971), 189–211.

7. See Kinkley's attempt to place Shen within Republican China's tradition of literary modernism: "Shen Congwen Among the Modernists," *Monumenta Serica* 56 (2006): 311–41. In his typology of modernisms, Kinkley draws up a new category for Shen:

"academic modernism," that is, writers who were at least partially supported by educational institutions and developed modernist subjects and techniques in ways different from their commercially independent Shanghai counterparts (327–29).

8. For an alternative definition, see John Seely Brown and Paul Duguid's contemporary business study *The Social Life of Information* (Boston: Harvard Business School, 2002).

9. I thank Wu Xiaodong at Peking University for originally calling my attention to this work's extensive exploration of communication, as well as for sharing his scholarship with me. I discuss his work later herein.

10. "Communication as a person-to-person activity became thinkable only in the shadow of mediated communication. Mass communication came first," writes John Durham Peters in *Speaking into the Air: A History of the Idea of Communication* (Chicago: University of Chicago Press, 1999), 4. This insight helps distinguish Shen's interest in *xiaoxi* from comparable cases such as the movement of *xiaoxi* in late imperial novels: the social life of information takes on a different significance following the advent of mass media and modern propaganda, as we will see.

11. If one brackets the primitivist elements of classical anthropology pervading Malinowski's essay, what remains is an articulation of the dialogistic dimension of a living language that is strikingly similar to Bakhtin's notion of heteroglossia. See Bronislaw Malinowski, "The Problem of Meaning in Primitive Languages," Supplement I in I. A. Richards and Charles Kay Ogden, *The Meaning of Meaning: A Study of the Influence of Language upon Thought and of the Science of Symbolism* (New York: Harcourt, Brace, 1923), 296–336.

12. On the origins of this latter formulation, see the diachronic study of mass media's impact on public opinion in Ohio during the 1940 presidential election: Paul F. Lazarsfeld, Bernard Berelson, and Hazel Gaudet, *The People's Choice: How the Voter Makes Up His Mind in a Presidential Campaign* (New York: Columbia University Press, 1944).

13. See Jean-François Lyotard's much-debated articulation of the "grand narrative" in his *The Postmodern Condition: A Report on Knowledge*, trans. Geoff Bennington and Brian Massumi (Minneapolis: University of Minnesota Press, 1984). My analysis of Shen Congwen's eclecticism and adoption of a "small narrative" form draws inspiration from Lyotard's notion of "small narrative," but it is not my intention that we read any sort of postmodern element into Shen's work.

14. *SCQJ*, 5:425–30. The story originally appeared in the journal that Shen Congwen cofounded with Ding Ling, *Hong hei* 紅黑, no. 8 (1929).

15. This story has been ignored in subsequent criticism. It originally appeared in the short-lived journal, *Weiyin yuekan* 微音月刊 2, no. 7–8 (1932): 171–83.

16. For a full account of Shen's fraught relationship with Ding Ling during her pivot to Communism and her consequent capture by the GMD in 1933, see Jeffrey C. Kinkley's landmark biography of Shen, *The Odyssey of Shen Congwen*, 76, 202–7, particularly his extensive endnotes where he speculates about the reason for the falling out between the two friends.

17. See Kinkley, *The Odyssey of Shen Congwen*.

18. Besides the example of "Unemployed," another fascinating story is "Knowledge" (*Zhishi* 知識), published in *Shuixing* in 1934, in which a foreign-educated youth's trip to his home region results in his disavowal of modern knowledge in favor of

the Buddhist insight that all is pain and suffering. Both in its repetition of Buddhist tropes and in its subject of a May Fourth youth's fraught return to his hometown, "Knowledge" strongly resembles Lu Xun's masterful story "Prayers for a New Year's Blessing" (*Zhufu* 祝福). Lydia Liu has pointed out the latter story's complex connections to Buddhism in her article "Life as Form: How Biomimesis Encountered Buddhism in Lu Xun," *Journal of Asian Studies* 68, no. 1 (2009): 21–56.

19. On the relationship between the newspaper and the literary supplement, see Shen's wartime exhortation for newspapers to foster more May Fourth-style social debate and literary production in "Transform the Way It's Done" ("Bianbian zuofeng" 變變作風), originally published in the *Dagongbao* 大公報 literary supplement, *Wenyi* 文藝1051 (March 15, 1941); republished in *SCQJ*, 14:158–61. Also, see Shen's postwar article on newspaper publishing in Kunming, "Zenyang ban yi fen hao baozhi" 怎樣班一份好報紙, *SCQJ*, 14:239–44. The original appeared in *Shanghai wenhua* 上海文化, no. 8 (September 1946).

20. Shen Congwen, "Yi ge dubaozhe dui baozhi de xiwang"一個讀報者對報紙的希望, *SCQJ*, 14:91–92. This short *zawen* essay originally appeared in the July 7, 1935, issue of the *Shibao*. Shen ostensibly wrote this piece after reading an article in a Shanghai newspaper that included statistics on Chinese newspaper circulation and sales.

21. In a 1980 postscript, Shen notes how he wrote the book in merely three weeks while working as a teacher in Qingdao. *SCQJ*, 16:366–68. Here I rely on the original 1934 publication, which in places differs from later editions. See *Congwen zizhuan* 從文自傳 (Shanghai: Diyiban chubanshe, 1934). Subsequent page numbers are given parenthetically in text.

22. Referring to the *Romance of the Three Kingdoms* (*Sanguo yanyi* 三國演義) chapters 51, 55, and 56, where the masterful general Zhuge Liang outmatches his rival from the state of Wu.

23. Meng Yue, *Shanghai and the Edges of Empires* (Minneapolis: University of Minnesota Press, 2006), 52–54. Meng observes that the *Ciyuan*'s compilers meant to reconcile Chinese and foreign terms relating to modern knowledge, along with explaining the somewhat more familiar-looking neologisms and loanwords that were flooding in from Meiji Japan (52).

24. This verb is again conspicuously present in the autobiography's later chapter, "A Place for Studying History" ("Xue lishi de difang" 學歷史的地方; *Congwen zizhuan* 149–50), where, stationed in Hunan and employed again as a secretary for a commanding officer, Shen has the opportunity to explore a trove of ancient cultural artifacts that are stored in the building where he works: a hundred scroll paintings dating back as early as the Song, multiple bronzes and porcelains, more than ten boxes of old books, and the *Siku congkan* 四庫叢刊. "When I didn't know what era the author of one of the books came from, I would flip through [*fan* 翻] the *Siku congkan*'s abstracts [*tiyao* 提要]" (*Congwen zizhuan*, 150). Shen concludes: "From this [experience], through a slice of color, a certain line, a piece of greened bronze or a pile [*dui* 堆] of clay, and a set of characters [*yi zu wenzi* 一組文字], I gained an elementary and general recognition of the various arts produced during this nation's long, long history" (150). The quantifier words that Shen uses (*pian* 片, *ba* 把, *kuai* 块, *dui* 堆, and *zu* 組) help to highlight the materiality of the art media at hand. This materiality would later permeate his conception of art—including literature, whose

essential medium is language. See his statement on art in a 1941 lecture in Kunming: "In even a very small work, if the author pours all of his highest ideals, his richest sentiments, arranges everything in the proper manner, then a single rock, a single thread, a dab of plain ink, a few splinters of bamboo assembled together, can all be overflowing with vitality." *SCQJ*, 16:504.

25. Which, materially speaking, has pre-Republican roots, *Shenbao* having been published since 1872 and the *Ciyuan* being a project conceived and initiated in 1908.

26. See the eponymous first chapter of *From the Tree to the Labyrinth: Historical Studies on the Sign and Interpretation*, trans. Anthony Oldcorn (Cambridge, MA: Harvard University Press, 2014), 3–94. See also Umberto Eco, *Semiotics and the Philosophy of Language* (Bloomington: Indiana University Press, 1984), 80–82.

27. David Der-Wei Wang, *Fictional Realism in Twentieth-Century China: Mao Dun, Lao She, Shen Congwen* (New York: Columbia University Press, 1992), 254.

28. The essay was first published in the *Xiao gongyuan* 小公園 supplement to the August 31, 1935, issue of the Tianjin newspaper, *Dagongbao*. It is reprinted in *SCQJ*, 16:470–73. For a similar statement on technique, see also Shen's "Gei yi ge duzhe" 給一個讀者, originally published as "Yi feng xin" 一封信 in the journal *Zhongxuesheng* 中學生 in June of 1935. Reprinted in *SCQJ*, 17:225–30.

29. See Shen's "Fengya yu suqi" 風雅與俗氣 (1935) for an expansion of this notion (*SCQJ*, 17:211–15). In this essay, Shen's primary target seems to be the works of humorists (*youmo xiaopin* 幽默小品) such as Lin Yutang 林語堂 (1895–1976).

30. Shen clarified this much when he brought up the issue of technique in a 1941 lecture at the National Southwestern Associated University in Kunming. See his "On the Short Story," republished in *SCQJ*, 16:492–507, particularly 502. See also Kinkley, *The Odyssey of Shen Congwen*, 194–95.

31. I have slightly modified the translation from "Universal or Restricted?" (*Yiban huo teshu* 一般或特殊), trans. Jeffrey Kinkley, in *Modern Chinese Literary Thought: Writings on Literature, 1893–1945*, ed. Kirk A. Denton (Stanford, CA: Stanford University Press, 1996), 451–52 (my emphasis). This piece originally appeared in vol. 1, no. 4 of *Jinri pinglun* 今日評論. It is reprinted in *SCQJ*, 17:260–64.

32. See Johanna Drucker, "Art," in *Critical Terms for Media Studies*, ed. W. J. T. Mitchell and Mark B. N. Hansen (Chicago: University of Chicago Press, 2010), 10 (emphasis in original).

33. This formulation was used as early as the mid-Qing to describe the sprawling form of the vernacular novel *The Scholars* (*Rulin waishi* 儒林外史). See Shuen-fu Lin's "Ritual and Narrative Structure in *Ju-lin wai-shi*," in *Chinese Narrative: Critical and Theoretical Essays*, ed. Andrew Plaks (Princeton, NJ: Princeton University Press, 1977), 244–65. This "all branch" framework is positioned in contrast to the traditional Chinese model of the "root and branch" (*benmo* 本末), which expresses relations between origin and effect and places them along a hierarchy of value. On this concept and its illustration as a principle of literary creation, see Stephen Owen's translation and explication of "The Poetic Exposition of Literature" ("Wenfu" 文賦) by Lu Ji 陸機 (261–303 CE), in *Readings in Chinese Literary Thought* (Cambridge, MA: Harvard University Press, 1992), 107, 113–15.

34. Wang Zengqi 汪曾祺, "Xingdou qi wen, chizi qi ren" 星斗其文，赤子其人, in *Wang Zengqi sanwen* 汪曾祺散文 (Zhengzhou: Henan wenyi chubanshe, 2020).

35. He Yubo, *Xiandai Zhongguo zuojia lun*, 2:139.

36. He Yubo, *Xiandai Zhongguo zuojia lun*, 2:122, 124. In a similar vein, the Taiwanese critic Su Xuelin 蘇雪林 opines: "Though in choice of diction and in the arrangement of his sentences he tries to achieve terseness, his descriptions are still verbose and cumbersome. Sometimes, several hundred words fail to yield the 'central idea.' . . . We can abbreviate a thousand-word passage into a hundred words without losing the original import. For this reason his language cannot pierce a reader's heart like a rapier, however pathetic or tragic his stories are, they cannot stay in the reader's mind as an ineradicable memory." From Lillian Chen Ming Chu, "*The Long River* by Shen Ts'ung-wen: Introduction and Partial Translation" (MA thesis, Columbia University, 1966), 11. Su's critique echoes the comparison between Shen's literary aesthetic and propaganda literature, where the latter is piercing, tragic/pathetic, ineradicable, abbreviated, and communicates one central idea.

37. The place of Shen's drawings, doodling, and photography in his literary practice (as well as in his literary representation in such stories as "Chuanshibing" 傳事兵 [1927]) falls outside the scope of this chapter. For an analysis of Shen's later drawings, see Zhang Xinying's 张新颖 masterful biography, *Shen Congwen de houban sheng* 沈从文的后半生 (Guangxi: Guangxi shifan daxue chubanshe, 2014). See also Wang Dewei [David Der-wei Wang], "Shen Congwen de san ci qiwu" 沈从文的三次 启悟, in *Shuqing chuantong yu Zhongguo xiandaixing: Zai Beida de ba tang ke* 抒情 传统与中国现代性: 在北大的八堂课 (Beijing: Sanlian shudian, 2010), 98–131.

38. In this regard, He Yubo's frustration with Shen Congwen's work is anticipated in criticism of *Rulin waishi* by a slightly earlier generation of May Fourth critics, including Hu Shi, "who often described the eighteenth-century satirical work as a series of loosely connected short stories without a grand integrative design. This general criticism has derived . . . from a predilection for centralized and monolithic plot structure, which is more typical of the Western novel." See Lin, "Ritual and Narrative Structure in *Ju-lin wai-shi*," in Plaks, ed., *Chinese Narrative*, 244–45.

39. Kinkley, *The Odyssey of Shen Congwen*, 3.

40. Wang, *Fictional Realism*, 230, 202, 203, 206, 217.

41. Wang, *Fictional Realism*, 252.

42. I have adapted this translation from Anthony J. Prince's translation, "The Life and Works of Shen Ts'ung-wen" (PhD diss., University of Sydney, 1968), 49. The original passage is located in *SCQJ*, 11:230.

43. Bakhtin, *The Dialogic Imagination*, 276–77.

44. In a 1982 preface to a partial English translation of his Xiangxi works, Shen explains that he wrote *West Hunan* after a meeting with local powerholders (many of whom had historical ties with Shen's family), including the "Miao King," Long Yunfei, who were eager to hear Shen's appraisal of the national situation. They collectively resolved that the countryside had an important role to play in relocating refugees and organizations to the interior by offering them space and local resources. See his "Preface to *Random Sketches of a Trip to Western Hunan*," in *SCQJ*, 16:387–94.

45. *Changhe* 长河, ed. Zhang Xinying 张新颖 (Guangzhou: Huacheng chubanshe, 2010), 101–2. Subsequent in-text citations of the novel come from this version of the text.

46. Wang, *Fictional Realism*, 260.

47. Zhang Xinying argues that Shen first conceived of the novel as an elaboration of the themes of change and constancy in *Border Town*. See "Changhe: 'chang' yu 'bian'" 《长河》:"常"与"变," in *Changhe*, 286, 287–88.

48. In speculating why Shen never finished the work, David Wang suggests "the ominous vision of West Hunan's future may have proved an unbearable strain for Shen Congwen at the time and disabled him from writing and personally fulfilling its doom. Leaving *Long River* unfinished, therefore, might have meant for Shen Congwen both a political gesture, 'saying' in silence what was unsayable in a policed literature, and a psychological self-censorship, blocking the textual manifestation of a[n] unbearable trauma." See *Fictional Realism*, 276.

49. Regarding Shen's early distaste for the pomp and display of a united front among writers, see his essay "Wentan de 'tuanjie' yu 'lianhe'" 文壇的'團結'與'聯合,' in *Guowen zhoubao* 國聞週報13, no. 45 (1936; reprinted in *SCQJ*, 17:114–18), which eschews making a political stand and depicts the literary institution as self-obsessed with a series of discursive civil wars in which ultimately the loser is the reader.

50. Shen, "Universal or Restricted?," 452.

51. Of course, the characterization of propaganda as "causing a stir" resonates with the reflections of propaganda in contemporary leftist art and literature that I discussed in chapter 3. On the longer history of *renao* in literature, see Paize Keulemans, *Sound Rising from the Paper: Nineteenth-Century Martial Arts Fiction and the Chinese Acoustic Imagination* (Cambridge, MA: Harvard University Press, 2014).

52. Shen, "Universal or Restricted?," 451–52.

53. Arguably the degree to which this position was apolitical is something of a straw man, constructed and directed by advocates of May Fourth realism in the 1920s seeking to promote a socially engaged alternative of "art for life's sake." See Marston Anderson, "Introduction," in *The Limits of Realism: Chinese Fiction in the Revolutionary Period* (Berkeley: University of California Press, 1990), 1–26, along with Guo Moruo's revival of this position as an object of attack in his influential manifesto on the politicization of literature, *Wenyi yu xuanchuan* 文藝與宣傳 (Guangzhou: Shenghuo shudian, 1938).

54. For an expansion of this view, see Shen's 1938 essay, "Tan jinbu" 談進步 (*SCQJ*, 16:479–88), in which he discusses at length the role of writing (*wenzi* 文字) in igniting political passion and literature's function for neutralizing this sort of passion while promoting social change in its own manner. Together with "Universal or Restricted?" "Tan jinbu" leaves little doubt that *Long River* is Shen's attempt to demonstrate literature's place outside of propaganda. On Shen's reaffirmation of the May Fourth spirit, but a critique of the "misuse" (*lanyong* 濫用; *wuyong* 誤用) of the tool of writing, see also his essay "'Wusi' ershiyi nian" "五四"二十一年 (1940) in *SCQJ*, 14:133–35.

55. Shen, "Universal or Restricted?" 453.

56. Interestingly, Shen took up the topic directly in a short story named "Country Village" (*Xiangcheng* 鄉城; 1940), reprinted in *SCQJ*, 10:287–94. Told from the point of view of villagers, the story narrates the arrival of a unit of student propagandists and their eager pursuit of "stirring up" (*re'nao* 熱鬧) the local population. The village head treats the students as a kind of occupying force who must be properly received (*zhaodai* 招待) with a banquet. This puts a strain on village resources. The actual propaganda of the students, including writing slogans and acting out a patriotic play, is described only in passing, thus suggesting that such activities leave little mark on the bemused villagers. The theme of miscommunication is exemplified by the letters written by student volunteers on behalf of villagers; intended for villagers' relatives fighting in the war, the letters are full of empty slogans. Worse

yet, the villagers do not know the exact address to which they should be sent. The story ends ironically, noting that after the event, local newspapers reported the all-around success of the propaganda campaign. Shen also appends an admonition telling his readers that, in going to the countryside to propagate, one's "enthusiasm" (*reqing* 熱情) is not enough—what is required instead is the kind of sensitivity to local conditions as they are portrayed in the story.

57. As Kinkley explains, Shen experimented with Buddhist ideas during the 1930s, as evident in stories such as "Knowledge" (1934), where he seems to "have borrowed Buddhist plots, symbols, and perhaps the pantheistic idea of Indira's web . . . [to] focus on higher ideals [and] describe Life as a pantheistic spirit: a flame, radiating into the lives of others," *The Odyssey of Shen Congwen*, 222–23.

58. Shen, "Universal or Restricted?," 452. Despite its narrowly local scope, Shen argues in the preface that the novel offers a sort of case study whose lessons would be applicable to rural China elsewhere (*Changhe*, 102–3).

59. Where possible, I draw from and adjust the excerpted translation of Lillian Chen Ming Chu. See her "*The Long River* by Shen Ts'ung-wen: Introduction and Partial Translation" (MA thesis, Columbia University, 1966). Hereafter I cite first the page number of her work and then the page number of the Chinese version, Zhang Xinying, *Changhe*. The preceding excerpt is from Chu, "*The Long River*," 49; Zhang, *Changhe*, 136.

60. This distinction is Wu Xiaodong's. He further notes that *Shenbao* appears a total of sixteen times in the text, where it is shown attracting both direct readers (such as Teng Changchun and other well-to-do merchants, and petty officials), as well as "indirect readers" such as the old boatman. See "*Changhe* zhong de chuanmei fuma—Shen Congwen de guojia xiangxiang he xiandai xiangxiang" 《长河》中的传媒符码：沈从文的国家想象和现代想象, *Shijie* 世界, no. 12 (2003): 198–213. Jeffrey Kinkley has recently translated Wu's essay into English; see "Code Words for Communications Media in *Long River*: Shen Congwen's Imaginaries of the Nation and of the Modern," in *Routledge Companion to Shen Congwen*, ed. Gang Zhou, Chen Sihe, Zhang Xinying, and Jeffrey Kinkley (New York: Routledge, 2019), 134–50. Per Wu, the New Life Movement appears in the original text over fifty times (3). Wu's argues that ultimately the mass media in the narrative connect the periphery to the national center (7) and enable a sort of national imaginary under print capitalism (or, more precisely, "mass media capitalism"). I would argue, however, that Shen's text also stresses the additional mode of interpersonal connection and exchange.

61. See, e.g., Amand Mattelart, *The Invention of Communication*, trans. Susan Emanuel (Minneapolis: University of Minnesota Press, 1996).

62. James W. Carey, "A Cultural Approach to Communication," in *Communication as Culture: Essays on Media and Society* (Boston: Unwin Hyman, 1989), 13–36.

63. This is not to say, however, that oral *xiaoxi* and the printed *Shenbao* are regarded as equally authoritative. The disjuncture between these sources reinforces the elevated social status of literate newspaper readers. The narrative also introduces an even more informed group of news consumers: local missionaries, who have access to radio (*Changhe*, 161).

64. To Daren and Manman we can add three more characters: the grandfather in *Border Town*, who, as a ferryman, serves as an intermediary of information between passers-by (which in turn makes him a rich source of local hearsay and knowledge)

but who fails in his role as a go-between for the marriage between his granddaughter, Cuicui, and the handsome son of a local well-to-do family; the old military messenger in Shen's short story "Mountain Passer" ("Guofengzhe" 過峰者; 1934), whose job is to transmit messages and serve as a kind of information hub between spies; and the eponymous protagonist of "Staff Adviser" ("Guwenguan" 顧問官; 1935). Alongside these fictional characters we might also include Shen himself (or, as he imagined himself) and his own background as a clerk for a regional military troop, where, at the age of sixteen (in 1918), he was responsible for copying reports and keeping records. The position allowed Shen to fraternize with a much wider slice of society than he would have had access to as a regular soldier, and many of his stories are drawn from this experience (*Congwen zizhuan*, 62–63).

65. That Shen Congwen intended to use this string of interrogations as a frame for communicating information to his reader is particularly spotlighted in this chapter. Manman's conversation with the last boatman reveals in passing that the boatman formerly worked as a teacher and witnessed the white terror in Changsha in the late 1920s. His tongue loosened by wine, the boatman begins to speak about the corruption he has seen and read about, but is interrupted by a textual ellipsis, followed by a parenthetical statement merely saying that a "significant paragraph has [here] been excised by the Central Propaganda Bureau" (*Changhe*, 201). Such an interpolation certainly calls our attention to the multiple purposes of Manman's information gathering.

66. I have translated these terms quite literally, but, alternatively, the term "eyes that see a thousand miles" (*qianliyan* 千里眼) is a rendering of "telescope," a translation that dates back to the late Ming.

67. Bakhtin, *The Dialogic Imagination*, 263.

68. On the possibility that Shen was struggling with schizophrenia, see Xiaojue Wang, "From Asylum to Museum: The Discourse of Insanity and Schizophrenia in Shen Congwen's 1949 Transition," *Modern Chinese Literature and Culture* 23, no. 1 (Spring 2011): 133–68.

69. Quoted in Zhang Xinying, *Shen Congwen de houbansheng*, 24. The original diary entry is in *SCQJ*, 19:22.

70. Zhang, *Shen Congwen de houbansheng*, 69, 74.

71. Zhang, *Shen Congwen de houbansheng*, 69, 83.

72. Zhang, *Shen Congwen de houbansheng*, 70. Shen's interest in arts education in fact extends back to the 1930s. See his treatment of contemporary art and artistic training in "'Yishi zhoukan' de dansheng" 《藝術週刊》的誕生, *SCQJ*, 16:464–69, and "Yishu jiaoyu' 藝術教育, *SCQJ*, 16:474–78, published in 1934 and 1937, respectively.

73. Reprinted in Zhang, *Shen Congwen de houbansheng*, 38. The full text is from *SCQJ*, 27:23. Shen states that he learned about himself through music, but that he learned about others through art. The first "art" that he remembers impacting him was the sight of bees building nests and spiders weaving webs: "Their painstaking work and their integrated structures led me to realize the honesty and cleverness [*qiaozhi* 巧智] of these small lives" (*SCQJ*, 27:22).

74. For an illuminating survey of the modern history of craftsmanship in China, see the introduction to Jacob Eyferth's *Eating Rice from Bamboo Shoots: The Social History of a Community of Handicraft Papermakers in Rural Sichuan, 1920–2000* (Cambridge, MA: Harvard University Press, 2009), 1–22.

75. Xiaojue Wang emphasizes continuity across the 1949 gap as well. While I agree with her that Shen's museological turn represents a kind of tacit resistance to the monumentality of the new socialist revolutionary regime that arose in the late 1940s, I dispute her interpretation of Shen's labor at the museum as a form of engagement with "dead" objects. In fact, Shen saw craft as a *living* form of tradition. I also disagree with Wang's assertion that Shen's latter career was not a genuine attempt on his part to contribute to the socialist state. See Wang, "From Asylum to Museum," as well as the second chapter to her monograph, *Modernity with a Cold War Face: Reimagining the Nation in Chinese Literature Across the 1949 Divide* (Cambridge, MA: Harvard University Press, 2013), 57–58. On Shen's survival strategies during this period, see also Jenny Huangfu Day, "Roads to Salvation: Shen Congwen, Xiao Qian, and the Problem of Non-Communist Celebrity Writers, 1948–1957," *Modern Chinese Literature and Culture* 22, no. 2 (Fall 2010): 39–87.

76. On the longer history of weaving and female labor, see Francesca Bray, *Technology and Gender: Fabrics of Power in Late Imperial China* (Berkeley: University of California Press, 1997).

77. The original essay was printed in *Zhuangshi* 装饰, no. 3 (1959).

78. Beijing: Zhongguo gudian yishu chubanshe, 1957. Shen produced the study in collaboration with a recent graduate of the Central Academy of Art named Wang Jiashu 王家树 (b. 1929).

79. Wang, *Modernity with a Cold War Face*, 101.

83. See W. J. T. Mitchell, *Picture Theory* (Chicago: University of Chicago Press, 1994), 35–82.

CONCLUSION: SEEING THROUGH ABSTRACTION

1. "One could. . . . ask if the storyteller's relationship to his material, human life is not that of a craftsman, if the storyteller's role does not consist precisely in reworking the raw material of experience in a solid, useful, and unique way." Walter Benjamin, *The Storyteller Essays*, trans. Tess Lewis, ed. Samuel Titan (New York: New York Review of Books, 2019), 73.

2. More than simply a style of writing, Mao-style prose is both a discourse in the Foucauldian sense and a material linguistic form. See Li Tuo 李陀, "Ding Ling bu jiandan: Geming shiqi zhishifenzi zai huayu shengchanzhong de fuzaxing" 丁玲不简单：革命时期知识分子在话语生产中的复杂性, and "Wang Zengqi yu xiandai Hanyu xiezuo: Jian tan Mao wenti" 汪曾祺与现代汉语写作：兼谈毛文体, which are reprinted in his volume of collected essays, *Xuebeng he chu* 雪崩何处 (Beijing: Zhongxin chubanshe, 2015), 128–57 and 156–94, respectively.

3. Li Tuo, "Wang Zengqi yu xiandai Hanyu xiezuo," 185.

4. Julia F. Andrews and Kuiyi Shen, "The Modern Woodcut Movement," in *A Century in Crisis: Modernity and Tradition in the Art of Twentieth Century China*, ed. Julia F. Andrews and Kuiyi Shen (New York: Guggenheim Museum, 1998), 234.

5. Andrew F. Jones, "Quotation Songs: Portable Media and the Maoist Pop Song," in *Mao's Little Red Book: A Global History*, ed. Alexander C. Cook (Cambridge: Cambridge University Press), 43–60.

6. Ji, Xing, "Standing Between Entertainment and Politics: A Study on Chinese Anti-Spy Fiction, 1951–1965" (MA thesis, National University of Singapore, 2012), especially 142–50.

7. Yomi Braester, *Witness Against History: Literature, Film, and Public Discourse in Twentieth-Century China* (Stanford, CA: Stanford University Press, 2003), 117–20.

8. Richard Jean So, "Literary Information Warfare: Eileen Chang, the US State Department, and Cold War Media Aesthetics," in *American Literature* 85, no. 4 (2013): 719–44.

9. Xiao Liu, *Information Fantasies: Precarious Mediation in Postsocialist China* (Minneapolis: University of Minnesota Press, 2019), 1–38.

10. "Investment bankers like Goldman," writes Matt Taibbi, "created vehicles to package shitty mortgages and sell them en masse to unsuspecting insurance companies and pension funds. . . . then they sold investors on the idea that, because a bunch of those mortgages would turn out to be OK, there was no reason to worry so much about the shitty ones." As a graduate student living in New York, I barely knew what a mortgage was, let alone a subprime one, which made Taibbi's lucid analysis of the chain of events really eye-opening. See "The Great American Bubble Machine," *Rolling Stone*, April 5, 2010.

11. John Durham Peters, "Information: Notes Toward a Critical History," *Journal of Communication Inquiry* 12, no. 2 (1988): 15. Walter Benjamin similarly gestures toward the importance of modern statistical seeing in his seminal essay "The Work of Art in the Age of Mechanical Reproduction." But if Peters somewhat reverentially characterizes such vision as a "mystic transcendence of individuality" and deixis, Benjamin emphasizes the direct threat that such perception poses to the form of unique presence or "aura" of an individual work: "To pry an object from its shell, to destroy its aura, is the mark of a perception whose 'sense of the universal equality of things' has increased to such a degree that it extracts it even from a unique object by means of reproduction. This is manifested in the field of perception what in the theoretical sphere is noticeable in the increasing importance of statistics." Walter Benjamin, *Illuminations*, trans. Harry Zohn (New York: Schocken, 1968), 223.

12. James C. Scott, *Seeing Like a State: How Certain Schemes to Improve the Human Condition Have Failed* (New Haven, CT: Yale University Press, 1998).

13. Scott, *Seeing Like a State*, 11–52.

14. In a brilliant essay about the author Eric Ambler (1909–1998), Rob Horning describes a parallel development in English literature. With the rise of fascism and the accompanying onset of "total war" and permanent mobilization, Horning argues, the genre of detective and spy fiction changed during the 1930s. Horning argues. Whereas before, the detective or spy protagonist (and, through them, the reader) was equipped with a "special transcendental capacity to discern the truth," Ambler's work registers a new paradigm for the genre where the detective or spy came to discover themselves as a pawn within a large game by virtue of their being in possession of some key bit of knowledge. They thus find themselves "in the midst of an epistemological shift that would seem to accompany the growing logistical complexity of the economy and the globalized interconnection of states and firms . . . [where] their actions constitute information (knowing what) without knowledge (knowing how or why)." See "Agents Without Agency," *New Inquiry* 5 (2012), http://thenewinquiry.com/essays/agents-without-agency/.

APPENDIX: TRANSLATIONS

1. The essay's original title was simply "Stock Exchange" (*Zhengquan jiaoyisuo* 證券交易所). It was first published in the spring of 1936 in an issue of the widely read *Liangyou huabao* 良友畫報 pictorial magazine, number 114. Later that decade, Mao Dun renamed the essay "Sketch of the Stock Exchange" and republished it in a collection of his essays, *Impressions, Associations, Memories* (*Yinxiang, ganxiang, huiyi* 印象，感想，回憶) (Shanghai: Wenhua shenghuo chubanshe, 1939).

   This is the Shanghai Huashang (Merchants') Stock and Bond Market (Shanghai Huashang zhengquan jiaoyisuo 上海華商證券交易所). It was chartered in 1919 and began operation in 1920. In 1933, following a general consolidation of stock exchanges in Shanghai, the Huashang Exchange became much more powerful. The exchange closed between during the Japanese occupation from 1937 to 1946 but quickly reopened after the war with one billion yuan worth of capital in the postwar period, only to close permanently on the eve of the Communist takeover.

2. That is, those who ride the short-term fluctuations of stock prices looking to quick make profit by buying low, selling high.

3. This story appears in the February 1935 (vol. 4, no. 2) *Shenbao Monthly* (*Shenbao yuekan* 申報月刊) literary supplement.

4. Interestingly, this is an atypical usage of *xiaoxi* to mean "information" in the sense of statistics, rather than as a bit of personal and ephemeral news.

5. This short story originally appeared in *Mercury* (*Shuixing* 水星) 2, no. 3. It is reprinted in *Collected Works of Shen Congwen* (*Shen Congwen quanji* 沈从文全集) (Taiyuan: Beiyue wenyi chubanshe, 2002), 8: 311–18.

BIBLIOGRAPHY

1935 Shanghai Yearbook. Shanghai: Municipal Archive, 1992.

Alber, Charles J. *Enduring the Revolution: Ding Ling and the Politics of Literature in Guomindang China*. Westport, CT: Praeger, 2002.

Alekna, John. *Seeking News, Making China: Information, Technology, and the Emergence of Mass Society*. Stanford, CA: Stanford University Press, 2024.

Anderson, Marston. *The Limits of Realism: Chinese Fiction in the Revolutionary Period*. Berkeley: University of California Press, 1990.

Andrews, Julia F. *Painters and Politics in the People's Republic of China, 1949–1979*. Berkeley: University of California Press, 1994.

Andrews, Julia F., and Kuiyi Shen. "The Modern Woodcut Movement." In *A Century in Crisis: Modernity and Tradition in the Art of Twentieth Century China*, ed. Julia F. Andrews and Kuiyi Shen, 213–27. New York: Guggenheim Museum, 1998.

Auerbach, Erich. *Mimesis: The Representation of Reality in Western Literature*. Trans. Willard R. Trask. Princeton, NJ: Princeton University Press, 1953.

Baark, Erik. *Lightning Wires: The Telegraph and China's Technological Modernization, 1860–1890*. Westport, CT: Greenwood Press, 1997.

Bakhtin, M. M. *The Dialogic Imagination: Four Essays*. Ed. Michael Holquist. Trans. Caryl Emerson and Michael Holquist. Austin: University of Texas Press, 1981.

Bao, Weihong. *Fiery Cinema: The Emergence of an Affective Medium in China, 1915–1945*. Minneapolis: University of Minnesota Press, 2015.

——. "In Search of a 'Cinematic Esperanto': Exhibiting Wartime Chongqing Cinema in a Global Context." *Journal of Chinese Cinemas* 3, no. 2 (2009): 135–47.

——. "'A Vibrating Art in the Air': Cinema, Ether, and Propaganda Film Theory in Wartime Chongqing." *New German Critique* 41, no. 2 (Summer 2014): 171–88.

Barthes, Roland. "The Reality Effect." In *The Rustle of Language*, trans. Richard Howard, 141–48. Berkeley: University of California Press, 1989.

Bateson, Gregory. *Steps to an Ecology of Mind: Collected Essays in Anthropology, Psychiatry, Evolution, and Epistemology*. Northvale, NJ: Jason Aronson, 1987.

Battle-Baptiste, Whitney, and Britt Rusert, eds. *W. E. B. Du Bois's Data Portraits Visualizing Black America: The Color Line at the Turn of the Twentieth Century*. New York: Princeton Architectural Press, 2018.

Bayly, C. A. *Empire and Information: Intelligence Gathering and Social Communication in India, 1780–1870*. Cambridge: Cambridge University Press, 1996.

BBVA. "The Five Vs of Big Data." Updated May 26, 2020. https://www.bbva.com/en/five-vs-big-data/.

Beniger, James. *The Control Revolution: Technological and Economic Origins of the Information Society*. Cambridge, MA: Harvard University Press, 1986.

Benjamin, Walter. *Illuminations*. Trans. Harry Zohn. New York: Schocken, 1968.

——. *The Storyteller Essays*. Trans. Tess Lewis. Ed. Samuel Titan. New York: New York Review of Books, 2019.

Berry, Mary Elizabeth. *Japan in Print: Information and Nation in the Early Modern Period*. Berkeley: University of California Press, 2006.

Bi, Shutang. "Shuping: Duojiao guanxi: Mao Dun zuo." *Yuzhou feng*, no. 36 (1936): 73–74.

Blair, Ann. *Too Much to Know: Managing Scholarly Information Before the Modern Age*. New Haven, CT: Yale University Press, 2010.

Boecking, Felix, and Monika Scholz. "Did the Nationalist Government Manipulate the Chinese Bond Market? A Quantitative Perspective on Short-Term Price Fluctuations of Domestic Government Bonds, 1932–1934." *Frontiers of History in China* 10, no. 1 (2015): 126–44.

Borges, Jorge Luis. *Collected Fictions*. Trans. Andrew Hurley. New York: Penguin Books, 1998.

Braester, Yomi. *Witness Against History: Literature, Film, and Public Discourse in Twentieth-Century China*. Stanford, CA: Stanford University Press, 2003.

Braudel, Fernand. *On History*. Trans. Sarah Matthews. Chicago: University of Chicago Press, 1980.

Bray, Francesca. *Technology and Gender: Fabrics of Power in Late Imperial China*. Berkeley: University of California Press, 1997.

Bray, Francesca, Vera Dorofeeva-Lichtmann, and Georges Métailié, eds. *Graphics and Text in the Production of Technical Knowledge in China: The Warp and the Weft*. Leiden: Brill, 2007.

Brown, John Seely, and Paul Duguid. *The Social Life of Information*. Boston: Harvard Business School, 2002.

Buenza, Daniel, and David Stark. "How to Recognize Opportunities: Heterarchical Search in a Trading Room." In *The Sociology of Financial Markets*, ed. Karin Knorr Cetina and Alex Preda, 84–101. Oxford: Oxford University Press, 2005.

Burnham, Jack. "Systems Aesthetics." In *Networks*, ed. Lars Bang Larsen, 42–46. Cambridge, MA: MIT Press, [1968] 2014.

Carey, James W. *Communication as Culture: Essays on Media and Society*. Boston: Unwin Hyman, 1989.

Chen, Heqin. "Tubiaoshi de tongji baogao fa." *Xin jiaoyu* 8, no. 1 (1924): 46–59.

——. *Yutiwen yingyong zihui*. Shanghai: Shangwu yinshuguan, 1928.

——. "Yutiwen yingyong zihui: Zihui yanjiu zhi lishi." *Xin jiaoyu* 5, no. 5 (1922): 74.

Chen, Jack W., Anatoly Detwyler, Christopher M. B. Nugent, Xiao Liu, and Bruce Rusk. *Literary Information in China: A History*. New York: Columbia University Press, 2021.

Chen, Yuxin. *Xuanchuan zhan*. Beijing: Guomindang lujun daxuexiao, 1931.

Cheng, Junying. "Shiren zhi zhuyi ji xingqu." *Xinli* 2, nos. 1 and 2 (1923): 1–30 and 1–32.

Chiang, Kai-shek. "The Object of a New Life Movement." In *Sources of Chinese Tradition*, compiled by Wm. Theodore de Bary, 801. New York: Columbia University Press, 1960.

China Telecom Shanghai Company, ed. *Dianxin de jiyi: Shanghai dianxin 138 nian*. Shanghai: Wenhui chubanshe, 2009.

Chou, Siegen K. "The Present State of Psychology in China." *American Journal of Psychology* 38, no. 4 (October 1927).

Chow, Rey. *Primitive Passions: Visuality, Sexuality, Ethnography, and Contemporary Chinese Cinema*. New York: Columbia University Press, 1995.

Chu, Chia-Hua. *China's Postal and Other Communications Systems*. Shanghai: China United Press, 1937.

Chu, Lillian Chen Ming. "The Long River by Shen Ts'ung-wen: Introduction and Partial Translation." MA thesis, Columbia University, 1966.

Ciyuan. Shanghai: Shangwu yinshuguan bianshenbu, 1915.

Clarke, Bruce. "Information." In *Critical Terms for Media Studies*, ed. W. J. T. Mitchell and Mark B. N. Hansen, 157–71. Chicago: University of Chicago Press, 2010.

Crespi, John A. *Voices in Revolution: Poetry and the Auditory Imagination in Modern China*. Honolulu: University of Hawai'i Press, 2009.

Cronk, Lee. *That Complex Whole: Culture and the Evolution of Human Behavior*. Boulder, CO: Westview Press, 1999.

Culp, Robert. "Rethinking Governmentality: Training, Cultivation, and Cultural Citizenship in Nationalist China." *Journal of Asian Studies* 65, no. 3 (2006): 529–54.

Dai, Jingsu, ed. *Zhongguo xuanchuan wenxuan*. Chongqing: Shangwu yinshuguan, 1939.

Day, Jenny Huangfu. "Roads to Salvation: Shen Congwen, Xiao Qian, and the Problem of Non-Communist Celebrity Writers, 1948–1957." *Modern Chinese Literature and Culture* 22, no. 2 (Fall 2010): 39–87.

DeDeo, Simon. "Information Theory for Intelligent People." September 9, 2018. https://wiki.santafe.edu/images/a/a8/IT-for-Intelligent-People-DeDeo.pdf.

Denton, Kirk A., ed. *Modern Chinese Literary Thought: Writings on Literature, 1893–1945*. Stanford, CA: Stanford University Press, 1996.

Des Forges, Alexander. *Mediasphere Shanghai: The Aesthetics of Cultural Production*. Honolulu: University of Hawai'i Press, 2007.

De Weerdt, Hilde. *Information, Territory, and Networks: The Crisis and Maintenance of Empire in Song China*. Cambridge, MA: Harvard University Asia Center, 2015.

DiGiorgi, Laura. "Communication Technology and Mass Propaganda in Republican China: The Nationalist Party's Radio Broadcast Policy and Organisation during the Nanjing Decade (1927–1937)." *European Journal of East Asian Studies* 13, no. 2 (2014): 305–29.

Ding, Ling. *Ding Ling lun chuangzuo*. Shanghai: Shanghai wenyi chubanshe, 1985.

——. "Duo shi zhi qiu." *Beidou* 1, no. 3 (1932); *Beidou* 2, no. 1 (January 20, 1932), and nos. 3–4 (July 20, 1932): 25–37, 153–66.

——. "The Flood." Trans. Agnes Smedley. *Asia Magazine* (October 1935).

——. *I Myself Am a Woman: Selected Writings of Ding Ling.* Ed. Tani Barlow with Gary Bjorge. Boston: Beacon Press, 1989.

——. "Xiaoxi." *Wenxue yuebao* 1, no. 2 (1932): 33–38.

Eco, Umberto. *From the Tree to the Labyrinth: Historical Studies on the Sign and Interpretation.* Trans. Anthony Oldcorn. Cambridge, MA: Harvard University Press, 2014.

——. *Semiotics and the Philosophy of Language.* Bloomington: Indiana University Press, 1984.

Ellul, Jacques. *Propaganda: The Formation of Men's Attitude.* Trans. Konrad Kellen and Lean Lerner. New York: Vintage Books, 1973.

Enns, Anthony, and Shelley Trower, eds. *Vibratory Modernism.* London: Palgrave Macmillan, 2013.

Eyferth, Jacob. *Eating Rice from Bamboo Shoots: The Social History of a Community of Handicraft Papermakers in Rural Sichuan, 1920–2000.* Cambridge, MA: Harvard University Press, 2009.

Farina, Jonathan. "'The New Science of Literary Mensuration': Accounting for Reading, Then and Now." *Victorians Institute Journal Digital Annex* 38 (2010). https://nines.org/exhibits/Literary_Mensuration.

Farquhar, Mary, and Chris Berry. "Shadow Opera: Toward a New Archaeology of Chinese Cinema." In *Chinese-Language Film: Historiography, Poetics, Politics,* ed. Sheldon Lu and Yueh-Yu Yeh, 27–52. Honolulu: University of Hawai'i Press, 2005.

Feng, Xuefeng. "Guanyu xin de xiaoshuo de dansheng." *Beidou* 2, no. 1 (1932): 240–44.

Ferlanti, Federica. "The New Life Movement in Jiangxi, 1934–1938." *Modern Asia Studies* 44, no. 5 (2010): 961–1000.

Feuerwerker, Yi-tsi Mei. *Ding Ling's Fiction: Ideology and Narrative in Modern Chinese Literature.* Cambridge, MA: Harvard University Press, 1982.

Fitzgerald, Devin, and Carla Nappi. "Information in Early Modern East Asia." In *Information: A Historical Companion,* ed. Ann Blair, Paul Duguid, Anja-Silvia Goeing, and Anthony Grafton, 38–60. Princeton, NJ: Princeton University Press, 2021.

Fitzgerald, John. *Awakening China: Politics, Culture, and Class in the Nationalist Revolution.* Stanford, CA: Stanford University Press, 1996.

Friendly, Michael. "The Golden Age of Statistical Graphics." *Statistical Science* 23, no. 4 (2008): 502–35.

Fu, Donghua. "Wenxue zhi jindai yanjiu." *Xiaoshuo yuebao* 17, no. 1 (1926): 14–43.

Gardella, Robert. "Squaring Accounts: Commercial Bookkeeping Methods and Capitalist Rationalism in Late Qing and Republican China." *Journal of Asian Studies* 51, no. 2 (1992): 317–39.

Geng, Jizhi. "Zenyang chuangzao wenxue de xingxiang." *Wenxue* 7, no. 2 (1936): 406–16.

Geoghegan, Bernard. "From Information Theory to French Theory: Jakobson, Lévi-Strauss, and the Cybernetic Apparatus." *Critical Inquiry* 38, no. 1 (Autumn 2011).

Gitelman, Lisa, ed. *"Raw Data" Is an Oxymoron.* Cambridge, MA: MIT Press, 2013.

Gleick, James. *The Information: A History, A Theory, A Flood.* New York: Pantheon, 2011.

Gluck, Carole. *Japan's Modern Myths: Ideology in the Late Meiji Period.* Princeton, NJ: Princeton University Press, 1985.

Godin, Benoit. "From Eugenics to Scientometrics: Galton, Cattell, and Men of Science." *Social Studies of Science* 37, no. 5 (2007): 691–728.

Goodman, Bryna. "Networks of News: Power, Language, and Transnational Dimensions of the Chinese Press, 1850–1949." *China Review* 4, no. 1 (2004): 1–10.

——. "Things Unheard of East or West: Colonialism, Nationalism, and Cultural Contamination in Early Chinese Exchanges." In *Twentieth-Century Colonialism and China: Localities, the Everyday, and the World*, ed. Bryna Goodman and David S. G. Goodman, 57–77. New York: Routledge, 2012.

Guo Moruo zhuzuo bianji chuban weiyuanhui, ed. *Guo Moruo quanji*. Beijing: Xinhua shudian, 1992.

Harris, Lane Jeremy. "The Post Office and State Formation in Modern China, 1896–1949." PhD dissertation, University of Illinois at Urbana-Champaign, 2012.

Harrison, Henrietta. "Newspapers and Nationalism in Rural China, 1890–1929." In *Twentieth-Century China: New Approaches*, ed. Jeffrey Wasserstrom, 83–102. London: Routledge, 2003.

Hashimoto, Satoru. "Liang Qichao's Suspended Translation and the Future of Chinese New Fiction." In *A New Literary History of Modern China*, ed. David Der-wei Wang, 161–65. Cambridge, MA: Belknap Press of Harvard University Press, 2017.

Hayles, N. Katherine. *How We Became Posthuman: Virtual Bodies in Cybernetics, Literature, and Informatics*. Chicago: University of Chicago Press, 1999.

Hayot, Eric. *On Literary Worlds*. New York: Columbia University Press, 2012.

Hayot, Eric, Anatoly Detwyler, and Lea Pao, eds. *Information: A Reader*. New York: Columbia University Press, 2021.

He, Yubo. "Mao Dun chuangzuo de kaocha." *Dushu yuekan* 2, no. 1 (1931): 268.

——. *Xiandai Zhongguo zuojia lun*. Shanghai: Guanghua shuju, 1932.

——. "Xiaoshuo de tujie." *Dushu yuekan* 2 (1931), nos. 4–5: 125.

Heinrich, Ari Larissa. *The Afterlife of Images: Translating the Pathological Body Between China and the West*. Durham, NC: Duke University Press, 2008.

Henderson, Linda Dalrymple. "Vibratory Modernism: Boccioni, Kupka, and the Ether of Space." In *From Energy to Information: Representation in Science and Technology, Art, and Literature*, ed. Bruce Clarke and Linda Dalrymple Henderson, 126–48. Stanford, CA: Stanford University Press, 2002.

Ho, Chun-yu, and Dan Li. "A Mirror of History: China's Bond Market, 1921–1942." *Economic History Review* 67, no. 2 (2014): 409–34.

Hobert, Michael E., and Zachary S. Schiffman. *Information Ages: Literacy, Numeracy, and the Computer Revolution*. Baltimore: Johns Hopkins University Press, 1998.

Hockx, Michel. *Questions of Style: Literary Societies and Literary Journals in Modern China, 1911–1937*. Leiden: Brill, 2002.

Holm, David. *Art and Ideology in Revolutionary China*. Oxford: Clarendon Press, 1991.

Hong, Xuecun. "Guanyu 'Duojiaoguanxi.'" *Chuangjin yuekan* 3, no. 8 (1936): 67–70.

Horning, Rob. "Agents Without Agency." *New Inquiry* no. 5 (2012). http://thenewinquiry.com/essays/agents-without-agency/.

Hsia, C. T. *A History of Modern Chinese Fiction*. 2nd ed. New Haven, CT: Yale University Press, 1971.

Hsia, Tsi-an. *Gate of Darkness: Studies on the Leftist Literary Movement in China*. Seattle: University of Washington Press, 1968.

Huabei Zhengwu Weiyuanhui. *Xuanchuan jishu*. n.p.: Huabei zhengwu weiyuanhui zongwu ting qingbao ju, 1944.

Hung, Chang-tai. *War and Popular Culture: Resistance in Modern China, 1937–1945*. Berkeley: University of California Press, 1994.

Huters, Theodore. *Bringing the World Home: Appropriating the West in Late and Early Republican China*. Honolulu: University of Hawai'i Press, 2005.

The I Ching or Book of Changes: The Richard Wilhelm Translation Rendered Into English by Cary F. Baynes. Princeton, NJ: Princeton University Press, 1950.

Isekenmeier, Guido. "Literary Visuality: Visibility—Visualization—Description." In *Handbook of Intermediality: Literature—Image—Sound—Music*, ed. Gabriele Rippl, 325–42. Berlin: De Gruyter, 2015.

Ji, Da. *Xuanchuanxue yu xinwen jizhe*. Jinan: Jinan daxue wenhuabu, 1932.

Ji, Xing. "Standing Between Entertainment and Politics: A Study on Chinese Anti-Spy Fiction, 1951–1965." MA thesis, National University of Singapore, 2012.

Johnson, Matthew David. "International and Wartime Origins of the Propaganda State: The Motion Picture in China, 1897–1955." PhD dissertation, University of California San Diego, 2008.

Joncich, Geraldine. *The Sane Positivist: A Biography of Edward L. Thorndike*. Middletown, CT: Wesleyan University Press, 1968.

Jones, Andrew F. "Quotation Songs: Portable Media and the Maoist Pop Song." In *Mao's Little Red Book: A Global History*, ed. Alexander C. Cook, 43–60. Cambridge: Cambridge University Press.

——. *Yellow Music: Media Culture and Colonial Modernity in the Chinese Jazz Age*. Durham, NC: Duke University Press, 2001.

Journal of Literary Theory 13, no. 1 (March 2019). Special issue, "Moscow Formalism and Literary History."

Judge, Joan. "The Power of Print: Print Capitalism and the News Media in Late Qing China and Republican China." *Harvard Journal of Asian Studies* 66, no. 1 (2006): 233–54.

Kataoka, Teppei. "The Linesmen." Trans. Gregory Golley. In *For Dignity, Justice, and Revolution: An Anthology of Japanese Proletarian Literature*, ed. Norma Field and Heather Bowen-Struyk, 159–71. Chicago: University of Chicago Press, 2016.

Kay, Lily E. *Who Wrote the Book of Life? A History of the Genetic Code*. Stanford, CA: Stanford University Press, 2000.

Keulemans, Paize. *Sound Rising from the Paper: Nineteenth-Century Martial Arts Fiction and the Chinese Acoustic Imagination*. Cambridge, MA: Harvard University Press, 2014.

Kinkley, Jeffrey C. *The Odyssey of Shen Congwen*. Stanford, CA: Stanford University Press, 1987.

——. "Shen Congwen among the Modernists." *Monumenta Serica* 56 (2006): 311–41.

Klein, Lauren, et al. "The Shape of History: Reimagining Elizabeth Palmer Peabody's Historical Visualization Work." http://shapeofhistory.net.

Knouf, Nicholas A. *How Noise Matters to Finance*. Minneapolis: University of Minnesota Press, 2016.

Krauss, Rosalind. *Grids: Format and Image in 20th Century Art*. New York: Pace Gallery, 1980.

Krysko, Michael A. "Forbidden Frequencies: Sino-American Relations and Chinese Broadcasting during the Interwar Era." *Technology and Culture* 45, no. 4 (2004): 712–39.

Kwok, D. W. Y. *Scientism in Chinese Thought, 1900–1950*. New Haven, CT: Yale University Press, 1965.

Laing, Ellen Johnston. "Reform, Revolutionary, Political, and Resistance Themes in Chinese Popular Prints, 1900–1940." *Modern Chinese Literature and Culture* 12, no. 2 (Fall 2000): 123–75.

Lam, Tong. *A Passion for Facts: Social Surveys and the Construction of the Chinese State, 1900–1949*. Berkeley: University of California Press, 2011.

Landsberger, Stefan. *Chinese Propaganda Posters: From Revolution to Modernization*. Armonk, NY: M. E. Sharpe, 1995.

Larson, Wendy. *From Ah Q to Lei Feng: Freud and Revolutionary Spirit in 20th Century China*. Stanford, CA: Stanford University Press, 2008.

Lasswell, Harold D. *Propaganda and Promotional Activities: An Annotated Bibliography*. Minneapolis: University of Minnesota Press, 1935.

——. *Propaganda Technique in the World War*. New York: Peter Smith, 1927.

Lau, Joseph. "Naturalism in Modern Chinese Fiction." *Literature East & West* 12 (1968): 149–56.

Laughlin, Charles. "The All-China Resistance Association of Writers and Artists." In *Literary Societies of Republican China*, ed. Kirk A. Denton and Michel Hockx, 379–412. Lanham, MD: Lexington Books, 2008.

——. "Narrative Subjectivity and the Production of Social Space in Chinese Reportage." *boundary 2* 25, no. 3 (1998): 25–46.

Lazarsfeld, Paul F., Bernard Berelson, and Hazel Gaudet. *The People's Choice: How the Voter Makes Up His Mind in a Presidential Campaign*. New York: Columbia University Press, 1944.

Lazich, Michael C. "The Diffusion of Useful Knowledge in China: The Canton Era Information Strategy." In *Mapping Meanings: The Field of New Learning in Late Qing China*, ed. Michael Lackner and Natascha Vittinghoff. Leiden: Brill, 2004.

Lee, Haiyan. *Revolution of the Heart: A Genealogy of Love in China, 1900–1950*. Stanford, CA: Stanford University Press, 2007.

Lee, Ou-fan. *The Romantic Generation of Modern Chinese Writers*. Cambridge, MA: Harvard University Press, 1973.

Lee, Leo Ou-fan, and Andrew Nathan. "The Beginnings of Mass Culture: Journalism and Fiction in the Late-Qing and Beyond." In *Popular Culture in Late Imperial China*, ed. David Johnson, Andrew J. Nathan, and Evelyn S. Rawski, 360–95. Berkeley: University of California Press, 1983.

Li, Tuo. *Xuebeng he chu*. Beijing: Zhongxin chubanshe, 2015.

Liang, Ch'i-ch'ao. *Intellectual Trends in the Ch'ing Period*. Trans. Immanuel C. Y. Hsü. Cambridge, MA: Harvard University Press, 1959.

Liang, Qichao. *Liang Qichao quanji*. Ed. Yang Gang and Wang Xiangyi. Beijing: Beijing chubanshe, 1999.

——. "Lun xiaoshuo yu qunzhi zhi guanxi." *Xin xiaoshuo* no. 1 (1902).

Liao, Shicheng. "Dufa ceyan." *Xinli* 1, no. 2 (1922): 1–20.

Lin, Chuanding. *Tang Song yilai sanshisi ge lishi renwu xinli tezhi de guji*. Beijing: Furen daxue xinlixi, 1939.

Lin, Shuen-fu. "Ritual and Narrative Structure in Ju-lin wai-shi." In *Chinese Narrative: Critical and Theoretical Essays*, ed. Andrew Plaks, 244–65. Princeton, NJ: Princeton University Press, 1977.

Liou, Wei-Chih. "An Analysis of Doctoral Dissertations from Chinese Students at Teachers College, Columbia University (1914–1929)." *Bulletin of Educational Research* 59, no. 2 (2013): 1–48.

Liu, Lu. "Away/With the Pest: Science, Visuality, and Socialist Subjectivities in Modern China's Biosocial Abjection." PhD dissertation, University of Wisconsin–Madison, 2019.

Liu, Lydia H. *The Freudian Robot: Digital Media and the Future of the Unconscious.* Chicago: University of Chicago Press, 2010.

——. "Life as Form: How Biomimesis Encountered Buddhism in Lu Xun." *Journal of Asian Studies* 68, no. 1 (2009): 21–56.

——. *Translingual Practice: Literature, National Culture, and Translated Modernity— China, 1900–1938.* Stanford, CA: Stanford University Press, 1995.

Liu, Xian. *Ziye zhi tu.* Shanghai: Weiming muke she, 1937.

Liu, Xiao. *Information Fantasies: Precarious Mediation in Postsocialist China.* Minneapolis: University of Minnesota Press, 2019.

Liu, Zhiying. *Jindai Shanghai Huashang zhengquan shichang yanjiu.* Shanghai: Xuelin chubanshe, 2004.

Liu, Zixiong. "Lun woguo xiandai xuanchuan yanjiu de di yi bo gaochao." *Sichuan ligong xueyuan xuebao* 23, no. 4 (August 2008): 7–10.

Long, Hoyt. *The Value of Numbers: Reading Japanese Literature in a Global Information Age.* New York: Columbia University Press, 2021.

Lu, Xun. "Wenyi yu geming." *Yusi* 4, no. 16 (1928): 38–46.

——. "Zailun Leifengta de daodiao." *Yusi* 1, no. 15 (1925): 1.

Luo Qingzhen muke zuopin xuanji. Shanghai: Renmin meishu chubanshe, 1958.

Lyotard, Jean-François. *The Postmodern Condition: A Report on Knowledge.* Trans. Geoff Bennington and Brian Massumi. Minneapolis: University of Minnesota Press, 1984.

MacKerras, Colin. *The Chinese Theatre in Modern Times: From 1840 to the Present Day.* Amherst: University of Massachusetts Press, 1975.

Malinowski, Bronislaw. "The Problem of Meaning in Primitive Languages." Supplement I in I. A. Richards and Charles Kay Ogden, *The Meaning of Meaning: A Study of the Influence of Language Upon Thought and of the Science of Symbolism*, 296–336. New York: Harcourt, Brace, 1923.

Mao Dun. "Bei kaowen le 'Zhongguo de yi ri.'" *Shenghuo xingqikan* 1, no. 18 (1936).

——. *Mao Dun quanji.* Beijing: Renmin wenxue chubanshe, 1984–2006.

——. *Midnight.* Trans. Hsu Meng-hsiung. Beijing: Foreign Languages Press, 1979.

——. *One Day in China: May 21, 1936.* Trans. and ed. Sherman Cochran and Andrew C. K. Hsieh, with Janis Cochran. New Haven, CT: Yale University Press, 1983.

——. *Spring Silkworms and Other Stories.* Trans. Sidney Shapiro. Beijing: Foreign Languages Press, 1979.

——. *Wo zouguo de daolu.* Beijing: Renmin wenxue, 1997.

——. "Zhengquan jiaoyisuo." *Liangyou Huabao*, no. 114 (February 1935): 24–25.

——, ed. *Zhongguo de yi ri.* Shanghai: Shenghuo shudian, 1936.

——. *Ziye.* Shanghai: Kaiming shuju, 1933.

Mao Zedong. *Selected Works of Mao Tse-tung.* Vol. 1. Beijing: Foreign Languages Press, 1967.

Marx, Karl. *Capital: A Critique of Political Economy.* Vol. 3. Trans. David Fernbach. New York: Penguin Books, 1991.

Masuda, Yoneji. *The Information Society as Post-Industrial Society.* Tokyo: Institute for the Information Society, 1980.

McLuhan, Marshall. *Cybernation and Culture.* Notre Dame, IN: University of Notre Dame Press, 1966.

——. *Understanding Media: The Extensions of Man.* New York: McGraw-Hill, 1965.

Mattelart, Amand. *The Invention of Communication.* Trans. Susan Emanuel. Minneapolis: University of Minnesota Press, 1996.

Meng, Yue. *Shanghai and the Edges of Empires.* Minneapolis: University of Minnesota Press, 2006.

Meng, Yue, and Dai Jinhua. *Fuchu lishi dibiao: Xiandai funü wenxue yanjiu.* Zhengzhou: Henan renmin chubanshe, 1993.

Menke, Richard. *Telegraphic Realism: Victorian Fiction and Other Information Systems.* Stanford, CA: Stanford University Press, 2008.

Merkel-Hess, Kate. *The Rural Modern: Reconstructing the Self and State in Republican China.* Chicago: University of Chicago Press, 2016.

Mitchell, W. J. T. *Picture Theory.* Chicago: University of Chicago Press, 1994.

Mittler, Barbara. *A Newspaper for China? Power, Identity, and Change in Shanghai's News Media, 1872–1912.* Cambridge, MA: Harvard University Press, 2003.

Moretti, Franco. "Conjectures on World Literature." *New Left Review,* no. 1 (January–February 2000): 54–68.

——. *Graphs, Maps, Trees: Abstract Models for Literary History.* London: Verso, 2005.

Moulton, Richard Green. *The Modern Study of Literature.* Chicago: University of Chicago Press, 1915.

Mu, Chao. *Feichang shiqi de xuanchuan zhengce.* n.p.: Zhengzhong shuju, 1938.

Mu, Shiying. *Mu Shiying quanji.* Beijing: Beijing shiyue wenyi chubanshe, 2008.

Mullaney, Thomas. "Quote Unquote Language Reform: New-Style Punctuation and the Horizontalization of Chinese." *Modern Chinese Literature and Culture* 29, no. 2 (2017): 206–50.

Natsume, Sōseki. *Theory of Literature and Other Critical Writings.* Trans. and ed. Michael K. Bourdaghs, Atsuko Ueda, and Joseph A. Murphy. New York: Columbia University Press, 2010.

North, Joseph. *Literary Criticism: A Concise Political History.* Cambridge, MA: Harvard University Press, 2017.

North, Michael. *Reading 1922: A Return to the Scene of the Modern.* New York: Oxford University Press, 1999.

Novak, David. "Noise." In *Keywords in Sound,* ed. David Novak and Matt Sakakeeny, 125–38. Durham, NC: Duke University Press, 2015.

Nylan, Michael. "Mapping Time in the Shiji and Hanshu Tables 表." *East Asian Science, Technology, and Medicine,* no. 43 (2016): 61–122.

Ogden, Charles Kay. *The Basic Vocabulary: A Statistical Analysis.* London: Kegan Paul, 1930.

——, ed. *The System of Basic English.* New York: Harcourt, Brace, 1934.

Ouyang, Xiang. "Zase." *Xinli* 2, no. 3 (1923): 1–15.

Owen, Stephen. *Readings in Chinese Literary Thought.* Cambridge, MA: Harvard University Press, 1992.

Pang, Laikwan. "Walking Into and out of the Spectacle: China's Earliest Film Scene." *Screen* 47, no. 1 (2006): 66–80.

Paulson, William R. *The Noise of Culture: Literary Texts in a World of Information.* Ithaca, NY: Cornell University Press, 1988.

Peng, Leshan. *Guangbo zhan.* Chongqing: Zhongguo bianyi chubanshe, 1943.

Peters, John Durham. "Information: Notes Toward a Critical History." *Journal of Communication Inquiry* 12, no. 2 (1988): 9–23.

——. *The Marvelous Clouds: Toward a Philosophy of Elemental Media*. Chicago: University of Chicago Press, 2015.

——. *Speaking into the Air: A History of the Idea of Communication*. Chicago: University of Chicago Press, 1999.

Plaks, Andrew, ed. *Chinese Narrative: Critical and Theoretical Essays*. Princeton, NJ: Princeton University Press, 1977.

Poovey, Mary. *Genres of the Credit Economy: Mediating Value in Eighteenth- and Nineteenth-Century Britain*. Chicago: University of Chicago Press, 2008.

——. *A History of the Modern Fact: Problems of Knowledge in the Sciences of Wealth and Society*. Chicago: University of Chicago Press, 1998.

Porter, Theodore M. *Trust in Numbers: The Pursuit of Objectivity in Science and Public Life*. Princeton, NJ: Princeton University Press, 1995.

Prince, Anthony J. "The Life and Works of Shen Ts'ung-wen." PhD dissertation, University of Sydney, 1968.

Qian, Xingcun. "Guanyu 'Ping Duankudang.'" *Taiyang yuekan*, no. 2 (1928).

Qian, Zhongshu. *Limited Views: Essays on Ideas and Letters*. Ed. and trans. Ronald Egan. Cambridge, MA: Harvard University Press, 1998.

Ramazani, Jahani. *Poetry and Its Others: News, Prayer, Song, and the Dialogue of Genres*. Chicago: University of Chicago Press, 2013.

Reed, Christopher. *Gutenberg in Shanghai: Chinese Print Capitalism, 1876–1937*. Honolulu: University of Hawai'i Press, 2004.

Ren, Baitao. *Riben dui Hua de xuanchuan zhengce*. Changsha: Shangwu yinshuguan, 1940.

Richards, Thomas. *The Imperial Archive: Knowledge and the Fantasy of Empire*. London: Verso, 1993.

Robinson, Michael. "Broadcasting, Cultural Hegemony, and Colonial Modernity in Korea, 1924–1945." In *Colonial Modernity in Korea*, ed. Gi-Wook Shin and Michael Robinson, 52–69. Cambridge, MA: Harvard University Press, 1999.

Rosha, Rekha. "Accounting Capital, Race and Benjamin Franklin's 'Pecuniary Habits' of Mind in *The Autobiography*." In *Culture, Capital and Representation*, ed. Robert J. Balfour, 35–48. London: Palgrave, 2010.

Sa, Kongliao. *Xuanchuan xinli yanjiu*. Shanghai: Gengyun chubanshe, 1948.

Sa, Mengwu, and Lin Yimin. "Xuanchuan zhi lilun ji qi shiji." *Duli qingnian* 1, no. 3 (March 1926): 13–17.

San, Mu. *Yu wusheng chu ting jinglei: Lu Xun yu wenang*. Nanchang: Baihuazhou wenyi chubanshe, 2002.

Sanft, Charles. *Communication and Cooperation in Early Imperial Culture: Publicizing the Qin Dynasty*. Albany: State University of New York Press, 2014.

Schaeffer, William. *Shadow Modernism: Photography, Writing, and Space in Shanghai, 1925–1937*. Durham, NC: Duke University Press, 2017.

Schulz, Katherine. "What Is Distant Reading?" *New York Times*, June 24, 2011.

Scott, James C. *Seeing Like a State: How Certain Schemes to Improve the Human Condition Have Failed*. New Haven, CT: Yale University Press, 1998.

Shanghai Lu Xun Jinianguan and Jiangsu Guji Chubanshe, eds. *Banhua jicheng: Lu Xun cang Zhongguo xiandai muke quanji*. Nanjing: Jiangsu guji chubanshe, 1991.

Shannon, Claude. "A Mathematical Theory of Communication." *Bell System Technical Journal* 27, nos. 3–4 (1948): 379–423, 623–56.

Shao, Peiren, ed. *Xuanchuanxue he yulunxue*. Shanghai: Fudan daxue chubanshe, 2002.

Sharma, Nikhil. "The Origin of [the] Data Information Knowledge (DIKW) Hierarchy." April 2008. https://www.researchgate.net/publication/292335202_The_Origin_of_Data_Information_Knowledge_Wisdom_DIKW_Hierarchy.

Shen, Congwen. *Changhe*. Ed. Zhang Xinying. Guangzhou: Huacheng chubanshe, 2010.

——. *Congwen zizhuan*. Shanghai: Diyiban chubanshe, 1934.

Shen, Congwen, and Zhang Zhaohe, eds. *Shen Congwen Quanji*. Taiyuan: Beiyue wenyi chubanshe, 2002.

Shi, Tuo. *Jiehun*. Beijing: Huaxia chubanshe, [1947] 2010.

Shiroyama, Tomoko. *China During the Great Depression: Market, State, and the World Economy, 1929–1937*. Cambridge, MA: Harvard University Press, 2008.

So, Richard Jean. "Literary Information Warfare: Eileen Chang, the US State Department, and Cold War Media Aesthetics." *American Literature* 85, no. 4 (2013): 719–44.

——. *Transpacific Community: America, China, and the Rise and Fall of a Cultural Network*. New York: Columbia University Press, 2016.

Strand, David. *An Unfinished Republic: Leading by Word and Deed in Modern China*. Berkeley: University of California Press, 2011.

Sun, Xiangji. "Zayin." *Xinli* 1, no. 3 (1922): 1–3.

Sun, Xupei. *Huaxia chuanbolun*. Beijing: Renmin chubanshe, 1997.

Taibbi, Matt. "The Great American Bubble Machine." *Rolling Stone*, April 5, 2010.

Tang, Xiaobing. *Chinese Modern: The Heroic and the Quotidian*. Durham, NC: Duke University Press, 2000.

——. *The Origins of the Chinese Avant-Garde: The Modern Woodcut Movement*. Berkeley: University of California Press, 2008.

Tang, Xiaobing, with Michel Hockx. "The Creation Society (1921–1930)." In *Literary Societies of Republican China*, ed. Kirk A. Denton and Michel Hockx, 103–36. Lanham, MD: Lexington Books, 2008.

Tao, Deyi. "Shan'e zihui." *Xinli* 3, no. 2 (1924): 1–33, and 3, no. 3 (1924): 1–44.

Tenen, Dennis. "Stalin's Powerpoint." *Modernism/Modernity* 21, no. 1 (2014): 253–67.

Thorndike, Edward. *The Teacher's Word Book*. New York: Teachers College, Columbia University, 1921.

Ting, Lee-hsia Hsu. *Government Control of the Press in Modern China, 1900–1949*. Cambridge, MA: Harvard University Press, 1974.

Underwood, Ted. "A Genealogy of Distant Reading." *Digital Humanities Quarterly* 11, no. 2 (2017).

Wagner, Rudolf, ed. *Joining the Global Public: Word, Image, and City in Early Chinese Newspapers, 1870–1910*. Albany: State University of New York Press, 2007.

Wang, Chelsea Zi. "More Haste, Less Speed: Sources of Friction in the Ming Postal System." *Late Imperial China* 40, no. 2 (2019): 89–140.

Wang, David Der-Wei. *Fictional Realism in Twentieth-Century China: Mao Dun, Lao She, Shen Congwen*. New York: Columbia University Press, 1992.

——. *Fin-de-Siècle Splendor: Repressed Modernities of Late Qing Fiction, 1849–1911*. Stanford, CA: Stanford University Press, 1997.

Wang, Dewei [David Der-wei Wang]. "Shen Congwen de san ci qiwu." In *Shuqing chuantong yu Zhongguo xiandaixing: Zai Beida de ba tang ke*, 67–85. Beijing: Sanlian, 2010.

Wang, Xiaojue. "From Asylum to Museum: The Discourse of Insanity and Schizophrenia in Shen Congwen's 1949 Transition." *Modern Chinese Literature and Culture* 23, no. 1 (Spring 2011): 133–68.

——. *Modernity with a Cold War Face: Reimagining the Nation in Chinese Literature Across the 1949 Divide.* Cambridge, MA: Harvard University Press, 2013.

Wang, Xinqi. *Lu Xun meishu nianpu.* Guangzhou: Lingnan Art Press, 1986.

Wang, Xipeng. "Xiaoshuo de tujie." *Wenyi yuekan* 6, no. 3 (1934): 16–23.

Wang, Yizhi. *Zonghe xuanchuanxue.* Chongqing: Guomin tushu chubanshe, 1944.

Wang, Zengqi. "Xingdou qi wen, chizi qi ren." In *Wang Zengqi sanwen.* Zhengzhou: Henan wenyi chubanshe, 2020.

Wei, Juxian. *Lishi tongjixue.* Shanghai: Shangwu yinshuguan, 1934.

——. "Yingyong tongjixue de fangfa zhengli guoxue." *Dongfang zazhi* 26, no. 14 (1929): 73–84.

——. "Lishi tongjixue di genben wenti." *Yanjiu yu pipan* 1, no. 1 (1935): 75–78.

Welsh, Alexander. *George Eliot and Blackmail.* Cambridge, MA: Harvard University Press, 1985.

Wiener, Norbert. *Cybernetics and Society: The Human Use of Human Beings.* Boston: Houghton Mifflin, 1954.

Wollaeger, Mark. *Modernism, Media, and Propaganda: British Narrative from 1900 to 1945.* Princeton, NJ: Princeton University Press, 2006.

Wong, Wang-chi. *Politics and Literature in Shanghai.* Manchester: Manchester University Press, 1991.

Wright, David. "Tan Sitong and the Ether Reconsidered." *Bulletin of the School of Oriental and African Studies* 57, no. 3 (1994): 551–75.

Wu, Silas. *Communication and Imperial Control in China: Evolution of the Palace Memorial System, 1693–1735.* Cambridge, MA: Harvard University Press, 1970.

Wu, Xiaodong. "Changhe zhong de chuanmei fuma—Shen Congwen de guojia xiangxiang he xiandai xiangxiang." *Shijie,* no. 12 (2003): 198–213.

——. "Code Words for Communications Media in *Long River*: Shen Congwen's Imaginaries of the Nation and of the Modern." Trans. Jeffrey C. Kinkley. In *Routledge Companion to Shen Congwen,* ed. Gang Zhou, Sihe Chen, Zhang Xinying, and Jeffrey Kinkley, 134–50. London and New York: Routledge, 2019.

Xiao, Jiwei. *Telling Details: Chinese Fiction, World Literature.* New York: Routledge, 2022.

Xiao, Tie. *Revolutionary Waves: The Crowd in Modern China.* Cambridge, MA: Harvard University Press, 2017.

Xie Liuyi. "Qingnian yu xinwen." *Qingnianjie* 6, no. 2 (1934): 49–51.

——. *Xie Liuyi ji.* Liaoning: Liaoning renmin chubanshe, 2009.

——. *Xie Liuyi wenji.* Ed. Chen Jiang and Chen Gengchu. Beijing: Shangwu Yinshuguan, 1995.

Xinbo banhua ji. Beijing: Remin meishu chubanshe, 1978.

Xu Dongping, ed. *Shiyong xuanchuanxue cidian.* Anhui: Anhui remin chubanshe, 1989.

Xu Yi. *Xuanchuanshu yu qunzhong yundong.* Shanghai: Zhonghua shuju, 1931.

Yang, Daqing. *Technology of Empire: Telecommunications and Japanese Expansion in Asia, 1883–1945.* Cambridge, MA: Harvard University Press, 2011.

Yarkho, Boris I. "Speech Distribution in Five-Act Tragedies (A Question of Classicism and Romanticism)." *Journal of Literary Theory* 13, no. 1 ([1935–38] 2019): 13–76.

Ye Shengtao. *Ni Huanzhi*. Shanghai: Kaiming shuju, 1978.

—— [Yeh Sheng-tao]. *Schoolmaster Ni Huan-chih*. Trans. A. C. Barnes. Beijing: Foreign Languages Press, 1978.

Yeh, Michelle. *Modern Chinese Poetry: Theory and Practice since 1917*. New Haven, CT: Yale University Press, 1991.

Yokomitsu, Riichi. *Shanghai*. Trans. Dennis Washburn. Ann Arbor: University of Michigan Press, [1935] 2001.

Yu Dafu. "Jieshao yi ge wenxue de gongshi." *Chenbao fukan: Yilin xunkan* 15 (1925): 3–4.

Yu Lie. "Shuping: Duojiao guanxi: Mao Dun zuo." *Qinghua zhoukan* 45, nos. 10–11 (1936): 102–5.

Yu Pingbo. "Shehui shang duiyu xinshi de gezhong xinliguan." *Xinchao* 2, no. 1 (1919): 163–72.

Yun Zhen and Wang Chongzhi. *Wuxiandian yu Zhongguo*. Shanghai: Wenrui yinshuguan, 1931.

Zeleny, Milan. "Management Support Systems: Toward Integrated Knowledge Management." *Human Systems Management* 7, no. 1 (1987): 59–70.

Zhang Hui mukehua di er ji. Shanghai: Kaiming shudian; Beiping: Lijian shuju, 1935.

Zhang, Jingyuan. *Psychoanalysis in China: Literary Transformations 1919–1949*. Ithaca, NY: Cornell University Press, 1992.

Zhang Xinying. *Shen Congwen de houban sheng*. Guangxi: Guangxi shifan daxue chubanshe, 2014.

Zhang Yaoxiang. "Baihuashi zhong gantanfu." *Chenbao fukan*, September 22, 1924, 2–3.

——. "Beijing shangdian zhi zhaopai." *Chenbao liu zhounian zengkan*, December 1924, 137–44.

——. "Da moujun chao baihuashi." *Liumei xuesheng jikan* 6, no. 1 (1919): 237–38.

—— [Yao-Chiang Chang]. "Factors Affecting the Speed and Clearness of Reading Chinese." MA thesis, Columbia University, 1919.

——. "Qingxu shiyan." *Xinli* 1, no. 4 (1922): 1–12.

——. "Shizi shiyan." *Xinli* 1, no. 1 (1922): 113–133.

——. "Wenxuejia zhi xiangxiang." *Xinli* 1, no. 3 (1922).

——, ed. *Xinli zazhi xuancun*. Shanghai: Zhonghua shuju, 1932.

——. "Xinshiren zhi qingxu." *Xinli* 2, no. 3 (1924): 1–14.

——. "Zayin." *Xinli* 1, no. 2 (1922).

——. "Zhihui celiang." *Beijing nügao shi youzhi jiaoyu de yanjiu* 1, no. 1 (1920): 92–97.

——. "Zhihui celiang: Shi gaizao." *Jiaoyu congkan* 1, no. 4 (1920): 1–8.

——. "Zhili ceyan: Zhili ceyan yuanqi." *Xinli* 1, no. 1 (1922): 87–89.

Zhang, Yingjin. *Chinese National Cinema*. New York: Routledge, 2004.

Zhang Yiping. "Gantan fuhao yu xinshi." *Chenbao fukan*, September 15, 1924, 3–4.

Zhang Zhen. *An Amorous History of the Silver Screen: Shanghai Cinema, 1896–1937*. Chicago: University of Chicago Press, 2006.

——. "Teahouse, Shadowplay, Bricolage: Laborer's Love and the Question of Early Chinese Cinema." In *Cinema and Urban Culture in Shanghai, 1922–1943*, ed. Yingjin Zhang, 27–50. Stanford, CA: Stanford University Press, 1999.

Zhang Zhizhong. "Xinwen zhanzheng yu Propaganda." *Liudong xuebao* 2, no. 2 (1936): 95–100.

Zhao, Henry Y. H. *The Uneasy Narrator: Chinese Fiction from the Traditional to the Modern*. Oxford: Oxford University Press, 1995.

Zhao Jingshen. "Yuanqu shidai xianhou kao." *Xiandai* 5, no. 4 (1932): 580–92.

Zhong, Yurou. *Chinese Grammatology: Script Revolution and Literary Modernity, 1916–1958.* New York: Columbia University Press, 2019.

Zhongguo Gongchandang xinwen gongzuo wenjian huibian. Ed. Zhongguo Shehui kexue yuan xinwen yanjiusuo. Beijing: Xinhua chubanshe, 1980.

Zhonghua xinli xuehui. "Ben zazhi zongzhi." *Xinli* 1, no. 1 (1922): 1.

Zhou Yongming. *Historicizing Online Politics: Telegraphy, the Internet, and Political Participation in China.* Stanford, CA: Stanford University Press, 2006.

INDEX

GPSR Authorized Representative: Easy Access System Europe, Mustamäe tee
50, 10621 Tallinn, Estonia, gpsr.requests@easproject.com

www.ingramcontent.com/pod-product-compliance
Lightning Source LLC
Chambersburg PA
CBHW031218050326
40689CB00009B/1380